Dad,

Happy Birthday, 1981.

Love,

Mark + family

THE
FIRST
FRONTIER

THE INDIAN WARS
AND AMERICA'S ORIGINS
1607–1776

by David Horowitz

Simon and Schuster
New York

Published by Simon & Schuster
A Division of Gulf & Western Corporation
Simon & Schuster Building
Rockefeller Plaza
1230 Avenue of the Americas
New York, New York   10020

Designed by Irving Perkins
Manufactured in the United States of America
1   2   3   4   5   6   7   8   9   10

Library of Congress Cataloging in Publication Data

Horowitz, David, date.
The first frontier.

Bibliography: p.
Includes index.
1.   Indians of North America—Wars. 2.   United
States—History—Colonial period, ca. 1600-1775.
I.   Title.
E82.H84   973.2   78-13174
ISBN   0-671-22534-0

Acknowledgments

I am indebted to Alice Mayhew for a skillful editorial hand, which helped to shape the style of this work. Bob Rafelson gave me encouragement in the early stages of writing when I needed it most. Moss Roberts read the final section of the manuscript and made useful criticisms. Peter Loewenberg and Daniel Ellsberg gave me the benefit of their insight and experience.

To Elissa

Contents

Introduction   13

PART I   THANKSGIVING IN NEW ENGLAND

     1   Patuxet   17
     2   *Magnalia Christi Americana*   36
     3   Metacomet   55

PART II   DEMOCRACY IN VIRGINIA

     1   Seed of the Plantation   85
     2   Bacon's Rebellion   104
     3   *Durante Vita*   128

PART III   THE CAUSE OF FREEDOM

     1   Forest Wars   143
     2   Battle for Empire   157
     3   Declaring Independence   189

     Selected Bibliography   228
     Index   243

If we carefully examine the social and political state of America, after having studied its history, we shall remain perfectly convinced that not an opinion, not a custom, not a law, I may even say not an event is upon record which the origin of that people will not explain.

ALEXIS DE TOCQUEVILLE

Introduction

THE story of America's origins, which is told in these pages, is an unfamiliar one. Its wars are uncelebrated, its heroes unsung, its causes unremembered. The source of this failure is not a loss of the historical evidence. It lies in the nature of the memory itself. America is a nation self-conceived. Its sense of nationhood and the memory of its origins are almost indivisible. The memory is one of innocence: a pilgrimage to freedom and a self-defining struggle for independence in a wilderness frontier.

There may be laments for the Indian tribes who were once a presence in the pre-American landscape. There may be regret for the Africans who were owned by the founding fathers, and for the unfulfilled promises of the revolutionary faith. But this remorse is an afterthought, a recollection of native peoples who prevented the land from being empty when the first settlements were established, and free. It is a recognition that rarely touches on the essential American character and its achievement.

That character is ordinarily attributed to an expanding territory of opportunity and freedom. "The existence of an area of free land, its continuous recession, and the advance of American settlement westward, explain American development," wrote Frederick Jackson Turner at the close of the continental frontier. "This perennial rebirth, this fluidity of American life, this expansion westward with its new opportunities, its continuous touch with the simplicity of primitive society, furnish the forces dominating American character."

The expanding territory was undoubtedly a force in America's early development. If the Pacific is seen as the frontier's extension in the west, it was a formative factor for the modern experience as well.

But the real frontier of flesh and blood is different from the frontier of accepted legend. The land the Pilgrims came to was not free; the opportunity they sought was not innocent. The forests and plains of the continent were inhabited by more than six hundred Indian nations. Not a square mile was unclaimed.

It is the memory of the struggle with these peoples that has been nearly forgotten. For almost two hundred years, from the founding of the first settlements through the establishment of the Republic, almost continuous warfare raged on the American continent, its conflicts more threatening than any the nation was to face again. Americans remember the end of the frontier, when the Indian tribes were a vanishing remnant on the western outskirts of their own civilization. But they forget its beginning, when the conflicts challenged the very existence of America's settlements and determined their future course.

The repression of the first memory has obscured and colored a second: the memory of Independence and the nation's birth. America was created in a struggle with England for control of the continental domain. The conflict is remembered now as an Old World tyranny versus a New World freedom. Its legends are invoked to justify the nation's contemporary crusades. "Our cause," declared President John F. Kennedy on the threshold of a new frontier in Vietnam, "is the cause of all mankind." These were words first uttered by Tom Paine, as a battle cry of America's revolutionary birth. Yet that struggle was no more a "cause of all mankind" than America's crusade in Asia; no more than the Indian frontier was free.

The effort to recapture historical memory is a quest for the complexity of the nation's past. If such a search has a moral purpose, it is to restore the sense of historical limit. To know the past, to weigh not only its achievements but its crimes, not merely its victories but its defeats, is a first step toward relinquishing the passion to relive it.

PART I

THANKSGIVING
IN
NEW ENGLAND

1

Patuxet

IN the winter of 1616 an infection ravaged the natives of the coastal territory known as New England with a virulence that made its chroniclers think of smallpox and yellow fever. An unprecedented force in the wilderness region, the plague was brought by European traders and adventurers, whose ships had touched land with increasing frequency, as the advance guard of a maritime empire.

In the two years during which the fever spread through their villages, perhaps a third of the peoples living between the Narragansett Bay and the Piscataqua River died. Tribes that had been flourishing and strong grew weak; weak tribes disappeared. "The hand of God fell heavily upon them with such a mortall stroake," wrote Thomas Morton, an Englishman who had visited the New World, "that they died on heapes, as they lay in their houses, and the living, that were able to shift for themselves would runne away and let them dy, and let there Carkases ly above the ground without buriall. For in a place where many inhabited, there hath been but one a live, to tell what became of the rest, the livinge being (as it seems) not able to bury the dead, they were left for Crowes, Kites, and vermin to pray upon. And the bones and skulls upon the severall places of their habitations, made such a spectacle after my coming into these partes, that as I travailed in that Forrest, nere the Massachussets, it seemed to mee a new found Golgotha."

Among the tribes that were nearly swept out of existence
was a tawny strong-limbed people called Massachusetts. Before
the plague they had been one of the most powerful of the
Algonquin peoples, whose dialects could be heard from the
Virginia Tidewater to the rim of the Canadian Arctic. South
of the Massachusetts on the curve of a sheltered bay, lived the
Wampanoags, who had also been decimated by the fever.
Whole villages had perished on the shoreline, leaving the land
open for settlement.

In England, King James hailed "the wonderful plague among
the salvages" as a divine favor to the colonial mission, and
those who came to settle shortly afterward regarded the
catastrophe as a special grace: "By this meanes Christ ... not
onely made roome for his people to plant but also tamed the
hard and cruell hearts of these barbarous Indians," wrote an
early colonist, "insomuch that halfe a handfull of his people
landing not long after in Plimoth-Plantation, found little resistance."

Europeans had fished and traded on the northern coasts of
the New World for years, but the first to settle and survive
were the pilgrim "Saints" of a separatist church. Persecuted by
the Anglican state for their religion, they had fled England
across the North Sea to Leyden. For twelve years they lived
and labored piously in Holland. But poverty and the "hardnes"
of the place discouraged them and began to drive their children
from the fold. As their sufferings increased, they concluded
that their burdens might be eased and their spirits raised if they
moved elsewhere. Many who now preached against them would
join their ranks (their pastor John Robinson declared) "if they
were in a place wher they might have libertie *and* live com-
fortably."

Their hopes were directed to the New World on the other
side of the ocean to the west: "These vast and unpeopled
countries of America which are fruitfull and fitt for habitation
being devoyd of all civil inhabitants; wher ther are only salvage
and brutish men which range up and downe, little otherwise
then the wild beasts of the same."

The Crown had entrusted the colonizing of the New World

to joint stock companies. The Leyden parishioners now applied to the Virginia Company for a patent to settle. For capital to underwrite their voyage and plantation, they appealed to a group of merchants headed by an ironmonger named Thomas Weston, who was impressed by their claim that they were "as industrious and frugal...as any company of people in the world." A contract was signed binding them into a partnership for seven years; profits from trade, fishing and other activities were to remain in the common stock until the contract's term. A ship was chartered, and on September 6, 1620, the Pilgrims set sail in the *Mayflower* for Virginia.

The party consisted of forty-one "Saints" of their own church and forty "Strangers" who had joined the venture in hopes of improving their earthly lot. Five hired hands and eighteen bondslaves were attached to these groups, including four waifs plucked off the streets of London (a common practice for reducing the population of the urban poor). Though the Saints were the more substantial subjects, owning most of the servants on board the *Mayflower*, they were all commoners "from the cottages and not the castles of England."

For two months the small ship, buffeted by the fall weather, was carried westward over the endless menacing ocean. Then, on November 9 or 10, a thin edge of land appeared over the horizon. As they drew close, they saw that it was "Cape Cod," which had been discovered about eighteen years before. They thanked their God for their safe passage and deliverance, and took stock of their situation. "If they looked behind them," William Bradford recorded, "ther was the mighty ocean which they had passed, and was now as a maine barr and goulfe to separate them from all the civill parts of the world." If they looked before them, "what could they see but a hidious and desolate wildernes, full of wild beasts and willd men?"

A sandy curve cradled the bay which the *Mayflower* had entered. From the ship the Pilgrims could observe a school of whales at play. The beaches and the sky were crowded with birds ("the greatest store of fowl we ever saw"); and woods of sassafras, juniper and oak crested the shoreline to the sea edge. The land was hard and flat, a glacial clay studded with rocks;

thickets and vines stripped of their summer leafage gave the country "a wild and savage heiw."

Winter was already upon them and a chill air promised snow. But before they could go ashore to construct some shelter, a serious matter had to be settled. When the *Mayflower* had approached harbor and the Strangers on board had seen that the land was not Virginia, where the Saints had their patent and authority, some of them began to declare their independence. When they went ashore, they said, they "would use their owne libertie; for none had power to command them."

Yet, exposed to the elements and the hidden dangers of a wilderness land, their liberty was limited. The Saints offered a compromise in the form of a covenant of all the adult males present. It established an authority of "just and equall lawes," among Saints and Strangers alike, the first self-government in the New World. After signing the compact, they elected a governor by unanimous vote, John Carver, the richest man on board.

The Pilgrims scouted the cape and its environs for a month. After setting out the first day and walking about a mile from the ship, they saw five or six Nauset Indians with a dog coming toward them. The Nausets fled at their approach and disappeared after a chase of several miles. Later the Pilgrims stumbled on a recently vacated Indian camp and unearthed an underground corn barn. They took the precious seed and continued on. The ground was now covered with snow, the weather so cold that the spray of the sea glazed their coats.

One night while camping near the place where they had seen the natives, they were wakened by a "hideous great crie" and the shouts of their sentinel calling "Arme, arme." Jumping to their feet, they fired their muskets and the noise stopped. The next morning after prayer they heard the cries again, and all of a sudden one of their company came running from the beach shouting, "Men, Indeans, Indeans," and at that moment arrows came flying into their midst. Snatching their muskets, they fired at the attackers and easily routed them. Then they prayed and "gave God sollemne thanks and praise for their deliverance."

Two days later they crossed the bay in a freezing rainstorm to a harbor they thought suitable for settling. On Christmas Day they began to erect the first house of their colony, which they called Plymouth.

Situated on the high ground, it had a commanding view of the harbor. There was no forest adjacent—a protection from attack—while the fields around were already cleared and had been cultivated for corn. This fortune was linked to a previous providence. As they soon learned, they had settled in a village which four years earlier had been called Patuxet, one of the communities obliterated by the plague.

The first winter in the New World was harsh. Weakened by their ordeal at sea, the settlers were wracked by scurvy and pneumonia, and dropped with somber regularity through the season's cold. When the thaw came and they took inventory of the dead, they counted four whole families, thirteen of eighteen wives, and twenty-nine of the single men, hired hands and servants. In three months, half of all those who had come with them had been buried in graves beneath the New England snow.

Military considerations had already assumed a central place in the Pilgrims' affairs. All through the winter they had buried their dead at night, at Cole's Hill, leveled the graves and planted corn over them to prevent the unseen natives from learning of their losses. For although they had won their first skirmish, they were now in such sore straits and so weakened by disease that the outcome of another battle would not be so certain.

Then, about March 16, as they gathered to discuss their defenses, a tall raven-haired warrior, naked except for a leather fringe around his waist, strode into their midst and began to welcome them in broken English. His name was Samoset, sagamore of Pemaquid. His English was learned from the fishermen and adventurers who frequented the northern coast in the early years of the century. Eight months previous, one of their vessels had carried him to the cape to stay among the Wampanoags, the principal tribe of the surrounding region. Now he explained to them that they had planted their New Plymouth in the destroyed Patuxet village of this tribe.

Samoset's talk extended into the evening, and the amiable flow of conversation was encouraged by a festive dinner of pudding, duck and "strong water." The native's observations were valued intelligence to the settlers; they included descriptions of the tribes of the area, their names and strength, and who was chief among them. When Samoset left the following morning, he promised to return with members of the Wampanoag tribe and their sachem, Massasoit, and to bring beaver for trade. The colonists presented Samoset with a ring, a bracelet and a knife as tokens of gratitude.

Four or five days after Samoset's visit, the Wampanoag sachem arrived at the outskirts of Plymouth with sixty of his warriors. Their faces were painted and some wore skins, while others were naked. A long knife hung from Massasoit's bosom, his face was painted red with deep mulberry, and as his special mark he had "a great chain of white bone beads about his neck." Behind his head hung a little bag of tobacco, which he offered to the Pilgrims as they came to meet him with gifts.

After some negotiations and an exchange of hostages, the sachem and twenty of his warriors set down their bows and followed Edward Winslow to the settlement. They were greeted at the Town Brook by Captain Miles Standish, the Pilgrims' military commander, and half a dozen musketeers. Along the north bank of the brook the main street of the town extended all the way to Fort Hill, where Standish had mounted his cannon. On either side stood a dozen wooden structures with thatched roofs, the largest of which was twenty feet square. This was the Common House, which also served as hospital and church.

Standish conducted the sachem to a building not yet completed, where a green rug and several cushions were laid out for him. Then Governor Carver appeared at the head of three or four musketeers to a flurry of drums and a fanfare of trumpets. He offered Massasoit some liquor and drank a toast and Massasoit took "a great draught," which caused him to sweat. When the preliminaries were over, they sat down together to draw up a treaty of peace.

Before all else, the signatories to the treaty agreed that neither Massasoit nor any of his people would harm the English. If any did, Massasoit agreed that he would send the offender to Plymouth to be punished. If anything was stolen from the colonists, Massasoit pledged to see that it was restored; the Pilgrims pledged the same. They further agreed that they would be allies in any war, that the Indians would leave their weapons behind when they visited the colony and "lastly, that doing thus, King James would esteem of him [Massasoit] as a friend and ally."

When Massasoit departed, he left behind his interpreter, Squanto, a native of Patuxet. Squanto's English was better than Samoset's. He had been kidnapped six years earlier by an English adventurer named Hunt, who had abducted twenty Patuxet and seven Nauset braves and sold them into slavery in Spain for twenty pounds a head. Later Squanto had been released from captivity and shipped to England, where he was taken in by the treasurer of the Newfoundland Company. In 1619, he had returned home to find his family and entire community wiped out by the plague.

Squanto showed the Plymouth settlers how to plant and tend the seed they had taken from the Nausets four months earlier, so that a crop would be ready for the next winter. He showed them how to set the seed and fertilize it with fish caught in the Town Brook. Soon they came to regard him as "a spetiall instrument sent of God for their good beyond their expectation."

In April, as the Pilgrims were busily engaged in planting, Governor Carver came from the field out of the hot sun complaining of a pain in his head. A few hours later he died, and William Bradford was elected Governor.

About the beginning of July, the Pilgrims decided that it was time to return Massasoit's visit. Such a visit, Bradford thought, would provide them with an opportunity to give him a present "to bind him the faster unto them." It would also be a chance to explore the country, to see the manner in which the sachem lived and "what strength he had aboute him," and to learn "the ways . . . to his place, if at any time they should have the occasion." The envoys were Edward Winslow and Stephen Hopkins. Squanto was their guide.

Setting out at nine in the morning, the three men followed

a river rising through stony uplands, and about six hours later reached Namasket, a village subject to Massasoit. They were warmly greeted by the Nemascheuks, who gave them bread and the spawn of shad to eat. Afterward they continued on their journey to Massasoit's village, following a river which they would later name Taunton and which flowed into the bay called Narragansett, after the great tribe that dwelled on its western shore.

At this river they were welcomed by Nemascheuks who had come to fish and who offered them bass from their day's catch. Winslow noted that the soil on both sides of the river was good, and had been cleared for growing: "Thousands of men have lived there, which died in a great plague long since," he reported, "and pity it was and is to see so many goodly fields, and so well seated, without men to dress and manure the same."

The following day, after traveling nearly twenty miles through country overgrown with trees, they arrived in Poka-noket. Massasoit's village was on the eastern shore of a neck of land that jutted twelve miles into Narragansett Bay. In the distance they could see the green elevation the Indians called Monthaup, and the colonists later called Mount Hope.

Massasoit was away but returned shortly. They greeted him by firing their weapons, and presented him with a red coat. After he put it on, they sat down to business. The Pilgrims began by saying they wished above all to continue the peace between them. They appealed to Massasoit to control his sub-jects, who were now coming often to Plymouth with their wives and children, draining the colony's meager supplies. They gave him a copper chain, saying that they would receive the bearer as his emissary, and that if he were pleased to come to Plymouth himself, they would welcome him. They also wished to make restitution to the Nausets whose corn they had taken, and whom they understood to be his subjects. Finally they asked his cooperation in setting up a beaver trade.

Massasoit agreed to their requests. Among all the villages and tribes that were his subjects, the people would be at peace with Plymouth and bring their skins to trade. Following his speech, they smoked tobacco and talked; and during their con-

versation the Plymouth emissaries heard Massasoit say, or so
Squanto interpreted, that the entire region "was King James
his country, and he also was King James his man."

Although the travelers were hungry, no food was served, for
Massasoit had none. When they retired for the night, the
sachem invited his guests to his plank bed to sleep with him
and his wife. The Pilgrim envoys spent two nights and a day
at Pokanoket, complaining later that they had but one meal
and were kept awake by the crowded bed and "the savage's
barbarous singing (for they use to sing themselves a sleep),"
so that they were more weary from their lodging than from
their journey.

As Massasoit became an ally of Plymouth's nascent empire,
Squanto began to acquire for himself a portion of its expanding
power. On one occasion he told some Wampanoags that the
colonists had buried the plague, which they had brought with
them, under the floor of their storehouse in Plymouth. As
the Pilgrims' servant, he could prevail on them to release the
killer at will. Asked about Squanto's boast, the Pilgrims (who
in fact had buried their gunpowder in the spot) admitted that
they did not have the ability to send the plague, but added,
"the God of the English had it in store, and could send it at
his pleasure to the destruction of his and our enemies."

The peace which Massasoit and Squanto negotiated with the
English was not welcomed by all the natives of the region.
Among those who opposed it was Corbitant, sachem of the
Pocassets, whose country spread across the cedar swamps and
sloping fields on the eastern shore of Narragansett Bay and up
beyond the Taunton estuary. Corbitant was Massasoit's most
powerful tributary. His seat in Mattapoisett was on a neck
that extended three miles into the bay and faced across the
water toward Mount Hope.

In the late summer, an English-speaking Indian named Hobomok, who also served the colonists as an interpreter, came running
into Plymouth in a sweat. He had come from Namasket with
alarming news. Corbitant had made an alliance with the Narragansetts and had gone to Namasket to draw Massasoit's subjects
away from him and turn them against the English. Finding

Squanto and Hobomok there, Corbitant had seized them both. Hobomok had managed to escape, but Squanto had not and was probably killed, for Corbitant had said "if he were dead, the English had lost their tongue."

When Hobomok finished his report, the colonists dispatched ten of their men to Namasket under the command of Captain Standish. Entering the village without resistance, they demanded to know if Corbitant was there, but no one would answer them. They assured the Nemascheuks that Corbitant alone was their reason for coming, and commanded everyone to remain still while they searched for him. Three braves disregarding the command were fired at and wounded. Finally the colonists were told that Corbitant was gone and Squanto alive, and were offered food and tobacco. They then discharged two of their guns at random, "which much terrified all the inhabitants," and celebrated their success.

Following this episode, Governor Bradford noted that the Colony had "many gratulations from diverce sachims, and much firmer peace . . . and this Corbitant him selfe used the mediation of Massassoyte to make his peace, but was shie to come neare them a longe while after." On September 13, 1621, Corbitant and eight other sachems signed a formal instrument of submission: "Know all men by these Presents, that we whose Names are under-written do acknowledge our selves to be the Loyal Subjects of King *James*, King of *Great Britain*, *France* and *Ireland*, Defender of the Faith, Etc." New Plymouth was now recognized as the agent of English sovereignty by all the inhabitants of the region from the ocean coast of Cape Cod to the eastern shores of Narragansett Bay.

A month later, Massasoit and ninety of his braves were invited to Plymouth for a three-day feast of Thanksgiving, to celebrate the peace and the harvest that Squanto had sown. (Squanto himself died less than a year afterward. Stricken suddenly with the plague, he bequeathed his possessions to Bradford and other Pilgrims, as "remembrances of his love," desiring the Governor "to pray for him, that he might goe to the Englishmen's God in heaven.")

As they celebrated their Thanksgiving, the Pilgrim founders

had much to be grateful for; they had survived the wilderness and established title to a new world. "Yea, it hath pleased God so to possess the Indians with a fear of us, and love unto us," wrote Winslow, "that not only the greatest King amongst them, called Massasoit, but also the princes and peoples around about us, have either made suit unto us, or been glad of any occasion to make peace."

About a month after the celebration, a ship anchored in Plymouth harbor with thirty-five new settlers. Among the passengers on board was Deacon Cushman, who came with a letter of commiseration from their pastor ("the death of so many of our dear friends and brethren, oh! how grievous hath it been to you to bear, and to us to take knowledge of"), and a letter of complaint from Thomas Weston, their chief investor. The *Mayflower* had returned to England without skins or other marketable goods ("I know your weaknes was the cause of it," Weston wrote testily, "and I believe more weaknes of judgmente than weaknes of hands"); moreover, the Pilgrims had not yet signed amendments that had been made to the original contract, granting the investors a share in the colony's houses and fields as well as its barter and produce.

This demand, distasteful enough to the Saints, who had made the agreement, was unacceptable to the Strangers, who had not. They were already clamoring for their rights in the common lands, which under the original terms were not to be theirs until the end of seven years. To quiet these demands and to preserve the contract with the investors, Cushman preached to the Pilgrim company on *The Dangers of Self-Love*. It was delivered in the Common House on December 9, 1621, and printed on his return to England, as the first sermon of the New World:

"*Israel* was seven years in Canaan, before the land was divided into tribes." Why, then, were they clamoring for their individual portions now, unless it was because they thought to live better than their neighbors? Had they forgotten the originator of such "particularizing" in the world? Was it not Satan, "who was not content to keep that equall state with his fellows, but would set his throne above the stars?" Just as nothing so resembled heavenly happiness as for people to be of one heart and soul, so nothing more resembled "hellish horror than for every man to shift for himself." If seeking one's own share were a good thing, "then it should be best also for God to provide one heaven for thee and another for thy neighbor."

Whether they were persuaded by Cushman's eloquence, or the difficulty of their circumstances and their continuing dependence on Weston, the colonists agreed to accept the new terms, and Cushman departed with a shipload of beaver skins and otter pelts.

But before the ship reached England, it was waylaid by a French privateer off the coast of Poitou and its cargo confiscated. Already impatient with the lack of returns from his Plymouth investment, and contemptuous of the sufferings of its Saints, Weston sold his interest and with an eye to the burgeoning fur trade obtained a patent for a colony nearby. Convinced that the failure of the Plymouth venture stemmed from a needless encumbrance of women and children and religious ideals, he rounded up fifty or sixty "stout knaves" from the streets of London ("not fitt for an honest man's company," as one of his partners remarked), and in the summer of 1622 he shipped them aboard the vessel *Charity* to seek a quick fortune in beaver and the other bounties of the New World.

Although they were hardly welcome when they arrived at Plymouth, Weston's men were hospitably received, remaining there while their ship continued its journey to Virginia with a load of freight and passengers. Soon, however, there were complaints that they often went into the field pretending to help with the corn, but "spared not day or night to steal the same." There was considerable relief when the *Charity* returned and took them north, where they hoped to establish a foothold colony at Wessagusset on the south shore of Boston Bay.

It was not long after the Wessagusset colony was begun, however, that the weakness of Weston's conception became evident. While his men were not burdened by women, children and religious scruples, they lacked the moral discipline of the Pilgrim community. As the winter cold settled on the New

England countryside, they became increasingly desperate. When food supplies ran out, they turned to plundering the local Indians, though the natives had little to offer. Remnants of the Massachusetts tribe that had been destroyed by the plague, they were themselves hard pressed.

Observing the extremities into which the Wessagusset colonists had fallen in such a short time, Governor Bradford laid it to their lack of thrift and foresight. They had squandered what they had and reduced themselves to destitution; "many sould away their cloathes and bedcoverings; others (so base were they) became servants to the Indeans, and would cutt them woode and fetch them water, for a cap full of corne; others fell to plaine stealing, both night and day, from the Indeans, of which they greevosly complained."

Weston's colonists had jeopardized their own survival. Worse, they had endangered the white presence in the New World. The terror inspired by the God of the Plague and by the Pilgrim arms was dissipated by the spectacle of their distress. The Wessagusset adventurers, Bradford complained, were condemned and scorned by the Indians, who "begane greatly to insulte over them in a most insolente maner."

As the situation in Wessagusset deteriorated, the Pilgrims became convinced that a conspiracy was being organized among the Indians to destroy Plymouth. Evidence of their intention was provided by Miles Standish, the colony's red-haired military captain, after a visit among the Cape tribes. While a guest of one of their sachems, he had been affronted by a Wessagusset brave, a "notable insulting villain" named Wituwamat, who had expressed a low opinion of whites because they "died crying, making sour faces, more like children than men." His suspicions aroused by these remarks, and by the warm reception the warrior received from his hosts, Standish decided that a conspiracy had been formed between Wituwamat and the Cape Indians to "ruinate" Weston's colony and then—because they know the planters "would never leave the death of their countrimen unrevenged"—to attack Plymouth.

"A little chimney is soon fired," wrote a colonial historian not many years later, "so was the Plymouth Captain, a man of very little stature, yet of a very hot and angry temper." Taking eight soldiers, Standish set out for Wessagusset, where he found to his dismay that the settlers mingled freely with the Massachusetts natives and had no fear of them. Standish announced that he had come to trade for beaver, and bided his time.

A few days after the Pilgrims' arrival, a towering Massachusetts warrior named Pecksuot approached Hobomok, who was acting as guide for the Plymouth force, and informed him that he knew Standish had come to kill them. "Tell him we know it: but fear him not, neither will we shun him. But let him begin, when he dare." Shortly afterward, Pecksuot encountered the Captain himself and taunted him. "Though you are a great Captain, yet you are but a little man, and though I be no Sachem; yet I am a man of great strength and courage."

Meanwhile, Standish was still unable to gather the Indians together in one place as he had planned. Abandoning this strategy, he invited their spokesmen Wituwamat and Pecksuot to dinner, together with Wituwamat's eighteen-year-old brother and another Massachusetts brave. The Indians accepted. When they were seated, a signal was given, the door locked, and Standish lunged at the unsuspecting Pecksuot, seized the knife which hung about the Indian's neck, and plunged it into his breast. The other Pilgrims then drew their weapons and fell on the unarmed Wituwamat and the others. ("It is incredible," wrote Winslow afterward, "how many wounds these two ... received before they died, not making any fearful noise but catching at their weapons and striving to the last.") Only the boy survived the assault, and he was hanged afterward.

As soon as it was over, Standish ordered his soldiers to seize and kill every Indian male that could be found. Though most of the natives had fled the vicinity, a few were captured and executed. As a symbol of the Pilgrims' restored prestige, the severed head of Wituwamat was placed on a pike and brought to Plymouth, where it was prominently displayed for the next twenty years.

The massacre assured the final disintegration of Wessagusset. The defenseless inhabitants now lived in fear of Indian reprisals, and when Plymouth offered them passage home, they welcomed the opportunity. It was a satisfactory outcome for the Pilgrims, who were at the same time rid of their principal competitors in the beaver trade, and a menace to their colonial peace.

News of the incident traveled as far as Leyden, reaching the pastor of the Pilgrim Church. "Concerning the killing of those poor Indeans," John Robinson wrote his flock, "how happy a thing had it been if you had converted some before you had killed any." It was "more glorious in mens eyes, then pleasing in Gods, or conveniente for Christians, to be a terrour to poore and barbarous people;... Me thinks one or two principals should have been full enough, according to that approved rule, The punishmente to a few, and the fear to many."

Although he thought the Plymouth Captain was an instrument sent by the Lord "in great mercie and for much good ... if you use him aright," events had shown he "may be wanting that tendernes of the life of man (made after Gods image) which is meete." They must be mindful of the danger, he cautioned, that through these precedents, "others should be drawne to affecte a kind of rufling course in the world."

Yet the Captain, whom these words chastised, remained an indispensable figure of the New England frontier (though alone among Plymouth's leaders he never joined the Pilgrim Church). For thirty years, Standish's voice was rivaled only by those of Winslow and Bradford in Plymouth's councils. Although embarrassing to some, the terror he instituted was an important factor in the peace which made possible Plymouth's early progress and ensured stability in the region for a long time to come. When Thomas Morton settled there two years later, he found the event had entered the language of the Massachusetts, who "did from that time afterwards, call the English Planters *Wotawquenange*, which in their language signifieth stabbers or Cutthroates, and this name was received by those that came after for good."

After the destruction of Wessagusset, the Indian problem receded, but the problem of survival remained. As they entered the third planting season in the New World, the Pilgrims turned their attention to ways by which they might obtain a better crop to overcome the scarcity that had plagued their first winters. After deliberating, they decided that production might be increased by giving up their communal organization. The land held in common was parceled out as private property to each family according to its numbers. Every man would now plant "for his owne perticuler" and rely on himself for his portion.

Later, Governor Bradford judged the plan a success. Under its terms all hands became industrious, and more corn was sown. The women, for example, "now wente willingly into the feild and tooke their little-ones with them to get corne, which before would aledg weaknes, and inabilitie; whom to have compelled would have bene thought great tiranie and oppression." The success of this course showed

> [the] vanitie of that conceite of Plato's and other ancients, applauded by some of later times; that the taking away of propertie, and bringing in communitie into a comone wealth, would make them happy and flourishing; as if they were wiser then God. For this communitie (so farr as it was) was found to breed much confusion and discontent, and retard much imployment that would have been to their benefite and comforte.... Let none objecte this is men's corruption, and nothing to the course it selfe. I answer, seeing all men have this corruption in them, God in his wisdome saw another course fiter for them.

The course of this new individualism was allowed only within the lawful limits of the colonial enterprise. The men of Wessagusset had posed one kind of challenge to the colonial order. Shortly after their departure, Thomas Morton arrived to pose another.

A lawyer and poet, Morton had made a brief journey to the New World in 1622, probably aboard Weston's ship *Charity*. Three years later he returned with a party of fortune seekers who established a plantation and trading post at Passonagessit, two miles north of Wessagusset's empty remains. Within a short time after its settlement, however, the plantation at Passonagessit was disbanded, having failed to realize the expectations of its investors, who had hoped to become "great men and rich all of a sudaine." Its leader, Captain Wollaston, departed for Virginia with the intention of selling most of the indentured servants they had brought with them.

When Wollaston was gone, Morton invited the remainder of the servants and hired hands to a feast. After everyone was sufficiently "merie," he began to encourage the revelers to rebel. If they waited until their captain returned, he told them, they too would be carried off and sold into servitude. As a shareholder in the plantation, he offered to make them "my partners and consociates," if they agreed to his plan. They would then be free to "converse, trade, plante, and live to-geather as equalls, and supporte and protecte on[e] another, or to like effecte."

Morton's proposal was accepted, and a new community was born at Passonagessit. To signify the break with the past, the site that had been christened Mount Wollaston was renamed "Ma-re Mount," or "Mountain by the Sea," an event which Morton and his followers celebrated "with Revels and merri-ment after the old English custom." The Indians were also invited. Morton, with a classical flourish, regarded them as remnants of the "scattered Trojans" that had been dispersed "after such time as Brutus left *Latium*."

An eighty-foot pine Maypole was erected as the centerpiece of the revels. To the clatter of "drumes, gunnes, pistols and other fitting insturments," they danced, celebrated and sang:

> Drinke and be merry, merry, merry, boyes;
> Let all your delight be in Hymen's joyes;
> Io to Hymen, now the day is come,
> About the merry Maypole take a Roome.

From then onward, the community Morton founded was known by friends and foes as Merrymount, a warm pagan symbol, burning its light irreverently against the austere Plymouth cold.

To the Pilgrims, Morton and his "idle or idoll Maypole" were anathema. Bradford complained of him as a "Lord of Misrule," whose subjects spent their time vainly, in drinking and frivolity, "inviting the Indean women for their consorts, dancing and frisking togither (like so many fairies, or furies rather), and worse practises. As if they had anew revived and celebrated the feasts of the Roman Goddes Flora, or the beas[t]ly practieses of the madd Bacchinalians." As if there were no debt to higher power, no thought of the morrow, as if their "joylity would have lasted ever."

The Pilgrims saw a wilderness of trials for the Christian spirit in the New World; Morton envisioned a garden of earthly delights. To the Saints, America was the "Devil's territory," and they entered it as a terrain on which they would vanquish Satan's allies and establish a "new English Israel." Morton found in America a paradise, where nature's riches and natural humanity revealed the poverty of progress and the vanity of worldly goods.

What need had anyone of anything more than food and clothing? he asked in an account he wrote of *The New English Canaan:* "Why should not the Natives of New England be sayd to live richly having no want of either?" If the beggars of London could with so much ease "furnish themselves with foode, at all seasons, there would not be so many starved in the streets, neither would so many gaoles be stuffed, or gallouses furnished with poore wretches, as I have seene them." The natives of New England may have lacked the benefit of the civilized arts like navigation—"which is the very sinnus of a flourishing Commonwealth." Yet, they were supplied with "all manner of needfull things, for the maintenance of life and lifelyhood," and indeed they led "the more happy and freer life, being voyde of care, which torments the mindes of so many Christians."

Merrymount was a threat to Plymouth's order not only by its mischievous example, but as a refuge for those who joined its rebellion. against the Puritan design. If Merrymount thrived, Bradford complained, the Pilgrims could not hope to keep their servants. For Morton "would entertaine any, how vile soever, and all the scume of the countrie or any discontents would flock to him from all places." Worse yet, to maintain Merrymount's "riotous prodigallitie and profuse excess" Morton sold arms to the Indians, instructed them in their use and employed them to hunt game and beaver.

O the horiblness of this vilanie! [lamented the Governor
of Plymouth]. How many both Dutch and English have
been latly slaine by those Indeans, thus furnished; ... Oh!
that princes and parlements would take some timly order
to prevente this mischeefe, and at length to suppress it, by
some exemplerie punishmente upon some of these gaine
thirstie murderers, (for they deserve no better title,) before
their collonies in these parts be over throwne by these
barbarous savages, thus armed with their owne weapons,
by these evill instruments, and traytors to their neighbors
and cuntrie.

It was not long before Bradford and the Pilgrims determined
to rid themselves of Morton and his "turbulente" company.
For the safety of themselves, their wives and children, the
Plymouth leaders resolved to send an armed troop to Merrymount, under their military commander, Miles Standish, dubbed
by Morton "my Captaine Shrimpe."

Between Plymouth's stern force and the anarchic impulse of
Morton's Merrymount, there was little contest. Taken by
stealth while his confederates were dispersed in their daily
tasks, Morton was quickly overcome and made a prisoner. In
Plymouth, Miles Standish spoke long and earnestly for his
execution, but Morton was an aristocrat with powerful friends
in London, and policy dictated banishment instead.

While waiting for a ship to transport him to England, the
prisoner was secured for safekeeping on the Isles of Shoals off
the mouth of the Piscataqua River. There the Pilgrims left him
for a month in the dead of winter without food or shelter and
clad only in the "thinne suite" which he was wearing. In this
plight the founder of Merrymount might have perished, if not
for "the Salvages," who, as he later recorded in a poignant
observation, "tooke notice that mine Host was a Sachem of
Passonagessit." The Indians brought bottles of strong liquor
and food to him, and came to "unite themselves into a league
of brotherhood," he wrote, "so full of humanity are these infi-
dels before these Christians."

2

Magnalia Christi Americana

THE settling of Plymouth Plantation and a score of colonies
along the New England coastline in the following years was
like a fragile rain before a flood. The "good news" from
America arrived in the mother country in an hour of shrinking
prospects and threatening trials, and its promise of opportunity
soon spurred a great migration to the new-found vineyards to
the west. In 1628, Plymouth contained more colonists than all
of New England. Two years later it was not even the largest
of the settlements.

On a summer day in 1630, the board of directors and the
major stockholders of the Massachusetts Bay Company arrived
in Boston to take possession of their recently founded colony.
On board their flagship, the *Arbella*, Governor John Winthrop
proclaimed a frontier covenant between God and the colonizing force: "We shall finde that the God of Israell is among us,
when tenn of us shall be able to resist a thousand of our enemies,
when hee shall make us a prayse and glory, that men shall say
of succeeding plantacions; the Lord make it like that of New
England."

These settlers were a more substantial group than their Pilgrim predecessors. Reformist rather than radical in religion,
they were from the landed gentry and commercial classes.
Their settlement at once supplanted Plymouth as the dominant
colonial authority in the north.

That same year, the vessels bearing the builders of the Bay Colony were joined by others bringing in their hulls a thousand English Israelites to the wilderness Zion. As ship after ship laid its cargo on the shoreline, settlements sprang up along the inlet-laced coast and then inland along the waterways. Within a decade, eight thousand colonists were engaged in various trades and were asserting varying claims within the boundaries of the Massachusetts Bay Plantation. This still constituted less than half those who had arrived during the migration to swarm "as from an hive overstocked with bees" through the forests and rock-encrusted fields of New England.

At first the native tribes inhabiting the region were as accommodating to the bay settlers as the Wampanoags had been to the *Mayflower* party at Plymouth and for the same reasons. For the site of the new "Bible Plantation" was the heart of that devastated region through which Thomas Morton had traveled ten years earlier. Like the Plymouth natives, the pathetic remnants of the once powerful Massachusetts tribe were vulnerable to their unscathed rivals—Tarrantines to the north, Narragansetts and Pequots to the south, Nipmucs to the west. They had cause as well to remember the stabbers and cutthroats of Wessagusset and their red-haired Captain Miles Standish.

But as the stream of settlers reached further and further into the wilderness, the natives began to resist it. Conflicts ruptured the forest silence, and rumors of conspiracy raced through the settlement outposts. Just as the currents seemed ready to plunge the sides into combat, however, plague struck the heart of the native communities and the tension subsided. "God ended the Controversy," a Puritan chronicler observed, "by sending the Small-pox amongst the Indians."

Not for seventeen years had there been a scourge of illness such as now descended on the native villages in the vicinity of the bay plantation. Before the fever had run its course, thousands of natives had vanished from the valleys and uplands of southern New England, including seven hundred of the Narragansetts, its most potent and numerous tribe.

The disease affected only two of the English families settled in the region. While offering care to the native sick and aid in burying their dead, the colonists meditated on their fortune: "If God were not pleased with our inheriting these parts," observed Winthrop, the principal shareholder of the Massachusetts Bay Company, "why did he drive out the natives before us and why doth he still make roome for us, by diminishinge them as we increase?" To this reflection, the keeper of the Charlestown records added his own accounting: "Without this remarkable terrible stroke of God upon the natives, [we] would with much more difficulty have found room, and at a far greater charge have obtained and purchased land."

If the plague lessened the charge on land, the act of purchase was itself a means of diminishing the costs of military conquest. In the planters' eyes, legal title to the New World was established in the very act of its discovery by a Christian King, and colonizers came already endowed with patents, as agents of the royal Crown. To this pre-emptive claim they added another: the "right of possession" over land not colonized or cultivated—*vacuum domicilium credit occupanti.* "As for the Natives of New England," Winthrop wrote, "they enclose noe land, neither have any setled habytation, nor any tame Cattle to improve the Land by ... soe as if we leave them sufficient for their use, we may lawfully take the rest."

Patent and possession established the legal basis of the English colonization. The "right of purchase" was its *modus operandi.* For the most part, the colonists found the natives willing collaborators. Whether the tribes understood the transactions which alienated their lands is doubtful. They lived by communal traditions and their commerce did not include purchase and trade of their ancestral dwelling places. The purchasers offered them guarantees of liberty for fishing, hunting and "convenient planting" so that in the end, for hoes, knives and assorted trinkets the colonizers bought the woods, fields and valleys in which the Indians had lived for thousands of years.

So pliable were the inhabitants and so eager the purchasers, that governmental control was necessary to keep the pace of exploitation from outstripping the power to enforce it. While the weaker tribes accommodated, bargained and affixed their signs to the official deeds, the stronger watched and waited, and in the end waited too long.

Among those who cast a cold eye on this progress were the Pequots, a proud and powerful tribe inhabiting the spacious river valley on Massachusetts' southwestern frontier. The Pequots were originally Mohicans of the upper Hudson River, and had only recently migrated to the region. A fierce and feared people, they had quickly established their primacy over the other tribes of the valley.

It was into this territory that the bay settlers now extended their claims. For years the traders of New England had searched in vain for a phantom "Lake of the Iroquois," which was thought to be the source of all northern furs, and from which it was believed all the rivers of the north flowed to the sea. By moving west, the Puritan merchants hoped to reach the source and cut off all their competitors.

At first the Mystic River was thought to lead to the fabled lake, and then the Merrimac. But the greatest efforts and the highest hopes were directed toward the stream the Indians called *Quinatucquet* (meaning "At the Long Tidal River"), whose course divided New England in the west. In 1633, following the lead of the trader John Oldham and the Pilgrim Edward Winslow, the Massachusetts fur traders set up posts on the banks of the river, which they called Connecticut. At the same time, the flow of immigrants from the migration was creating an increasing appetite for new territory. In 1635, for "want of land" in the Bay Colony, three Massachusetts settlements relocated themselves a hundred miles away along the river at Matianuck, Pyquag and Saukiog, which they rechristened Windsor, Wethersfield and Hartford. At Hartford, which was founded by Thomas Hooker, the most famous preacher in New England, the General Court of Connecticut met for the first time in 1637 and resolved "that there shalbe an offensive warr agt the Pequoitt."

As in other frontier wars, the events which led to the conflict did not appear to pose the land question directly. It seemed instead to hinge on the mysterious death of a Virginia trader named John Stone. Stone had made himself *persona non grata* in virtually every community of the northern patent and had once come close to stabbing the Governor of Plymouth. In the spring of 1634, he and his eight-man crew were en route to

Virginia, when they paused to explore the trading prospects of the Connecticut River. There they kidnapped some Indians for ransom, but were then attacked themselves and killed. The natives involved were assumed by the colonial authorities to be Pequots.

Embroiled with the Dutch to the west and the Narragansetts to the east, the Pequots were eager to avoid a third major antagonist. When they learned of the colonies' concern for the dead men, they approached the Bay Colony in a spirit of conciliation. When they arrived in Boston, their emissaries denied responsibility, saying that Stone had attacked his assailants first and provoked his own undoing. Moreover, the natives involved were not Pequots and their sachem had since been killed by the Dutch, while all the rest "were dead of the pox, except two." But the General Court held that even if the culprits were not Pequots themselves, they were tributaries and the Pequots were responsible.

Since they were not ready to go to war with the formidable Bay Colony, the Pequots had no choice but to sign the treaty they were now offered. It provided for the surrender of those guilty of Stone's death and the payment of a large indemnity; it also stated their willingness to accept commercial relations with the bay traders and "to yield up Connecticut."

While signing the document, the Pequots kept their own counsel. Only part of the required indemnity was ever paid; the alleged assassins were not surrendered; and when a trader, John Oldham, arrived in Pequot territory the following spring to test its commercial provisions, he found them disinclined to do business—"a very false people."

The Puritan leaders viewed this defiance as a dangerous challenge to their authority on the frontier. Reiterating their demands, they readied themselves to terminate the league with the Pequots and "revenge the blood of our Countrimen as occasion shall serve." Before any action could be taken, however, news came that John Oldham had been killed in his boat off Block Island.

A frontier trader like Stone, Oldham had been twice banished from Plymouth for unscrupulous dealings, but since then had become a prominent figure in Bay Colony politics and commerce. This time the Pequots were clearly innocent of the deed. Twelve of Oldham's assailants, killed at the scene, were identified as Block Island Indians, a tribe subordinate to the Narragansetts. Governor Winthrop and the Massachusetts authorities identified the Narragansetts as "contrivers" of his death. The motive, they reasoned, was that "he went to make peace, and trade with the Pekods," their bitter enemies.

Still suffering from the devastations of the recent plague, the Narragansetts were anxious to maintain a friendly posture toward the Bay Colony. Their principal sachems, Canonicus and Miantonomo, had not been privy to the killing of Oldham and indicated their readiness to make satisfactory restitution to the Puritan authority. At the same time, the Pequots and their sachem, Sassacus, were said to be harboring two surviving perpetrators of the deed and unwilling to cooperate. Thus, the focus of Massachusetts' policy shifted once again to the Pequot problem.

A force of ninety volunteers was assembled under Captain John Endicott, whose orders were to put to death all the native men on Block Island, seize the women and children, and take possession of the area. He was then to proceed to the Pequot territory to demand the "murderers" of Oldham and Stone, the payment of a new and harsher indemnity, and the surrender of several Pequot children as hostages to ensure the Indians' good faith.

When they reached Block Island, Endicott's troops met sporadic resistance and killed fourteen natives. But the main body of the inhabitants had fled before their advance. For two days, Endicott and his men burned the empty wigwams, mats and provisions of the departed villagers, destroying their harvested corn and smashing their beached canoes. Finally, in frustration, they "destroyed some of their dogs instead of men."

Endicott then proceeded along the sound to Pequot Harbor at the mouth of the Pequot River. On his arrival, he challenged the Pequots to battle, which they declined, retreating under fire. The Block Island ritual was then repeated. The expeditionary force laid waste the Pequot village, staved the canoes and wounded some of the defenders, killing two before departing the valley for home.

War was now unavoidable and the Pequots began to look for allies. Their principal hopes were directed toward their rivals, the Narragansetts, who were still able to summon more than a thousand warriors to battle. With the Pequots they shared primacy throughout the wilderness that was now pressed between the boundaries of the Plymouth and Massachusetts plantations.

Appearing before the Narragansett sachems, the Pequot emissaries drew the lessons of the sixteen years that had passed since Samoset had welcomed the English and Massasoit made his Pilgrim peace. "The English were strangers," they warned, "and begane to overspread their countrie, and would deprive them therof in time, if they were suffered to grow and increse; and if the Narigansets did assist the English to subdue them, they did but make way for their owne overthrow, for if they were rooted out, the English would soone take occasion to subjugate them."

To overcome the supremacy in arms which the English possessed, the Pequots proposed a strategy of attrition. If the Narragansetts would but join them, they explained, "they would not come into open battle with [the English] but fire their houses, kill their katle, and lye in ambush for them as they went abroad upon their occasions; and all this they might easily doe without any danger to them selves. The which course being held, they well saw the English could not long subsiste, but they would either be starved with hunger, or forced to forsake the countrie."

At first the Narragansetts inclined to this counsel. They had been suspected of Oldham's murder by Massachusetts. Their tributaries, the Wampanoags, had been seduced from them by Plymouth, and they themselves suspected the colonists of sending the recent plague among them. If the Narragansetts had persisted, the Bay Colony might have been faced with an overwhelming opponent and suffered an early demise. But a diplomatic stroke undermined the Pequot strategy. The Massachusetts authorities summoned Roger Williams from exile in Providence to undertake a mission to the Narragansett sachems, who were his friends, and detach them from the Pequot enemy.

It was an irony that made Williams the savior of New England. Half a year earlier he had been cast out of the Bay Colony as a heretic and subversive, his views publicly refuted by Thomas Hooker, the spiritual father of the Connecticut River settlements.

A separatist minister, Williams had arrived in Boston in 1631, just after the Bay Colony builders. Almost at once, however, he had come into uncompromising collision with the Puritan oligarchy and its mission to Zion: "the first rebel [as Cotton Mather later said] against the divine church-order established in the wilderness."

Williams had rebelled against the theological foundations of the Puritan state: the idea of a Chosen People and the ambition to build God's Kingdom on earth. He had denied the King's patent to the New World territories, denouncing as "sinfull" the notion "that Christians have a right to Heathans Lands." "The world lies in wickedness... like a wilderness," he contended, irremediably separate from the "garden of the church." Ever since the crucifixion, there could be no covenanted nation, no divinely guided state. To attempt to follow "that pattern of Israel" was inevitably to embrace a world of "bloody, irreligious and inhuman oppressions and destructions," to become a nation persecuting others in the name of Christ.

The Court of Massachusetts banished Williams, driving him, as he later recalled, "unkindly and unChristianly... from my house and land and wife and children" into the New England cold. In the dead of winter 1636, he fled for his life to find the only refuge the New World offered him—among the wilderness natives.

Some years earlier, while residing in Plymouth, Williams had stayed with Massasoit and spent many hours among the Wampanoags "in their very wild houses and by their barbarous fires," learning their language and customs. He had brought them gifts and become a respected and trusted friend. Unlike many of his countrymen, Williams did not regard the natives as a race inferior by birth or (as some men believed) children of the devil. For him, their "barbarism" lay in the fact that they lacked the arts and artifacts of civilization and the saving grace of Christian truth. "They have no books, nor letters," he reported, "and conceive their fathers never had, and therefore they are easily persuaded that the God that made Englishmen is a greater God, because he hath so richly endowed the English above themselves."

It was to Massasoit and the Wampanoags that Williams turned in his darkest hour. He lived in their "filthy smoakie holes" for three bitter winter months. When the spring came, Massasoit gave him a grant to settle on the Seekonk River, which fed into the northern end of Narragansett Bay. His plans for a settlement were not welcomed by the Plymouth and Massachusetts authorities. They feared that if a colony were planted so near, "the infection would easily spread" to their own churches. A short time after Williams had begun to clear his fields, he received a letter from Edward Winslow, then Governor of Plymouth, noting that he was still within the colony's boundaries and advising him to move across the water to the wilderness, where he might be "as free as themselves."

The western shores of the Seekonk River were ruled by the Narragansetts. There, on land ceded as an "act of love and favor" by the sachems Canonicus and Miantonomo, Williams founded a plantation which he called Providence, "in a Sence of Gods mercifull providence unto me in my destresse."

Williams planned his settlement as a shelter for other dissenters and seekers like himself. The government he created was secular, and freedom of conscience was the first principle of state. Soon Providence was followed by other towns in Narragansett—Portsmouth, Newport and Warwick—all founded by heretics and exiles from the theocratic oligarchies of the shore. In time they were united, becoming "The Colony of Rhode Island and Providence Plantations," the most democratic in the New World.

Dissent as he might from the theological premises of the Bay Colony fathers, Williams shared a basic sympathy of origins and purpose. While rejecting the gospel of the imperial state, he accepted its civil mission: the things of Caesar would be rendered unto Caesar. He had denounced the blasphemy under which the English King laid claim to the New World; but a few years after founding Providence, he traveled to England to secure a patent for Rhode Island. His reasons were practical, to protect his colony against others' claims. Yet, he too accepted the inevitability of native displacement, preferring only that it be by lawful purchase rather than sanctimonious plunder. The submergence of native culture was justified as the march of civil progress: not because the natives were heathens, but because they were "barbarians" who lacked the blessings of European learning and science.

In the late spring of 1636, as the foundations of Providence were being laid, the greatest peril to its survival was the imminent prospect of Massachusetts' war with the natives. If the Indians of Narragansett should join the Pequots in their conflict with the Bay, the infant settlements of Providence, lying in the frontier between them, would be in mortal jeopardy. When the Massachusetts Colony summoned Williams to employ "his utmost and speediest endeavors to break and hinder" the Narragansett and Pequot alliance, he gave himself wholeheartedly to the mission.

"The Lord helped me immediately to put my life into my hand," he recalled later, "and, scarce acquainting my wife, to ship myself, all alone, in a poor canoe, and to cut through a stormy wind, with great seas, every minute in hazard of life, to the Sachem's house." The destruction of the Indian villages at Block Island and Pequot Harbor by Endicott and his troops, and the questions surrounding Oldham's death, were far from the peacemaker's mind when he arrived at Miantonomo's dwelling. Only the fierce image of the Pequot warriors stirred his soul: "Three days and nights my business forced me to lodge and mix with the bloody Pequot ambassadors, whose hands and arms, methought, wreaked with the blood of my countrymen, murdered and massacred by them on Connecticut river, and from whom I could not but nightly look for their bloody knives at my own throat also."

The trust which Williams had built among the Narragansetts and their own rankling enmity with the Pequots worked to make his embassy a success. Their sachems rejected the Pequot proposal. Shortly afterward, a messenger came from the Narragansett camp bringing a severed Pequot hand to the Massachusetts governors as a sign of their allegiance. In September, Miantonomo and two of Canonicus' sons arrived in Boston to sign a formal treaty of peace, friendship and free trade with Massachusetts.

During the next months an air of insecurity hung over the Connecticut settlements and trading posts as scattered raids by bands of Pequots resulted in a mounting settler toll. Lion Gardiner, who commanded the Saybrook Fort near the mouth of the Connecticut, had complained bitterly of Endicott's expeditions: "You come hither to raise these Wasps about my ears and then you will take wings and flee away." Now he put a ban on all landings between Saybrook and Wethersfield. A settler named Tilley disobeying these orders was ambushed and captured. His Pequot captors cut off his hands and feet, after which he lived three days, impressing his tormentors as a brave man "because he cried not in his torture."

On April 18, the Bay Colony formally declared war on the Pequots. Five days later, at Wethersfield, two hundred natives attacked a small group of colonists at the request of a local tribe that felt its land rights had been abused. Nine colonists, including a woman and child, were massacred and two women were carried off (later released unharmed). On May 1, the Connecticut General Court declared war.

Plymouth held back. Bradford reminded Winthrop that in the past Massachusetts had taken advantage of its superior strength to deprive Plymouth of its trading post at Windsor on the Connecticut River. Endicott's actions "provoking the Pequots," he argued, were in fact the main cause of the war. Moreover, Plymouth had no responsibility for the deceased Captain Stone, and was under no obligation to revenge his death.

In answer, Winthrop invoked the frontier's imperative. Acknowledging that the man "for whom this war was begun" was not from Plymouth, the bay Governor observed that Stone and his men "were none of ours either." Yet, "in case of perill," he supposed that Plymouth would not stand upon such terms:

"we conceive that you looke at the Pequents, and all other Indieans, as a common enemie," he wrote. The Indians' rage might begin with only "one parte of the English," but should they prevail in such a struggle, they would surely pursue their advantage "to rooting out of the whole nation."

Plymouth accepted the argument. On June 7, 1637, its General Court resolved to send fifty armed men "at their owne charge" to add to Massachusetts' hundred and sixty and Connecticut's ninety for war "against the Pequin Indians, in revenge of the innocent blood of the English which the said Pequins have barbarously shed, and refuse to give satisfaction for."

It was the Connecticut forces, led by Captain John Mason, that launched the first assault and delivered the "main Stroak." They were supported by a contingent of twenty Massachusetts soldiers under John Underhill, and sixty Mohegan warriors. A year earlier, these natives had been Pequots themselves, but they had seceded with their sachem Uncas from the main tribe under Sassacus and revived the Mohegan name. In an initial skirmish with the Pequots at Saybrook, Uncas demonstrated his fidelity to the colonists by presenting them with four enemy heads and a captive who scornfully taunted them that they "durst not kill a Pequot." To refute him, the colonists tied one of his legs to a post and tore his limbs from his body until Underhill ended his misery with a shot. Afterward, the body was cooked and eaten by the Mohegans.

The main battle of the war took place in early June at the Pequot enclosure, a palisaded village containing some seventy wigwams. Situated on the Mystic River, the palisade covered almost an acre of ground and consisted of tree trunks sunk several feet in the earth and fastened together. Inside its walls were most of the Pequot tribe.

The night before the attack, the Connecticut soldiers and nearly three hundred Mohegan and Narragansett warriors lay in secret camp outside the perimeter of the palisade. Within the fortress they could hear sounds of celebration and song. The Pequots suspected nothing. At dawn the attackers entered the enclosure. As the bewildered natives scattered from their houses, Underhill, the portly Captain of the Connecticut troops, snatched a torch from inside one of the straw-roofed wigwams and with the aid of a strong wind set fire to the village. As the flames soared, the soldiers withdrew and formed a circle around the walls. From this vantage, they slew any Pequot who fled the inferno:

> Many courageous fellows were unwilling to come out, and fought most desperately through the palisadoes, so as they were scorched and burnt with the very flame, and were deprived of their arms—in regard the fire burnt their very bowstrings—and so perished valiantly. Mercy they did deserve for their valor, could we have had opportunity to have bestowed it. Many were burnt in the fort, both men, women, and children. Others forced out, and came in troops ... twenty and thirty at a time, which our soldiers received and entertained with the point of the sword. Down fell men, women, and children; those that scaped us, fell into the hands of the Indians that were in the rear of us. It is reported by themselves, that there were about four hundred souls in this fort, and not above five of them escaped out of our hands.

Some thought the victors had exceeded their commission. As Christians, should they not have shown more mercy and compassion? But Underhill referred such doubts to "David's warre." For by that Biblical precedent, when a people was grown to such "a height of bloud and sinne against God and man," God had "no respect to persons but harrowes them, and sawes them, and puts them to the sword." So Underhill concluded, "We had sufficient light from the word of God for our proceedings." Captain Mason agreed: "This was God seen in the Mount, crushing his proud Enemies and the Enemies of his People ... burning them up in the Fire of his Wrath, and dunging the Ground with their flesh; It was the Lord's doings and it was marvellous in our Eyes!"

The Massachusetts General Court set aside June 15 as a day of Thanksgiving "for the victory obtained against the Pequods and for other mercies," while the government of Connecticut rewarded Captain Mason with five hundred acres of Pequot

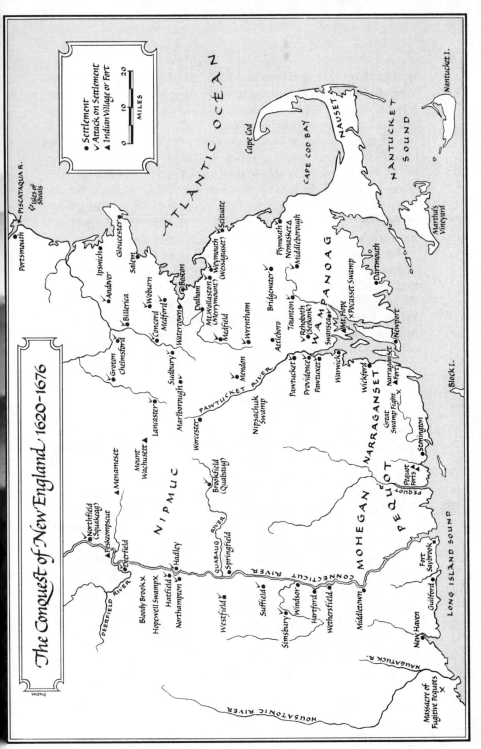

The Conquest of New England 1620-1676

Settlement •
Attack on Settlement ⋁
Indian Village or Fort ▲

MILES
0   10   20

WONG

land, and another five hundred to be divided among his troops.

Several hundred Pequots, including their sachem Sassacus, had not been in the Mystic palisade but in their camp at Pequot Harbor. At the urging of Roger Williams and others with knowledge of the Indians, this remnant was now made the object of general pursuit, lest they escape embittered to fight again. In the hunt for the Pequot survivors, the soldiers of the New England Zion were joined by Narragansett and Mohegan warriors, now incited by the blood of their once proud adversaries. "Sachem Head" on the map of modern Connecticut memorializes the fury of their revenge.

The bulk of the Pequot tribe fled west toward the Dutch plantation of New Netherland, but encumbered and slowed by their families, were quickly tracked to a swamp near Quinnipiac. As night fell, the circle of pursuers tightened around the survivors who huddled in the dense brush of the swamp. When morning came, the circle was closed. "They saw several Heaps of them sitting close together, upon whom they discharged their Peices laden with ten or twelve Pistol-bullets at a Time, putting the Muzles of their Peices under the Boughs within a few yeards of them; so as besides those that were found Dead (near twenty) it was judged that many more were killed and sunk into the Mire, and never were minded more by Friend or Fo."

Sassacus and about thirty of his warriors fled to the Mohawk country in the west, but found no refuge there. In August, the scalps of the Pequot sachem and five of his chiefs were brought to Hartford as a Mohawk offering to the victors.

Of the few Pequots that survived, about two hundred were divided between the Mohegan and Narragansett tribes as vassals, for which the colonies were paid an annual tribute. Others were sent to the Bermudas to be sold at auction, while some were distributed as chattels among the victors—the first slaves in New England. A month after the massacre, Roger Williams wrote to Governor Winthrop, requesting a Pequot servant: "Much honored sir: It having again pleased the Most High to put into your hands another miserable drone of Adam's degenerate seed, and our brethren by nature, I am bold (if I may not offend in it) to request the keeping and bringing up of one of the children. I have fixed mine eye on this little one but I will not be peremptory in my choice, but will rest in your loving pleasure for him or any, etc."

The Pequot chattels were shipped to the West Indies in the vessel *Desire*, which returned seven months later from Providence and Tortugas in the Caribbean with a cargo of "cotton, and tobacco and negroes." Thus the Pequot War marked also the appearance of black slavery in New England. The *Desire* became the region's first slaver, launching the triangular commerce in human cargo that would eventually promote the growth of a financial and industrial power unparalleled in the world.

The massacre at Mystic River and the victorious campaign that followed meant not only the defeat but the abolition of the Pequot Nation. When the peace was signed at Hartford, Miantonomo and Uncas were the sole native signatories to the pact. No representatives of that "insolent and barbarous" people were present, for it had been decided by the victors that "the remnant of that nation should not be suffered ... either to be a distinct people, or to retayne the name of Pequatts, or to settle in the Pequatt country."

Victory in the Pequot War removed the main obstacle to the colonists' expansion on the Connecticut frontier. An army of occupation was sent to the Pequot country to annex it as a spoil. At Pequot Harbor a settlement was built and named New London, and the Pequot River, which ran beside it, was christened Thames. Within two years the foundations were laid of settlements at Guilford, Milford, Stratford, Fairfield, Norwalk and Stamford in Connecticut, and New Haven at Quinnipiac, which became a colony in 1638.

The destruction of the Pequots also changed the balance of military power in New England. From Long Island Sound to the Piscataqua River there was hardly a tribe that failed to acknowledge the colonial authority. "This Overthrow given to the Pequots," summarized an official history, "struck such a Terror into all the *Indians* in those Parts ... that they sought our Friendship, and tendered to be under our Protection."

The prophecy the Pequots had made to the Narragansetts

began to be realized. As soon as the colonists' victory was complete, their suspicions shifted to their native allies. On several occasions Miantonomo was summoned to Boston to swear that the Narragansetts intended no conspiracy against the Bay Colony.

As he watched the spread of the English across the southern New England wilderness, the Narragansett sachem reconsidered the course he had taken. On a visit to Block Island, he told a gathering of Indians that they must regard themselves brothers, the way the English did, and be united as they were. "Otherwise we shall be all gone shortly, for you know our fathers had plenty of deer and skins, our plains were full of deer, as also our woods, and of turkies, and our coves full of fish and fowl. But these English having gotten our land, they with scythes cut down the grass, and with axes felled the trees; their cows and horses eat the grass, and their hogs spoil our clam banks, and we shall all be starved; therefore it is best for you to do as we, for we are all the Sachems from east to west... and we are all resolved to fall upon them all, at one appointed day."

Miantonomo's plans never materialized. The tribes remained divided, while his own forces alone were too weak to challenge the Bay Colony, whose inhabitants were now more numerous than all the native survivors of plague and warfare in the region.

Nevertheless, in 1643, the colonists formed a military alliance, calling themselves the United Colonies of New England. It was formed, explained Bradford, to answer "the plottings of the Narigansets, (ever since the Pequents warr,)" which had brought all the Indians "into a generall conspiracie against the English in all parts." Although Rhode Island was excluded, it was the first intercolonial pact among the states of the New World, and the forerunner of all their future unions:

> Wheras we all came into these parts of America with one and the same end and aime, namly, to advance the kingdome of our Lord Jesus Christ, and to injoye the liberties of Gospell in puritie with peace... and wheras we live encompassed with people of severall nations and strange languages, which herafter may prove injurious to us and our posterities; and for as much as the natives have formerly

committed sundrie insolencies and outrages upon severall plantations of the English, and have of late combined themselves against us ... That as in nation and religion, so in other respects, we be and continue one, according to the tenor and true meaning of the insuing artciles. (1) Wherfore it is fully agreed and concluded by and betweene the parties or jurisdictions above named, and they joyntly and severally doe by these presents agree and conclude, that they all be and henceforth be called by the name of THE UNITED COLONIES OF NEW-ENGLAND.

The first meeting of the United Colonies was in September. One month earlier, a battle had taken place between the forces of Uncas and Miantonomo. Betrayed by two of his captains, Miantonomo was captured. As a gesture to the English, Uncas then surrendered his prisoner to the authorities in Hartford.

This confronted the United Colonies with a dilemma. They agreed that it would not be safe to set Miantonomo at liberty, but as Winthrop observed, "neither had we sufficient ground for us to put him to death." In this difficulty, they called in five religious elders who gave their unanimous opinion that Miantonomo should die, because he had contrived "a general conspiracy among the Indians to cut off all the English" and also because "he was of a turbulent and proud spirit, and would never be at rest."

Although they now had religious sanction to kill Miantonomo, the United Colonies still balked at the act itself. Informing Uncas of their decision, they delivered Miantonomo into his hands. Taking him from Hartford, Uncas began the journey toward the Mohegan camp. Somewhere along the way, Uncas' brother came up behind the Narragansett sachem and "clave his head with an hatchet."

This was the end of Myantonomo, the most potent Indian prince the people of New-England had ever any concern with [wrote Stephen Hopkins, later Governor of the Rhode Island Colony], and this was the reward he received for assisting them seven years before, in their war with the Pequots. Surely a Rhode Island man may be permitted to mourn his unhappy fate, and drop a tear on the ashes of

Myantonomo, who, with his uncle Conanicus, were the best friends and greatest benefactors the colony ever had: They kindly received, fed, and protected the first settlers of it, when they were in distress, and were strangers and exiles, and all mankind else were their enemies; and by this kindness to them, drew upon themselves the resentment of the neighbouring colonies, and hastened the untimely end of the young king.

In February, the sachems Cutshamakin, Awan, Josias and Chikataubut came, in the name of all the Indians from Merrimac to Taunton, to tender themselves formally to the Governor of Massachusetts. Their covenant bound them to be ruled by the just laws and orders of the colony, "to give speedy notice of any conspiracy, attempt or evill intension" against the Puritan regime, and to abide by the Ten Commandments.

3

Metacomet

How oft have I heard both the English and Dutch (not onely the civill, but the most debauched and profane) say, These Heathen Dogges, *better kill a thousand of them then that we Christians should be indangered or troubled with them; Better they were all cut off, & then we shall be no more troubled with them: They have spilt our Christian bloud, the best way to make riddance of them, cut them all off, and so make way for Christians.*
—ROGER WILLIAMS,
Christenings Make Not Christians, 1645

LIKE the Jews of Exodus, the Puritan Saints had made a covenant with the God of wrath. "When God gives a speciall Commission," John Winthrop admonished during the dreadful passage to the New World, "he lookes to have it strictly observed." Like the children of the covenant, they were called not only to be holy in themselves, but to forge their holiness into a sword of grace. Conversion of the natives, proclaimed the Charter of Massachusetts, was "the principall Ende of this plantacion"; and the company's seal depicted an Indian pleading, "Come over and help us."

Who were these Indians, these red-skinned "naked Americans," who walked uncivil paths and worshiped dark pantheistic gods? In Puritan theology, they were remnants of the lost tribes of Israel, a race once white and now fallen into blackness to become the "bond slaves of Sathan." "Though we know not *when* or *how* these Indians became inhabitants of this mighty continent," wrote the Reverend Cotton Mather, "yet we may guess that probably the devil decoyed those miserable salvages hither in hopes that the Gospel of the Lord Jesus Christ would never come here to destroy or disturb his *absolute empire* over them."

Aboard the fleets of empire, politics and religion pursued an inseparable course. "Albeit faith be not wrought by the sword," proclaimed a Bay Colony edict, "neverthelesse . . . the blaspheming of the true God cannot be excused by any ignorance or infirmity of human nature . . . no person within this jurisdiction, whether Christian *or* pagan, shall wittingly and willingly presume to blaspheme his holy name . . . or reproach the holy religion of God as if it were but a polliticke devise to keepe ignorant men in awe. . . . If any person . . . shall breake this lawe, they shall be putt to death."

English Protestants scorned their Catholic competitors, who advanced the gospel under the flag of a trading empire. French Jesuits were content to raise a cross in native villages, sprinkle water and call it conversion. The Puritan errand was a more substantial mission to colonize, to purify and build. The purpose of the "Indian Worke," explained John Eliot, the chief Puritan apostle to the natives, was "to Civilize the wild people, thereby to prepare them for religion." Any work of grace to the natives, the Reverend Richard Mather agreed, had to be "accompanied with the Reformation of their disordered lives . . . their neglect of Labor, and their living in idelness and pleasure."

Those converted became known as "praying Indians" and were congregated in "praying towns" administered by the United Colonies. These were mainly the creation of Eliot, who had learned the Algonquin language from a servant taken captive in the Pequot War. In 1646, Eliot preached his first native sermon at the village of Waban, sachem of the Nonatums, a Massachusetts tribe. Soon other natives of Massachusetts came to observe the services at Waban's village. The sachem of Concord was "so farre affected" by what he saw, "that he desired to become more like to the English and to cast off those *Indian* wild and sinful courses."

Eliot was invited to preach at Concord, and in 1647 several sachems among the praying Indians there agreed to a code the colonists had drawn up for them. The rules adopted by the converts bound them to have no more than one wife, to pay their debts to the English, to observe the Lord's day, to knock on English doors before entering (and to expect the same), to abjure the sins of murder, theft and fornication, and "to weare their *haire* comely as the English do," and many similar strictures. "They desire they may bee a towne," their submission concluded, "and either to dwell on this side the *Beare Swamp*, or at the eastside of Mr. *Flint's Pond*."

The adoption of English styles and manners distinguished the praying Indians from the other natives as much as their English faith; the praying towns consolidated their separation.

The first praying town was created by Eliot at Natick in 1651 to be occupied by Waban and the Nonatum converts. Eventually there were fourteen such towns. In creating them, the Biblically minded Eliot invoked Jethro's advice to Moses, selecting the rulers of tens, fifties and hundreds from among the tribes at his command, "makeing the word of God theire only *magna charta*." Their governments were formally appointed by the colonies, who supplied them with tools, livestock and other useful goods and expected them to maintain order and report any "mischiefe" afoot against the English. Tithes to the church replaced tribute to the sachems.

The same Christian faith that stiffened the Saints for their trials in the wilderness, sapped the fibers of native strength. The Indian who accepted the gospel came to regard his people as conspirators with Satan, his ancestral ways as a fallen and inferior path. Tribes decimated by plague and war were most receptive to the Word; stronger tribes resisted. Among them were the Narragansetts led by Miantonomo's son, Canonchet, whom the colonists distrusted as an even prouder man than his father; also the Wampanoags, led by the Pilgrims' ally Massasoit, and afterward by his son, Metacomet.

For forty years the peace that Massasoit had made with the white men who came to settle in Patuxet provided the Plymouth Colony with a friendly and protected frontier. Although it never approached the dimensions of its Bay neighbor, Plymouth grew steadily on lands it purchased from Massasoit and his tributary sachems. Prospering modestly on beaver and fish, it was able to pay off its debts and leave behind the precarious uncertainty of its early years. The near starving winters were memorialized with other ghosts of the recent past. The constant disputes between Indian and settler that flared along its boundaries were arbitrated by its own court under the tenets of English law.

In 1639, a treaty provided that the natives within the patent could neither give nor sell their land without the colony's consent. Four years later it was decreed that no "stray" Indian was to be allowed in the Old Colony, and after 1656 it was forbidden to sell a native such coveted goods as boats, sails or horses, in addition to the already contraband liquor and weapons. Once an isolated enclave in the Wampanoag wilderness, Plymouth had extended its sovereignty so completely that the Indian tribes themselves appeared as alien fragments in its expanding civilization.

About 1660, when he had passed his eightieth year, Massasoit died, leaving his eldest son Wamsutta to inherit his dwindling domain. Wamsutta had married Weetamoo, daughter of Corbitant, the Pocasset sachem who forty years earlier had vainly challenged the Pilgrim peace. Now Corbitant too was dead, but the marriage of his daughter to Massasoit's son strengthened the bonds of all the native tribes between Cape Cod and Narragansett Bay.

After his father's death, Wamsutta made a pilgrimage to Plymouth. His purpose was to request English names for himself and his younger brother Metacomet, as a gesture of the continuing amity between their two peoples. The Plymouth Court gave him the name Alexander after Alexander the Great of Macedon. His younger brother, Metacomet, was named Philip, after Alexander's father. Later he was called King Philip, a nickname bestowed, it was said, "for his ambitious and haughty spirit."

Less than a year after his appearance at Plymouth, Alexander received a summons from the General Court following reports that he was making league with the Narragansetts. Suspicions were further aroused when Alexander failed to answer the summons. Two of the colony's most prominent military figures,

Major Josiah Winslow and Captain William Bradford, were dispatched with orders to bring him to court.

In Plymouth too there had been a passing of generations. Edward Winslow had died in 1655 on a flagship in the Caribbean, where he had been sent by the Crown to subdue the Spanish West Indies. A year later, Miles Standish "expired his mortal life." He had been Commander in Chief of the Pilgrim army for more than three decades, acquiring a modest but prosperous estate, and counting among his possessions five horses, fourteen head of cattle, a flock of sheep and a small library containing a well-thumbed copy of Caesar's *Commentaries*. Scarcely six months later, he was followed to the grave by the venerable William Bradford, who was still Governor, as he had been almost continuously since the first Plymouth spring. Then the richest man in the colony, a result in part of the official monopoly of trade which he had shared with Miles Standish and Isaac Allerton, he left behind a 300-acre farm, a large library and a unique historical record of the Plantation to which he had devoted himself until his final breath.

The sons of Winslow and Bradford made their way across the woodland trails toward Mount Hope to fetch the reluctant sachem. Long before reaching their destination, they came upon Alexander, his wife and eight of his people at one of their hunting lodges. Outside the structure, the guns of the natives were stacked where they had left them. The Pilgrims seized these first and then with their own weapons raised and ready, burst into the room and announced the purpose of their mission to the startled party.

At this intrusion, Alexander fell into a "raging Passion," saying that the Governor had no cause to send for him in such a manner, or to credit rumors, nor would he go to Plymouth until he saw reason to do so. Winslow stepped forward, placed a pistol to the sachem's chest, and said that his orders were to bring him back, and "if he stirred or refused to go, he was a dead Man."

Implored by his counselors to yield, Alexander consented to return to Plymouth. Yet, "such was the pride and height of his spirit that the very surprizal of him so raised his choler and indignation that it put him into a fever." When this fever failed to abate during the journey to Plymouth and the interrogations that followed, Alexander was permitted to return home on a litter, leaving his two sons as hostages. But as the party reached the Taunton River, midway between Plymouth and Mount Hope, he suddenly grew worse and died.

Grief for Alexander brought many Indians to Mount Hope for the death rites and mourning ceremonies. These were followed by a celebration in honor of his brother, Philip, who succeeded him.

The assembly of so large a body of Indians, many of whom were convinced that Alexander had been poisoned, alarmed the authorities at Plymouth. They summoned Philip to appear before them. Philip responded and renewed the covenant made by his father. He declared that he wished "the continuance of that amitie and friendship that hath formerly bine between this govment and his deceased father and brother," that to this end he desired that he and his successors would remain subject to the King of England, and he pledged that he would hold to all the conditions previously agreed on and would "indeavor to carry peaceably and inoffensively towards the English."

These declarations were signed by Philip, as sachem of Pokanoket, and his uncle Unkompowin, and witnessed by his interpreter and counselor, a former praying Indian named John Sassamon.

Nonetheless, over the years Philip had come to reflect painfully on the compact that his father had made with the Pilgrims. On one occasion, he spoke openly of his feelings to a Rhode Island settler named John Borden. He recalled how his father had welcomed the Pilgrims, and how they had been but a handful then. When his father's counselors saw that the first settlers would be followed by others, they had become uneasy and then alarmed. They feared that the English would eventually attempt "to give law to the Indians and take from them their country. They therefore advised him to destroy them before they should become too strong and daring and it should be too late."

But his father had disregarded this advice. Massasoit told

his counselors and warriors "that the English knew many sciences which the Indians did not; that they improved and cultivated the earth, and raised cattle and fruits, and that there was sufficient room in the country for both the English and the Indians." So the settlers were received in friendship and given aid. They prospered; more of them came, and more of the Indians' land became theirs. "[Only] a small part of the dominions of my ancestors remains," Philip concluded; "I am determined not to live till I have no country."

In 1667, Philip was summoned to the Plymouth Court and accused of conspiring with the French and Dutch to recover his lands through war. Two years later he was accused of conspiring with the Narragansetts to the same end. In 1671, warlike preparations were reported among the Wampanoags, "the repairing of guns, suspicious assemblings and impertinent bearing towards Englishmen in divers parts of the country." Once again Philip was called to Plymouth. This time he refused to come, but after a visit from the aging Roger Williams, he agreed to meet at Taunton. On April 10, armed colonists and natives gathered in their battle dress on either side of the town meeting house.

As the parley began, Philip protested the settlers' incursions on his planting grounds and claimed that his arms and preparations were solely for defense against the Narragansetts. The colonists dismissed this as mere pretense, observing that the Narragansetts and Wampanoags were on friendlier terms than ever. Superior force decided the argument. After several hours, Philip signed a formal statement of submission.

> Whereas my Father, my Brother and my self have formerly *submitted our selves and our people unto the Kings Majesty of England, and to this Colony of New-Plymouth,* by solemn Covenant under our Hand, but I having of late through my indiscretion, and the naughtiness of my heart violated and broken this my Covenant with my friends by *taking up Armes,* with evill intent against them, and that *groundlessly;* I being now deeply sensible of my unfaithfulness and folly, do desire at this time solemnly to renew my Covenant with my ancient Friends, above mentioned.

The Taunton agreements were followed by three years of relative calm. Plymouth continued its busy expansion; Philip held his peace. Then, in January 1675, the body of Philip's former counselor, John Sassamon, was discovered lying beneath the ice of Assawompsett Pond in Middleborough, near Namasket, about fifteen miles from the Plymouth settlement.

Before his death, Sassamon had played a prominent role in native-settler relations. A Christian Indian, he had served as an interpreter for the colonies during the Pequot War, and later became a schoolteacher and missionary at Natick, assisting Eliot. Then he suddenly left his vocation and church to live again as a heathen among the Wampanoags. Serving first Alexander and then Philip as secretary and interpreter, Sassamon had taken his place in the highest tribal councils. Once again, however, he had changed his allegiance. He had left Philip, made a public repentance, and had been rebaptized. During his new conversion, he informed the Governor of Plymouth that Philip was plotting a general conspiracy against the settlements. It was not long afterward that his body was found in Assawompsett Pond.

An investigation was ordered by the Plymouth authorities and a native was brought forward who claimed to have witnessed the murder. On the basis of his report, three Wampanoags were charged, among them Tobias, one of Philip's own counselors, and Tobias' son Wampapaquan. Their arrest and indictment were closely watched in the tribal councils of New England. All realized that the men who were to stand in the dock for Sassamon's death were surrogates for Philip.

The trial was held in June and the defendants convicted. On the eighth day of the month, they were hanged.

Even before the trial and execution, inhabitants of the Swansea area had begun to report the unusual and ominous presence of armed natives in their vicinity. In the week following the executions, there were other alarms—cattle killed, corn stolen, houses broken into and robbed. There were disturbing reports, in addition, that warriors from Narragansett, Cowesit, Pocasset and other areas were coming to join Philip in Mount Hope. In that week also, Awashonks and Weetamoo, squaw sachems of the Sakonnets and Pocassets, informed visitors that Philip was preparing for war.

On June 17, a last effort was made to avert the impending conflict. A delegation of Rhode Islanders, including Deputy Governor John Easton, met with Philip and forty of his men at Trip's Ferry on Narragansett Bay and proposed an arbitration of the dispute. The Indians replied that they had suffered greatly through arbitrations in the past, and insisted that the settlers hear their grievances instead. Recorded by the Quaker Easton, and uttered on the brink of New England's cataclysm, they constituted a final statement of the native cause:

"They said they had been the first in doing good to the English, and the English the first in doing wrong. They said when the English first came, their king's father was as a great man and the English as a little child. He constrained other Indians from wronging the English and gave them corn and showed them how to plant and freely did them any good, and had let them have a hundred times more land than now the king had for his own people. But their king's brother, when he was king came miserably to die by being forced to court [and], as they judged, poisoned.

"Another grievance was that if twenty of their honest Indians testified that an Englishman had done them wrong, it was as nothing, and if but one of their worst Indians testified against any Indian or their king, when it pleased the English that was sufficient.... They did not want any of their Indians to be called or forced to be Christian Indians. They said that such were in everything more mischievous, that they were only dissemblers, and that the English made them not subject to their kings, and by their lying to wrong their kings....

"Another grievance was that when their kings sold land, the English would later say that it was more than they agreed to, and the written deed was taken as proof against all of them. Moreover, some of their kings had done wrong to sell so much, leaving their people none. Some being given to drunkenness were made drunk by the English and then cheated in the bargaining. But now their kings were forewarned not to part with the land, for nothing compared to it in value. Now they

*would disinherit those whom the English had recognized as their
sovereigns and had done this, and they would make another king
who was willing to give or sell them back their land. For now
they had no hopes left to keep any land.*"

The Rhode Islanders listened with sympathy to these complaints, and when the Indians had finished they made a final
attempt to dissuade them from a resistance that seemed futile:

"We endeavored that ... they should lay down their arms for
the English were too strong for them. *They said then the
English should do to them as they did when they were too
strong for the English.*

"So we departed without any discourteousness, and suddenly
had a letter from the Plymouth Governor that they intended
in arms to subdue Philip. But there was no information as to
what they required or what terms he refused, that their quarrel
might be resolved. And in a week's time after we had been
with the indians, the war thus began."

The first blood was shed at Swansea, in the area above Mount
Hope Neck. As a result of the previous week's incidents, most
of the colonists living in the area had abandoned their homesteads. Meanwhile, soldiers from Plymouth had arrived to
establish their headquarters at the house of the Reverend John
Miles. Shortly afterward, an old man and a youth returning to
their home saw three Indians run out of it:

"The old man bid the young man shoot, which he did, and
one of the Indians fell down, but got away again. . . . [Later]
some Indians came to the garrison and asked why they had shot
the Indian. The men in the garrison asked whether he was dead.
The Indians said yes. An English lad present said it was no
matter. The men endeavored to inform them that it was but an
idle lad's words, but the Indians went away in haste and did
not listen to them. The next day the lad that shot the Indian,
and his father, and five other English were killed. So the war
began with Philip."

Almost simultaneously, similar incidents occurred in Mattapoisett and other parts of the garrisoned area at the entrance
to the Wampanoag refuge. A group of Swansea people returning from public worship were ambushed by natives, and one

man was killed. That night at Miles's garrison one of the sentries was shot dead and two others mortally wounded. Two men were dispatched to Massachusetts to get medical aid. The following day their mutilated bodies were discovered by emissaries from the Bay who had been sent to the Wampanoags to see if arbitration was possible. The emissaries returned to recommend immediate support for the war against Philip.

As soon as the forces from Massachusetts arrived in Swansea, the army marched into the neck, hoping to trap the Wampanoags in Mount Hope. Soon after crossing Miles's bridge some five hundred yards from the garrison, they were fired on by an "ambuscade" of a dozen Indians and suffered three casualties, one mortal. The Indians retreated and they resumed their advance. Passing the burnt shells of the recently abandoned English homes, they came to Kickamuit, the narrow of the neck. There, set on poles "after the barbarous manner of those savages," were the heads and limbs of the eight Swansea settlers who had been killed three days before. A break was ordered in the march so that the troops could take down what was left of the bodies and bury them. Then they marched the final distance to Mount Hope, but reaching their destination, they found the place abandoned. Philip and the Wampanoags had fled east across the water to Pocasset, hoping to find allies for their rebellion.

In Pocasset, the squaw sachem Weetamoo welcomed them and pledged her forces to the Wampanoag cause. But her husband Petonowowett, whom she had married after the death of Alexander, refused to join Philip and left Pocasset for the English camp.

Already about fifty Christian Indians from Natick and several Mohegans had joined the colonial forces as scouts. The Narragansetts, whose loyalty had been so pivotal during the Pequot War, once again became the focus of colonial concern. Within a week of Philip's flight from Mount Hope, the Bay Colony dispatched its entire army to the Narragansett country to enlist the support of Canonchet and his warriors. It was not the first embassy sent with this intention. At the end of June, just prior to the Swansea incidents, Roger Williams and a peace mission from Massachusetts had met with the Narragansett sachems to sound out their position in the conflict. At the time, the Narragansetts had professed to hold no agreement with Philip. Yet they questioned the intervention of Massachusetts and Rhode Island in a dispute between the Wampanoags and Plymouth.

"They demanded of us why Massachusetts and Rhode Island rose, and joined with Plymouth against Philip and left not Philip and Plymouth to fight it out," reported Williams. "We answered that all the Colonies were subject to one King Charles, and it was his pleasure, and our duty and engagement, for one English man to stand to the death by each other, in all parts of the world."

At the second parley, Williams again represented the colonial cause. But this time the principal Narragansett sachems did not appear, having left the vicinity with most of their people at the approach of the Massachusetts troops. Only a handful of tribal counselors remained to sign the covenant of peace and amity that the colonists drafted. In these articles, the Indians agreed to surrender any of Philip's people who fell into their hands, and to support the English cause. Additionally, they were made to confirm "all former grants, sales, bargains or conveyances of lands, meadows, timber, grass, stones, or whatever else the English have heretofore bought or quietly possessed and enjoyed, to be unto them, and their heirs, and assigns forever."

While the Massachusetts army was negotiating in the Narragansett country, Weetamoo and Philip had begun the war against the settlements. Attacking Middleborough in the Plymouth Colony, they set fire to its buildings, forcing the inhabitants to take refuge in a mill on the Namasket River and then flee to the safety of Plymouth. Middleborough stood midway between Plymouth and Pokanoket, a little more than a mile above Namasket, where Miles Standish had once pursued Corbitant. It was in Assawompsett Pond in Middleborough that the body of John Sassamon had been found.

Following this assault, the native forces attacked and fired Rehoboth, Taunton and Swansea, destroying most of the houses, carrying off the cattle and burning the hay and corn. In Dartmouth, thirty houses were set ablaze along the Apponagansett River and many of the inhabitants killed and dismembered. Panic spread through the settlements. When the fighting was over, 160 Indians who had taken no part in the attack were promised protection and persuaded to surrender. But when they arrived in Plymouth, they were sent out of the country and sold in the Indies as slaves. Many were to follow them in the months ahead.

Meanwhile, Philip's rebellion had begun to spread beyond the Narragansett country. Led by the war chief Matoonas, whose son had been executed by the colonial authority for the murder of an Englishman, the Nipmucs attacked the frontier town of Mendon, in western Massachusetts, killing five or six of the settlers and burning the village. Two weeks after the attack on Mendon, Matoonas ambushed a peace mission, killing or wounding eight of the party. The survivors retreated to the hilltop settlement of Brookfield, where Matoonas pursued them and laid siege to the outpost.

Meanwhile, the Massachusetts army returned to Pocasset to join Plymouth in an assault on the stronghold of Weetamoo and Philip. Their refuge was a dense wilderness known as the Cedar Swamp. Projecting into the Taunton River on its eastern shore, the swamp was tangled with a thick undergrowth that made it almost impenetrable. When the colonists entered it, they were fired on, and five at once fell dead, while several others were mortally wounded. The Indians then retreated, abandoning their freshly erected camp and drawing their attackers after them, deeper into the swamp. As dusk descended on the first day, the weary colonists were ordered to turn back. In the morning, their assault was abandoned altogether.

Deciding that Philip and Weetamoo were trapped in the recesses of the swamp, the colonial commanders divided their forces, sending some to Mendon and Dartmouth, and some to establish a base on the Mount Hope peninsula. The rest were left as a guard to prevent Philip from escaping. They immediately began to construct a fort with the aim of starving the Indians out. But the pause had given the Indians the respite they needed. On the night of July 29, about three hundred men,

women and children made their way up the eastern bank of the
Taunton River and crossed over into Swansea. Their goal was
the vast wilderness of the Nipmuc territory on Massachusetts'
western frontier.

The following day, attempting to cross the Seekonk plain,
Philip and his forces were spotted by a scouting party from
Taunton. Word passed quickly to the nearby towns of Rehoboth and Providence, and a company of settlers, joined by
a party of Mohegans led by Uncas' son Oneco, began pursuit.
They caught up with the rebels in the hilly country around
Nipsachuck swamp, some twelve miles northwest of Providence,
and the following morning struck Weetamoo's camp. About
thirty Wampanoags and Pocassets were slain in the battle
before they could regroup and make their retreat. Further losses
were avoided only when the Mohegans stopped to plunder the
abandoned camp and could not be induced by the colonists to
resume their advance.

While the pursuers hesitated over the spoils, Philip and
Weetamoo divided their forces and escaped. Taking the Pocassets south, Weetamoo fled to Narragansett while Philip set
out with fifty warriors, and many more women and children,
for the Nipmuc country. There he joined the Nipmucs fresh
from their siege of Brookfield. They met at an encampment just
four miles distant from where the ruins of the settlement
smoldered in the summer light.

The Nipmucs' welcome for Philip marked a change in attitude
toward the Wampanoag leader. Many natives had scorned his
signing of the Taunton Treaty as an abject surrender and disgrace. But the events following his escape to Pocasset—the
swamp fight, the firing of the Plymouth settlements and the
flight to the west—had cast a new aura about the sachem of
Mount Hope. Not since the death of Sassacus had anyone dared
so uncompromising a challenge to the colonial power.

For the colonists, too, the figure of Philip began to assume
symbolic dimensions. They saw his hand in every new outrage
against the settlements, every added fracture of the frontier
peace. Local acts of revenge over long-standing grievances took
on the appearance of a climactic conspiracy, pitting the agents
of native darkness against the bearers of the colonial light.

As their panic intensified, the colonists' suspicions turned on still friendly tribes, whose loyalty now seemed a mask of imminent betrayal. Not even the converts were exempt. On August 22, after seven Lancaster settlers were killed by natives, Massachusetts regulars raided the unarmed village of praying Indians at nearby Marlborough, seized eleven of the inhabitants and sent them, tied together by the neck, to Boston. Continuing their march into the Pennacook country, the troops burned the village and supplies of the friendly sachem Wannalancet, near Concord. Shortly afterward, reports came that the Nonatooks of the Upper Connecticut Valley had celebrated the native victories. A hundred troops, sent to subdue them, were ambushed in Hopewell Swamp. With this attack the conflict spread in earnest to the Nipmuc territory and the war against the river settlements of the upper valley began.

Now Pocumtooks, Nonatooks, Squakheags, Quabags and Nashaways—all tribes of the Nipmuc confederation that had long lived in peace with the colonists—rose in sudden vengeance against the river towns. One after another, they struck Northfield, Deerfield, Springfield, Hadley, Northampton and Hatfield. All through September and most of October they fired the settlement buildings, laid siege to the garrison houses and destroyed the crops ripening in the autumn sun. On September 18, a provision train of almost seventy men was trapped five or six miles south of Deerfield at a place thereafter called Bloody Creek. Almost the entire contingent, representing half the male population of Deerfield, died in the ambush.

Weeks earlier, the Algonquin tribes of the north had begun to harass the remote outposts of the frontier from Merrimac to Pemaquid. The day of the ambush at Bloody Creek, the Tarrantines launched a devastating assault against the settlements along the Saco River. Their leader Squando had once been a friend to the colonists, but his trust had been turned to bitter hatred by an incident some years before. Sailors from a vessel moored in the Saco River had seen his wife attempting to cross with her baby in a canoe. Having heard that the young of savages, like those of wild animals, would swim instinctively if thrown into the flood, the sailors upset the canoe and cast its occupants overboard. The mother dove to the bottom and recovered the infant still breathing, but shortly afterward it became ill and died. Squando never forgave the outrage.

Prior to the catastrophes in the Upper Connecticut Valley, the colonial soldiers had scorned the Indians as opponents; many had said, "One Englishman was sufficient to chase ten Indians; many reckoned it was no other but *Veni, vidi, vici.*" But now the flames of a wilderness Judgment were erupting out of the forest darkness all about the settlements, and there seemed no way to quell the holocaust that threatened to engulf them.

In Boston, a Day of Humiliation was declared with fasting and prayer ("that we may set our selves sincerely to seek the Lord, rending our hearts . . . and pursue the same with a thorough Reformation of what ever hath been . . . [that] the Lord may turn from his fierce anger, that we perish not"). But even as ways were sought to appease an angry Providence, suspicion and rage against the natives increased. On October 30, an order was given for the removal of Waban and all the Christian Indians living at Natick, and for their confinement on Deer Island in Massachusetts Bay.

A month later, in the dead of winter, the Indian agents John Eliot and Daniel Gookin made a visit to the island prison. There they found the internees humble and uncomplaining:

> . . . they lived chiefly upon clams and shell-fish, that they digged out of the sand, at low water; the island was bleak and cold, their wigwams poor and mean, their clothes few and thin; some little corn they had of their own, which the Council ordered to be fetched from their plantations, and conveyed to them by little and little; also a boat and man was appointed to look after them. I may say in the words of truth (according to my apprehension), there appeared among them much practical Christianity in this time of their trials.

The anxious colonists now turned their attention to the uncommitted tribes on the wilderness frontier. Under the July treaty, the Narragansetts had agreed to surrender any refugees from Philip's forces who came into their hands. Yet Weetamoo and her Pocassets had disappeared into their territory a month earlier and were still at large.

A meeting was called with the Narragansetts, and three weeks later their principal sachem came to Boston to sign a new agreement. This was Canonchet, the son of Miantonomo. The agreement committed the Narragansetts to surrender within ten days "all and every one of the said Indians, whether belonging unto Philip, the Pocasset Squaw, or the Saconett Indians, Quabaug, Hadley, or any other sachems or people that have bin or are in hostillitie with the English." On signing, Canonchet was given a silver-laced coat as a token of friendship.

When the deadline for delivering the refugees passed with no sign of compliance, the colonies met to determine their response. By mid-November they had reached a decision. An army of more than a thousand men, the largest ever seen in New England, was to be pressed into service to subdue the Narragansetts and compel their cooperation.

Josiah Winslow, the Governor of Plymouth, was chosen Commander General. There were 158 troops levied from Plymouth, 395 from Connecticut and 500 from the Bay Colony, including six companies on foot and a troop of horse. There were, besides, volunteers, teamsters and servants, and a contingent of 150 Mohegan and Pequot warriors. The force was to unite at Richard Smith's garrison on the western shore of Narragansett Bay, across the water from Pocasset.

Early in the morning of December 9, 1675, Winslow addressed the Massachusetts army in their base camp at Dedham. He promised his troops a bonus of free land if they drove the Indians from the Narragansett country, and then gave the orders to advance. That same day, Plymouth's army started out for Rehoboth, while the Connecticut force, swelled by the files of native allies, left New London and made its way eastward along the Pequot Path.

The Plymouth and Massachusetts contingents met in Rehoboth. It took them two more days to march the distance to Smith's Landing. While in transit, they encountered and captured several natives, and on one occasion attempted to surprise the sachem Pomham during the night, but had to abandon the effort when the guides lost their way in the darkness and the deep snow.

After their arrival, while waiting for the Connecticut troops, they made additional excursions into the surrounding wilderness, capturing several natives and burning 150 wigwams at the empty village of the "Old Queen," Quaiapen, a daughter-in-law of Canonicus and one of the six Narragansett sachems. Two days later, Winslow received word that the Connecticut troops were at Jireh Bull's garrison about seven miles south along the Pequot Path. With food supplies running low, he decided to push ahead to meet them and unite the three armies.

When they arrived at Bull's garrison, they discovered that it had been burnt to the ground in an ambush just before the arrival of the Connecticut forces. They spent the night in the open. It had begun to storm and the air was sharp with cold.

At dawn they set out eastward across the Chippuxet River. Before them stretched a wilderness territory of snow-covered woodland and swamp. Their fortunes now depended on a single Indian guide, a Narragansett named Peter Freeman, who had once lived among the English. He had been captured the previous week and to save his life had agreed to lead the colonists to their goal. Of the entire expedition, only "Indian Peter" was acquainted with the path to the Narragansett stronghold in the heart of the Great Swamp.

The stronghold was situated on an island between the Usquapaug River and Shickasheen Brook. Set on a rise of five or six acres, it was surrounded by a wall of stakes, reinforced by a rampart of rocks and brush several yards thick. The outwork was further protected by several blockhouses from which the defenders could fire on anyone who approached. Although Indian villages were sometimes stockaded, the Narragansett fort was unique in the dimensions of its construction. It was said to have been built with the advice of a renegade settler named Joshua Teft, who was subsequently captured and hanged. Within the wall more than a thousand men, women and children were sheltered from the winter frost, their bark wigwams stored with corn and dried fish and lined with animal furs and skins.

On December 19, shortly after noon, Indian Peter led the army of the United Colonies to the verge of the Great Swamp.

They were spotted by a party of natives, who fired at them and retreated. Following their attackers through the thick growth, the soldiers soon came to the rim of the fort. Its heavily guarded entrance could be approached over a fallen tree which had to be crossed a man at a time. Inclining to the right, they found a portion of the outwork that was not yet completed, the single weak point in its defenses. Like other good fortune, this was taken as a providential sign: "As he led Israel by the pillar of fire and the cloud of his presence to light a way through the wilderness," wrote the Reverend William Hubbard, "so [he] now directs our forces upon that side of the fort where they might only enter."

When they had assembled before the opening, the order was given and the Massachusetts contingent rushed the fort. A volley caught them as they crossed the ice, killing many. Another charge followed and then another, until finally a breach was made and the Connecticut troops, clambering over the bodies of the dead, poured through the space. The battle was now within the Narragansett enclosure. Its shelters were quickly torched, and the flames, whipped to a fury by the icy wind, set the entire village—five hundred dwellings—ablaze. "The shrieks and cries of the women and children, the yelling of the warriors, exhibited a most horrible and appalling scene," a witness reported; some of the soldiers were troubled by the spectacle, and "afterwards seriously inquired whether burning their enemies alive could be consistent with humanity and the benevolent principle of the gospel."

About a third of the Narragansett Nation, including more than three hundred old men, women and children, were thought to have perished in the fire. Those who escaped—among them Canonchet and Weetamoo—fled to the Nipmuc territory. Winslow made an effort to pursue them, but his own army had suffered greatly, many dying from the cold, and the pursuit was soon abandoned.

Most of the natives had gathered for the winter at Menameset on the Ware River, about ten miles above the ruins of Brookfield; others were at Squakeag, and further east at Mount Wachusett. But Philip was not among them. He had taken four or five hundred warriors beyond the Connecticut River to the region around Albany in hopes of enlisting support from the Mohawks. His efforts were unsuccessful; the Mohawks refused to consider war against the colonies.

Shortly after the arrival of Canonchet and the Narragansetts among the Nipmuc tribes, the Indians struck the exposed settlements of central Massachusetts. On the evening of February 9, they attacked and burned Lancaster, inflicting more than fifty casualties and taking as many prisoners. Eleven days later, they fell on Medfield, less than twenty miles southwest of Boston. Stealing into town after dark, they ambushed the inhabitants and two hundred troops garrisoned there as they emerged from their houses at dawn. Setting fire to the buildings, the attackers withdrew across the Charles River, firing the bridge by which they made their escape and leaving a note attached to the ruins: "Know by this paper, that the Indians that thou hast provoked to wrath and anger, will war this twenty one years if you will." Four nights after the attack on Medfield, a band of Indians burned several buildings at Weymouth, carrying the war to the coast.

In the beginning of March, a council of war was held near Squakeag, attended by the Nipmucs, Narragansetts and Wampanoags. Philip, Weetamoo and Canonchet were present, as well as the Narragansett sachems Pomham, Quinnapin, and Pessacus. When the council was over, a force of Wampanoags destroyed Clark's garrison three miles from Plymouth, killing eleven people. The following day the Nipmucs attacked Groton and burned a large number of buildings.

Meanwhile, Canonchet and the Narragansetts returned to their territory and burned the evacuated town of Warwick, leaving only one stone building erect. Following this they set fire to the abandoned settlements along the Narragansett shore all the way to Wickford and Smith's garrison.

On March 26, 1676, multiple disasters befell the settlers. In Simsbury, Connecticut, all forty houses of the abandoned town were put to the flame; in Marlborough, eleven barns and thirteen dwellings were burned; and in Plymouth, Captain Michael Pierce and fifty soldiers, pursuing Canonchet, walked into an

ambush and were destroyed. It took settlers from neighboring
Rehoboth three days to bury the dead.

On the morning of March 28, Canonchet burned Rehoboth
itself. On the 29th, he entered Providence. Of the two hundred
inhabitants of the town, only thirty had remained, among them
its aged founder, Roger Williams, who went out to speak to the
sachems. They told him that their principal quarrel was with
Plymouth, which they intended to burn. They intended also to
avenge the devastation they had suffered from the other colonies
and the destruction of their village in the Great Swamp.

"Mr. *Williams* reproved their confidence [one who was
present reported], minded them of their cruelties, and told them
that the Bay, viz. Boston, could yet spare Ten thousand men:
and if they should destroy all them, yet it was not to be doubted,
but our King would send as many every year from *Old England,*
rather than they should share the country; they answered
proudly, That they should be ready for them, or to that effect,
but told Mr. *Williams* that he was a good man, and had been
kinde to them formerly, and therefore they would not hurt
him." Then they fired the town.

As in the immolation of Rehoboth, only one inhabitant was
killed. This was a settler named Wright, "a man of a singular
and sordid Humour," who refused on principle to enter the
garrison house. He was convinced that if the Bible was in his
hand he would be safe from violence, but "the Enemy, finding
him in that Posture, deriding his groundless Apprehension, or
Folly therin, ripped him open and put his Bible in his Belly."

When the Massachusetts authorities heard of the disaster at
Providence, they lifted their forty-year ban against Roger
Williams and offered him refuge. But he declined, preferring to
follow the rest of the Narragansett settlers to the safety of
Aquidneck for the duration of the war.

By mid-April, the outer ring of the Massachusetts frontier
had collapsed. Groton, Lancaster, Mendon and Wrentham had
been abandoned, and Marlborough nearly so; assaults had been
made on Andover, Chelmsford, Billerica, Braintree, Woburn
and Bridgewater. Out of ninety settlements in New England,
fifty-two had been attacked and twelve completely destroyed.

It was the greatest devastation ever suffered by the colonies in America. Yet with the arrival of spring, the tide of Indian strength had reached its limit, and within a week of the destruction of Providence, it began a swift and fateful ebb.

Unable to hunt and fight at the same time, the Indians were increasingly short of food. As the new planting season arrived, they sent their braves to the territories from which they had been driven in an effort to recover the caches of seed they had hidden. It was partly for this purpose that the Narragansetts had returned to Providence.

On April 11, an expedition of Connecticut troops, accompanied by their Pequot and Mohegan allies, came upon a handful of Indians resting on the slope of a small hill. The Indians scattered at their approach, and they followed in pursuit. When one of the fleeing warriors cast off a blanket and then a silver-laced coat, the pursuers recognized at once the Narragansett sachem Canonchet. Escaping to the other side of the hill, Canonchet attempted to cross a nearby stream, but suddenly slipped into water so deep that his gun was soaked, a misfortune, he said later, at which "his heart turned within him, so as he became as a rotten stick." Heartsick and exhausted, he pushed through the water to the other side, but less than two hundred yards from the bank a Pequot named Monopoide caught up with him and captured him without a struggle.

His captors observed that Canonchet's carriage was "strangely proud and lofty." "Being examined why he did foment that war, which would certainly be the destruction of him and all the heathen Indians in the country, etc. He would make no other reply to any interrogatories, but this: —that he was born a prince, and if princes came to speak with him he would answer, but none present being such, he thought himself obliged in honor to hold his tongue, and not hold discourse with such persons, below his birth and quallity."

Canonchet was offered his life if he would use his influence to convince the Narragansetts to make peace. But he refused, saying the Indians would never yield. When told by his captors that he would be put to death, he replied that "he liked it well, that he should die before his heart was soft, or had spoken any thing unworthy of him." Then he asked that the Mohegan sachem Oneco, whose father, Uncas, had killed his own father, Miantonomo, more than thirty years earlier, should be his executioner.

After dispatching their other captives, the Connecticut volunteers took Canonchet to Stonington. There he was shot by Oneco and two Pequot sachems, according to his wishes. When he was dead, the Mohegans cut off his head and quartered his body, and the Niantics burned it, "that all might share in the glory of destroying so great a prince." Afterward, "as a token of their love and fidelity to the English," they presented the head to the Council of Hartford.

When word of Canonchet's death reached the Indians, their situation was already grave. Disease and the rigors of the winter flight had taken their toll, and the small stocks of powder on which they depended were nearly spent. The remaining settlements had been heavily garrisoned and would be costly to attack. On April 21, they launched their last major assault, on the frontier outpost of Sudbury. Their councils were now divided and uncertain, their defenses careless, as though the very will to struggle had been dealt a mortal blow.

As the warm May air melted the rivers, the embattled Indians were drawn in large numbers to the fishing grounds along their banks. One of the most favored of these spots was at Peskeompscut, on the Connecticut River, six miles south of Squakeag. There the stream was forced between banks of slabbed stone and an archipelago of rocks, which caused the water to speed before it spilled over a fifty-foot fall. Below the drop, the northern bank opened to admit the currents of the Fall River and then curved south toward Deerfield and the garrisoned settlements beyond. Gathered under a ridge at the head of the falls, were Wampanoags, Narragansetts, Nashaways, Quabags and even Tarrantines. Children played along the bank, while women and old men fished in the river. From time to time small bands of young braves returned with slaughtered livestock they had plundered from the settlement herds.

These raids soon alerted the river settlers to the Indians' presence. When a captive soldier escaped to report that the camps were unguarded, a military force was quickly organized. On May 18, the volunteers set off on horse for the site. Leaving at sunset, they went up the trail from Hatfield, past Hopewell Swamp and Bloody Creek, and through the black remains of the abandoned Deerfield settlement. When they crossed the Pocumtuck River, they were drenched by a storm which exploded bolts of lightning into the spring darkness. At daybreak, they reached the Fall River. After picketing their horses and proceeding to Peskeompscut on foot, they climbed the ridge of the northern bank above the Indian camp. From this vantage they could see that neither guards nor dogs had been posted by the Indians, who had withdrawn into their wigwams to shelter from the storm.

At a signal, the attack began. The colonists rushed the silent campsite, firing through the bark walls of the structures where the Indians slept. Some were able to scramble out and put up a token fight; others tried to find shelter under the rocky banks but were cut down by the attacking troops. Some rushed into the river: "Many of them were shot dead in the waters, others wounded were therin drowned, many got into canoes to paddle away, but the paddlers being shot, the canoes overset with all therin, and the stream of the river being very violent and swift in the place near the great falls, most that fell over board were borne by the strong current of that river, and carryed upon the falls of water from those exceeding high and steep rocks, and from thence tumbling down were broken in pieces."

The Indians never recovered from the blows at Peskeompscut. In all the wilderness they now had no refuge secure from attack. Their base camps at Wuchusett, Quabag and Squakeag were soon abandoned before the march of the colonial armies; their western frontier was closed by hostile Mohawks. As defections from their ranks became daily more numerous, the war ceased to be a contest between contending forces and became a hunt. "All the Indians were in a continual motion," reported Daniel Henchman to the Council of Massachusetts at the end of June, "some towards Narraganset, others toward Watchuset, shifting gradually, and taking up each others quarters, and lay not above a night in a place."

On July 2, five hundred Connecticut troops under Major John Talcott attacked a large encampment of Narragansetts in the Nipsachuck area. Taken by surprise, the Indians put up little resistance. Nearly two hundred of them were killed or made prisoner. Among the dead was the "Old Queen," Quaiapen. The following day, the Connecticut troops overtook another Narragansett party on the trail to Warwick and killed or captured nearly seventy.

There were greater losses to come. On June 29, Awashonks, squaw sachem of the Sakonnets, had surrendered to Major Bradford and Benjamin Church of Plymouth, and offered her services to their campaign against Philip. A week later, three hundred Cape and Plymouth Indians gave themselves up. The same day, the sachem of the Nashaways and other of the Nipmucs sent a letter to "Mr. *John Leverett* [Governor of Massachusetts], my Lord, Mr. *Waban*, and all the chief Men, our Brethren, Praying to God," and begging in the name of Jesus Christ to grant them peace. The Council rejected their plea, declaring that those "treacherous persons who began the war and those that have been barbarously bloody," could not expect to have their lives spared.

On July 27, Sagamore John marched into Boston with 180 Nipmucs and the aged Matoonas, who had led the first attack on Mendon, as his prisoner. He declared that he was sorry that he had fought against the English, and as a testament to his change of heart offered to kill his prisoner. The offer was accepted, and Matoonas was shot. Afterward the sachem's head was severed and placed on a pole on the town gallows opposite the skull of his son, who had been executed six years earlier.

Knowing that the end was near, Philip had returned with his people to the familiar swamps and woods around Plymouth. On July 30, some Bridgewater settlers encountered a group of Indians trying to cross the Taunton River. In the skirmish that followed, several of the Indians were killed. Among them was Unkompowin, Philip's uncle.

The following day, Captain Benjamin Church came to the spot with a company of volunteers and natives and saw an Indian sitting on a stump across the river. As Church took aim, one of the natives accompanying him urged him not to shoot, thinking it one of his own men. The noise caused the figure to look up, and the native, seeing that it was Philip, raised his gun and fired. But it was too late. Philip had leaped down the bank and escaped.

After crossing the Taunton, Church spread his men wide in pursuit of the Wampanoags, who scattered in every direction. A number of women and children who could not keep up with the rest were overtaken. Among those captured were Wootoneskanuske, Philip's wife, and his only son, a boy of nine.

Church tracked the Indians to a swamp, reaching their camp at dusk the following day. He drew his company in a ring around the campsite and waited for the morning light. But just before the attack was launched, the Indians were alerted, and Philip escaped. Nearly two hundred of his dwindling tribe were killed or captured in the assault.

That night, Church took his prisoners to Bridgewater and was told by them, "Sir, you have now made Philip ready to die, for you have made him as poor and miserable as he used to make the English; you have now killed or taken all his relations." Soon, they assured him, he would also have Philip's head, "for this bout had almost broke his heart."

A few days later, on August 6, an Indian deserter walked into the Taunton settlement and informed the inhabitants that the last remnant of the Pocasset tribe was not far off. Twenty soldiers were sent out and took the Indians without difficulty, but their squaw sachem Weetamoo escaped. Fleeing to the Taunton River, beyond which lay the country of Pocasset, she attempted to cross the water on a raft made of some pieces of broken wood. In midstream, her strength failed, from hunger or cold, and her naked body was found soon after in Mattapoisett near the river's mouth "not far from the water side."

Soon after, settlers from Taunton who found her corpse cut off her head and brought it to the town. "When it was set upon a pole in *Taunton*, the Indians who were prisoners there knew it presently, and made a most horrid and diabolical Lamentation, crying out that it was their Queen's head." Thus ended the career of Weetamoo, "who was next unto *Philip*" in making the war. Only a little more than a year had passed since she had joined the sachem and his cause not far from the place where her flight ended.

Now Philip was almost alone. With a handful of warriors he made his way back to Pokanoket and pitched his small camp in the shadow of Mount Hope.

On August 11, an Indian came to the colonists at Trip's Ferry and said that he had deserted Philip. He told them that Philip was at Mount Hope, that he had killed his brother for advising him to make peace, and that he would take them to Philip's camp. A force under Benjamin Church followed the Indian across the bay and arrived shortly after midnight at "a little spot of upland, that was in the south end of the miry swamp, just at the foot of the mount." Remaining in the darkness until morning, Church began to draw his men close about the sleeping Wampanoags. But as they approached the last stretch of distance, a shot was fired, waking the camp.

Grabbing his weapon, Philip leaped up and headed toward the brush and safety of the swamp. Waiting in his line of flight was a colonist named Cook and an Indian called Alderman. Cook raised his gun and pulled the trigger, but it misfired. He then called to the Indian to shoot, and the musket ball pierced Philip's heart.

When the battle was over, Church ordered the natives to pull Philip's body out of the mud and water where it had fallen. Then he gave instructions to cut off Philip's head and hand and to quarter his body. The pieces were hung from four trees at Church's instigation, so that "not one of his bones should be buried," for he had "caused many an Englishman's body to be unburied and to rot above ground." Church then gave Philip's hand as a bounty to the Indian who had shot him. It was said afterward that this Indian made "many a penny" in the colonies with the hand by charging the curious for a look.

Church then returned to Plymouth so that his company could receive their pay—four shillings and sixpence for the march and thirty shillings for each Indian killed or captured. The head of Massasoit's son Philip brought thirty shillings like all the rest.

In Plymouth, a "solemn day of Thanksgiving to Almighty God" was declared on August 17, and Philip's head was paraded through the streets. When the ceremonies were over, the Pilgrims placed it on a pole in the town center, like the skulls of Wituwamat and Pecksuot before, as a warning to all who passed.

The Wampanoags who escaped from the swamp surrendered shortly after. Their leader, Annawon, was slain. The last of the Narragansett sachems, Quinnapin, was also captured and shot. Those who were not executed were sold into slavery in Spain and the West Indies. Among these were Philip's wife and child. Some, more fortunate, fell into the hands of Providence and were reserved by Roger Williams and the colony's leaders for sale as indentured servants, the proceeds to be divided among the Providence settlers.

This ended "King Philip's War," and also the independent existence of the native peoples of New England. Twenty years later, a French Huguenot visiting the region reported, "There is Nothing to fear from the Savages ... The last Wars they had with the English ... have reduced them to a small Number, and consequently they are incapable of defending themselves."

The frontier wilderness, which had appeared so perilous for the colonists half a century before, was now open for peaceful expansion. The land God promised them was free.

PART II

DEMOCRACY
IN
VIRGINIA

1

Seed of the Plantation

IN the beginning, all of America was Virginia. The territorial claim which had been christened for England's Virgin Queen extended from Cape Fear in North Carolina to the Passamaquoddy Bay in Maine, from the Atlantic seaboard across a continent to the Pacific edge: an uncharted wilderness domain.

To the missionaries and the adventurers of the Elizabethan Court, the promise of Virginia was golden. In its harbors they sought a base against the Spanish empire, in its waterways a passage to the Orient and beneath its surface an English Peru.

Their first expedition landed on Roanoke Island off the Carolina coast in 1585. The prospect was paradisal: "The earth bringeth foorth all things in abundance," they reported, "as in the first creation, without toil or labor." The natives they encountered were "most gentle, loving and faithfull, void of all guile, and treason, and such as lived after the manner of the golden age."

Like other visions of the New World, this report reflected the visionaries' hopes. Within four years of the first planting, Virginia's wilderness had reclaimed its own. Of three expeditions, one returned to England in defeat after a year, the others vanished without a trace.

More than a decade elapsed before the attempts were renewed, and the Lost Colony passed into contemporary legend. But as the seapower of Spain receded under the blows of England's fleet, hopes revived. In 1604, Queen Elizabeth died and the Spanish monarch made peace with her successor. Two years later, King James I gave his official seal to a new colonial effort. "London" and "Plymouth" companies were chartered to settle the southern and northern parts of the patent, later to be called Virginia and New England.

On April 26, 1607, the *Susan Constant* and two companion vessels sailed into the broad bay the Indians called *K'tchisipik* or "Great Water" on the Virginia coast. The bay was fed by five navigable rivers. On the shores, dogwood and redbud trees were in bloom. The ground, covered with wild strawberries, was filled with strange plants and flowers: "Wee could find nothing worth the speaking of, but fair meadowes and goodly tall Trees, with such Fresh-waters running through the woods, as I was almost ravished at the first sight thereof," a member of the company recorded.

That night when they were returning to the ship, "there came the Savages creeping upon all foure, from the Hills, like Beares, with their Bowes in their mouthes, charged us very desperately in faces, hurt Captaine Gabrill Archer in both his hands and a sayler in two places of the body very dangerous. After they had spent their Arrowes, and felt the sharpnesse of our shot they retired into the Woods with a great noise, and so left us."

Other natives whom they encountered as they explored the waters and lands of the Chesapeake were less hostile. On the fifth of May, they were confronted with an exotic sight as the werowance (or chief) of the Rappahannocks came to greet them on the river bank. He was playing a reed flute and his hair was tied in a knot with a crown of deer hair dyed red and shaped like a rose. A copper plate was fastened on either side of his head, and two long feathers sprang like horns from his crown. His body was painted crimson, and his face was blue and sprinkled with silver. He wore a necklace of beads, and his ears were hung with bracelets of pearl, and in each was a bird's claw set with copper and gold. He invited the Englishmen to his village, and they accepted and were entertained in a friendly manner.

During their exploration of the Chesapeake, the English came on a formidable river which bore the name of the principal werowance of the region, Powhatan, whose confederacy ruled the Tidewater. In a solemn ceremony, the English planted a cross at the river's head and renamed it after their king. After sailing sixty miles up the James River, they discovered a peninsula that appeared defensible against Spaniards and natives alike. On May 24, amid high hopes and a fanfare of trumpets, they left their ships to take possession of the site, which they called James Towne.

They immediately began the construction of a triangular fort with a bulwark in the shape of a half-moon at each point. But before they completed it, the colony was attacked. Several casualties were inflicted, and only an artillery blast from the ships anchored in the river saved the settlement from burning. Yet, the real menace to Jamestown's early survival came not from hostile natives, who were scattered and few in number, but hunger and disease.

After the completion of Fort James, two of the ships of the expedition returned to England with their captain, leaving a hundred men in the heat and fevers of the Virginia summer to wait for the next "supply." Within two weeks, scarcely ten of them could stand. "There were never Englishmen left in a forreigne countrey in such miserie as wee were in this new discovered Virginia," complained George Percy, a gentleman among them. A single can of barley was the daily provision to be divided among five men. Water was taken out of the river, "which was, at a floud, verie salt; at a low tide, full of slime and filth," and quickly became a source of paralyzing sickness and death.

"If there were any conscience in men," wrote Percy, "it would make their harts to bleed to heare the pitifull murmurings and out-cries of our sick men without reliefe, every night and day, for the space of sixe weeks: some departing out of the World, many times three or foure in a night; in the morning, their bodies trailed out of their Cabines like Dogges, to be buried."

From June until September, almost fifty men were buried in

the Tidewater sun, nearly half those who had been left behind.
By the time their captain returned in January with the first
supply from England, only thirty-eight remained alive to greet
him.

The first season in the New World had proved a hard one for
Jamestown, but there were harder ones to come. By the beginning of the year 1609, a second and third supply had been
sent to the colony, swelling its population to nearly five hundred.
Its stores were well stocked with food and implements for
tilling the soil. But the Jamestown adventurers disdained labor
and squandered their reserves. When winter came, they were
helpless.

This second of Virginia's catastrophes was called "the Starving
Time" by its chroniclers. During its darkest hour, the settlers
descended to cannibalism, eating not only the flesh of their own
dead countrymen, but also that of an Indian who was dug out
of the grave where he had been buried three days. One man
murdered and ate his pregnant wife and, being discovered, was
hanged by his thumbs with weights on his feet until he confessed; then he was burned to death.

At the end of the winter, two small ships, the *Patience* and
the *Deliverance*, dropped their anchors in the James River.
Those who went ashore found sixty survivors of the five hundred settlers that had been left, looking "Lyke Anatomies Crye-
inge owtt we are starved We are starved."

Virginia's early misery and travail became a cautionary tale
for those who followed. As the Puritans justified their project
for the New World, they felt compelled to explain why New
England's fate should be better than Virginia's. Misfortune had
befallen the Virginia settlers, John Winthrop concluded, because "their mayne end was Carnall & not Religious ... they
used unfitt instruments, a multitude of rude & misgoverned
persons, the very scumme of the Land; [and] they did not
establish a right forme of government."

John Smith, the most forceful leader of the first Jamestown
expedition, agreed. "Idelnesse and carelesnesse," he told a royal
commission, "brought all I did in three yeares, in six months to
nothing." This he attributed to the goals of the Virginia ad-

venturers. For "though Religion was their Colour . . . their aime was nothing but present profit." Among the colonists "there was no talke, no hope, no worke," recalled another, "but dig gold, wash gold, refine gold, load gold."

The founders of Virginia were not a community like Plymouth's Saints, but a disparate collection of gentlemen-adventurers and their servants. From the outset, the colony was undermined by profiteering of food and other stores, and by political plots to control its meager authority and wealth. The colony was further jeopardized by an aristocratic contempt for labor. Devoting their energies and sparse supplies to the search for mineral treasures, passages to the Orient and other chimeras, the Virginians depended on barter with the hostile Indians for their food, and were left helpless when these sources were withdrawn.

As news of the successive Jamestown disasters spread to England, the Virginia Company took steps to protect its investment. In an effort to establish discipline in the colony's affairs, the company promulgated *Lawes Divine, Morall and Martial*. Death was prescribed for more than twenty kinds of offenses, including treason, sodomy, adultery, rape (whether "maid or Indian"), theft, lying, sacrilege, blasphemy, stealing, deriding the Bible, killing any domestic animal such as a cow or chicken, or taking so much as an ear of corn from a garden. Anyone slandering, criticizing or disobeying authority would be whipped three times and forced to acknowledge the crime on his knees for the first offense, condemned three years to the galley for the second, and executed for the third.

Under these codes, the harsh existence of Virginia's pioneers became even harsher. Their food allowance was only eight ounces of meal and half a pint of peas a day ("the one and the other mouldy, rotten, full of Cobwebs and Maggotts loathsome to man and not fytt for beasts"). Many fled to the Indians. Those unfortunate enough to be caught suffered "sundry deaths as by hanginge, shooting and breakinge upon the wheele."

Others resorted to theft to fight hunger. For them even more horrible fates were devised. One unfortunate caught with two or three pints of oatmeal had a needle thrust through his tongue, after which he was chained to a tree until he starved. Some who lacked the courage to steal, quietly chose not to live: " ... yf a man through his sicknes had not been able to worke, he had noe allowance at all, and soe consequently perished. Many through these extremities, being weery of life, digged holes in the earth and there hidd themselves till they famished."

If the colony did not disintegrate totally, it was only because of the size of its investment, its prominent sponsors, who included peers of the realm, and its conception as a strategic base against Spain's empire in America. But even these factors would have failed to save Virginia if it hadn't been for the discovery of a cash export in the "bewitching vegatable," tobacco.

On his first voyage to the New World, Christopher Columbus had been given the strange dried leaves by the natives of San Salvador, as a symbol of friendship. The Indians whom he and his men encountered chewed, snuffed and smoked tobacco and used it for ceremonial and medicinal purposes as well. Among the most important of these was the smoking of the calumet, the long-stemmed pipe of peace.

By the middle of the sixteenth century, tobacco was widely used in Europe as a miracle remedy, appearing in powders and unguents, cathartics and clysters. Meanwhile its pleasurable effects continued to make it a pastime of sailors and merchants plying the great trade routes from the Indies to the Orient.

In 1586 Sir Francis Drake returned to England with the survivors of Roanoke's second expedition, who had taken up the native custom of tobacco smoking. When their sponsor, Sir Walter Raleigh, took up the habit, he helped to transform it almost overnight into an institution for those who could afford its high prices on the European market. In a short space of time, "the joviall weed" became a favored vice in London's taverns and brothels; the Gulpe, the Retention and the Cuban Ebolition were symbols of initiation among the "reeking gallants" who made smoking an elaborate cult. Others regarded the "precious stinke" more somberly as a "chopping herbe of hell," or as "the Devil's revenge for his Indian children upon the white man."

The King himself opposed the addiction, describing it in his *Counter Blaste to Tobacco* as "A custom Lothsome to the eye, hateful to the Nose, harmful to the braine, dangerous to the Lungs, and in the black stinking fume thereof, neerest resembling the horrible Stigian smoke of the pit that is bottomlesse." Yet the Crown coveted the revenues that flowed from its production and were to make Virginia the most prized of its possessions.

Among the Indians of the Chesapeake, the tobacco plant was regarded as the fourth element of creation, following the appearance of earth, man and woman. Its leaf was smoked for pleasure and used in healing and in prayer: "In the morning by breake of day, before they eate or drinke, both men, women, and children (that be abouve tenne yeares of age) runnes into the water; there washes themselves a good while till the Sunne riseth: then offer Sacrifice to it, strewing Tobacco on the water or Land, honouring the Sunne as their God."

The colonists found Virginia's tobacco poor, weak and biting, unsuited for competition with the Spanish leaf. But shortly after the Starving Time, a Jamestown settler, John Rolfe, planted seeds he had imported from Trinidad and the Orinoco River Valley, and developed a tobacco that compared favorably with those sold on the London market. Rolfe had discovered a source of wealth beyond the gold of the Aztecs or the riches of Peru.

In the spring of 1614, the ship *Elizabeth* returned to England from Jamestown carrying four barrels of Rolfe's leaves in its hold. By 1616, the shipments had increased to two thousand pounds, and in Jamestown itself the marketplace and even the streets were planted with tobacco. By 1618, exports had reached fifty thousand pounds and a decade later more than a million. William Berkeley offered a sardonic view of these developments: "Our Governours by reason of the corruption of those times they lived in, laid the Foundation of our wealth and industry on the vices of men."

In John Rolfe's tobacco, the colony's sponsors had found a source of revenue; to tap it, they needed a supply of labor. The grim mortality rate was an obstacle. In 1616, the year

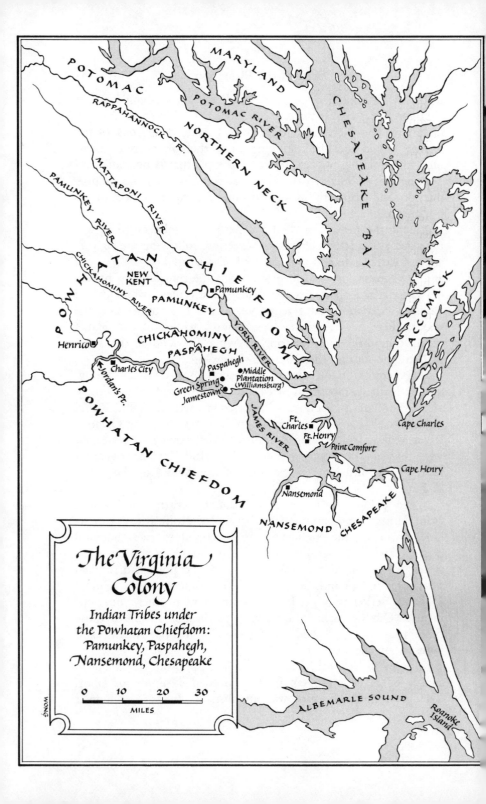

The Virginia Colony

Indian Tribes under the Powhatan Chiefdom: Pamunkey, Paspahegh, Nansemond, Chesapeake

0   10   20   30
MILES

WONG

production began in earnest, there were only 350 settlers in Virginia—"a small number [Rolfe lamented] to advance so great a worke." About the same time, a Spanish spy reported that roughly half the Jamestown settlers died annually of one cause or another.

To encourage immigrants and to retain their settlers, the Virginia Company now offered them an expanded stake in the New World. To planters who had paid for their passage and indentured servants who had completed their terms, they promised a hundred acres of land. A "headright" of fifty acres was also available for every immigrant brought by a planter at his own expense. With capital, a man could get both land and labor in abundance and the chance for wealth beyond his station.

Nor did the sponsors neglect the political dimension of the Virginians' hopes. In 1619, the Virginia Company liberalized the colony's legal code. The *Laws Divine, Morall and Martial* were abolished in favor of new laws which gave the colonists, as nearly as possible, the rights of Englishmen. At the same time, provision was made for a more representative and responsive government. A general assembly was created, with two burgesses to be elected from every settlement, the first representative legislature in the New World.

During this year of transformation, eight ships entered Jamestown harbor with twelve hundred immigrants in their holds. Among them were more than a hundred destitute children, paupers, convicted felons and impoverished laborers, the bulk destined for servitude in the colony under indentures of four years and more. In addition, the company sent a shipload of ninety young women so that "the Planters' mindes may be the faster tyed to Virginia by the bondes of wyves and children." In August, a Dutch man-of-war arrived and "brought not any thing but 20 and odd Negars, which the Governor . . . bought for victualls."

The wave of immigration, which lasted three years, brought 2500 settlers to the colony. When it subsided, more than twenty small settlements were scattered along the James River. Iron foundries, sawmills and shipyards had been constructed, and up river in Henrico, work on a college was begun.

The bustling expansion of activities, which meant hopeful possibilities for the colonists, assumed a different aspect in the villages inhabited by the Tidewater natives. These were Powhatans, Appomattocs, Mattaponis and Pamunkeys, members of the confederacy Powhatan had forged among the Algonquin tribes. From the outset, their relations with the intruders had been uncertain and marked by interludes of violence. By the Starving Time, incidents of conflict had deteriorated into bitter strife. In the midst of the suffering, fifty men from the colony were sent to Powhatan to barter for food. But during the negotiations, the company was slaughtered, with only sixteen surviving. Their captain was bound to a tree and "by woemen his fleshe was skraped from his bones with mussell shelles and before his face throwne into the fyer."

Not long afterward, when Powhatan refused to surrender men and arms captured from the colony, returning instead "prowde and disdaynefull Answers," George Percy led a punitive expedition against the local Paspaheghs. More than a dozen natives were killed in the surprise attack, and one brave was captured, along with their "queen" and her children. Percy ordered the village burned and its cornfields cut down. He scolded his lieutenant for taking a man prisoner and ordered the brave's head cut off. This failed to satisfy the soldiers, however, who began "to murmur becawse the quene and her Children were spared." A council was called and "itt was Agreed upon to putt the Children to deathe the which was effected by Throweinge them overboard and shoteinge owtt their Braynes in the water." The soldiers still clamored for the death of the mother, but Percy spared her until they returned to Jamestown, where she was put to the sword.

In 1613, relations took a more peaceful turn. In that year, Powhatan's daughter, Pocahontas, was kidnapped by the Governor of the colony, who held her hostage for a year. During her captivity, she was taught the Christian religion and then married to John Rolfe. The marriage promised to be a political stroke for the colony, but Rolfe's passion was derided by his peers. In a plaintive letter to the Governor, he defended himself, giving assurance that he was "no way led ... with the unbridled desire of carnall affection" in marrying an object "whose education hath bin rude, her manners barbarous, her generation accursed." He had sought the hand of the Indian princess, rather, "for the good of this plantation, for the honour of our countrie, for the glory of God, for my owne salvation, and for the converting to the true knowledge of God and Jesus Christ, an unbeleeving creature, namely Pokahuntas."

The wedding was followed by a series of treaties between the colony and the Powhatan tribes, signifying their submission to King James and his Virginia deputy. The peace lasted more than seven years, surviving both Powhatan and his daughter. Pocahontas was renamed Rebecca, and in 1616 her husband brought her to London, where she was presented to the Court. The following winter she was taken ill. As the illness progressed, she and her husband boarded a ship returning to the Chesapeake, but before they reached the mouth of the Thames, she had to be taken ashore. She died at Gravesend in 1617, aged twenty-two.

Her father, Powhatan, died the following year. His peace with the colony lasted until March 22, 1622, when his half-brother and successor, Opechancanough, abruptly ended the frontier calm.

On that Good Friday, the Indians came unarmed to the several plantations along the James, as was their habit, carrying "Deere, Turkies, Fish, Furres, and other provisions, to sell, and trucke ... for glasse, beades and other trifles." In some places, they sat down to breakfast with the settlers in their own houses, and then "with their owne [the settlers'] tooles and weapons, eyther laid downe, or standing in their houses ... basely and barbarously murthered [them], not sparing eyther age or sexe, man, woman or childe; so sodaine in their cruell execution, that few or none discerned the weapon or blow that brought them to destruction."

There were 347 colonists massacred, about a quarter of all the white settlers in Virginia (the few Africans bought from the West Indies were left unharmed). Jamestown itself was saved from destruction only at the last minute by a Christian Indian who warned his English master of the impending attack.

When the Virginia Company heard of the calamity, it dispatched a letter urging the survivors to rededicate themselves to the colonial effort. "We cannot but thinke, that the sheeding of this blood wilbe the Seed of the Plantation," they wrote; ". . . we conceave it a Sinne against the dead to abandon the enterprize, till we have fully settled the possession, for which so many of our Brethren have lost theire lives." This, they added, was "the first thing due from us and you," the next being "a sharp revenge upon the bloody miscreants, even to the measure that they intended against us, the rooting them out for being longer a people uppon the face of the Earth."

By the time the company's letter reached the colony, this rooting out had already begun. Punitive expeditions killed hundreds of the natives, destroying entire villages and their crops. "Our first worke," Virginia's Governor explained, "is expulsion of the Salvages to gaine the free range of the countrey for encrease of Cattle, swine etc. . . . for it is infinitely better to have no heathen among us . . . than to be at peace and league with them."

The massacre provided the colony with an opportunity to seize the natives' lands, and in particular the fields cleared for tobacco and corn. "We, who hitherto have had possession of no more ground than their waste, and our purchase . . . may now by right of Warre, and law of Nations, invade the Country, and destroy them who sought to destroy us," the government proclaimed; ". . . where by wee shall enjoy their cultivated places, turning the laborious Mattocks into the victorious Sword (wherein there is more both ease, benefit, and glory) and possessing the fruits of others labours. Now their cleared grounds in all their villages (which are situate in the fruitfullest places of the land) shall be inhabited by us, whereas heretofore the grubbing of woods was the greatest labour."

Although the revenge cleared the way for a new expansion of the Virginia settlement, it could not rescue the faltering fortunes of the colony's sponsors. Opechancanough's stroke did not dislodge the Virginia settlement, as he had hoped, but it proved fatal to the Virginia Company. Weakened by internal factions and a conflict with the King over tobacco duties, and financially drained by the recent expansion, the company had neither political nor economic resources to survive the calamity.

Following the March 22 massacre, a royal commission was appointed to investigate the colony and the abuses connected with its promotion and administration. The mortality figures alone condemned it. During the expansion that started in 1619, 3500 people had been sent to Virginia. Of these, it was now revealed, 3000 had died even before the massacre. Of 7000 immigrants to the colony since 1607, only 1000 had survived. On May 24, 1624, King James dissolved the Virginia Company and appointed his own governor, creating the first royal colony in the New World.

Under the new organization, no provision was made for the Assembly that the company had previously created. Yet, it never really ceased to exist. Whenever the royal Governor was confronted by such basic matters as defense, tobacco and taxes, he was compelled to revive the Assembly, which represented the principal planters of the James, until in 1640 it was legally restored. The separation of the frontier from its central authority created imperatives of government more binding than constitutions.

In these years, for the settlers survival was precarious. So great was the risk of death during the summer fevers that newly arrived servants were usually exempted from field work in the hot weather. A "seasoned" hand (one who had survived the first summer in Virginia) brought twice the price of an untested servant.

Meanwhile, the volume of the tobacco trade had made it a mainstay of Britain's imperial wealth. More than a million pounds were shipped annually to English and Dutch ports. Along the stream of tobacco, planters and merchants, shippers and pirates, government officials and legislators made their fortunes. Among these beneficiaries of the leaf, none surpassed the Crown itself. A duty imposed on every pound filled the royal coffers with sums exceeding £100,000 annually. Soon the revenues accruing to the royal treasury from Virginia were greater than from any other part of an empire which stretched from the Orient to the Antilles.

The government in Virginia rested even more completely on the staple. Within its authority fell land patents, exit and entrance permits, writs for elections, taxes and the regulation of the trade itself. All along the route, from plantation to port, charges were imposed and fees collected by colony officials. Percentages of these were often payable to the officials themselves. Public office in Virginia was a prime source of personal profit, and the pyramids of public and private power converged until they became indistinct.

Their apex was the Governor's office, which endowed its proprietor with an estate and salary, and afforded numerous privileges, gifts, taxes and tributes: a bushel of corn from every tithable in the colony, a fee of two hundred pounds of tobacco for a license to marry, five shillings for every permit to leave the colonial boundary.

Other offices were similarly enlarged. Every document and legal transaction required a fee and tribute. Taxation became a pervasive fact of colonial life, and corruption an indispensable element in its affairs. "There is not perhaps in all the King's Dominions," a Virginia councilor complained, "any place where the methods of Managing both the trade and the Revenues are so exactly calculated to defraud the Public and abuse the subject."

Sustaining the flow of tobacco wealth were the expanding plantations of the Tidewater settlements. Tracts for planting were made constantly available to planters through the continuing deaths and the unused headrights they released. But the bulk of the new plantations sprang up on space acquired from the surrounding wilderness. And in Virginia, as elsewhere in the New World, expansion and dispossession continued to be inseparable acts.

Although the natives of the Chesapeake had been decimated in the campaigns that followed the massacre, they had not been destroyed. Twenty years later, their leader, Opechancanough, was so aged and feeble that he could not open his eyes without assistance and had to be carried to battle on a litter. Still, in 1644 he summoned the remnants of the Powhatan tribes to a last rising against the intruders, killing five hundred

colonists in the attack. More numerous and stronger than before, the settlements survived the blow more easily, and struck
back with swift and devastating revenge.

Opechancanough was captured and taken to Jamestown. Until the end, it was reported, he held himself bravely. "He heard
one Day a great Noise of the Treading of People about him;
upon which he caused his Eye-lids to be lifted up; and finding
that a Crowd of People were let in to see him, he call'd in high
Indignation for the Governour; who being come, *Oppechan-
canough* scornfully told him, That had it been his Fortune to
take Sir *William Berkeley* Prisoner, he should not meanly have
exposed him as a Show to the People."

Governor Berkeley had planned to send the sachem to
England and present him to the Court of King Charles. But
the plan was aborted when a common soldier, enraged by the
sufferings which he had brought on the colony, shot him in
the back and killed him.

In 1646, a treaty of pacification declared all of the region
from the York River to the Blackwater, south of the James,
out of bounds to the Indians. Thereafter, natives could only
enter these lands with the colony's permission. A yearly tribute
from the defeated tribes was payable personally to Governor
Berkeley, whose approval was also required from that time
for the selection of tribal chiefs.

Virginia's expansion was now free to take its course. During
the next ten years, five new counties appeared on the colonial
map, and the settlers extended their claims to the "Northern
Neck," bounded by the Rappahannock and Potomac rivers. The
only limit to the colony's expansion in these years was the
grant that had been made to Lord Baltimore a decade earlier
of the land north of the Potomac. In that part of the Virginia
patent, he established Maryland as a proprietary colony for
himself, and a refuge for Catholics.

Although land was the symbol of wealth in the New World,
it was not in itself an avenue to riches. Its very abundance diminished the price and limited its value. In the middle of the
seventeenth century, an acre could be acquired for four cents,
or two pounds of tobacco. To transform base earth into precious

gold required labor. Consequently, during the first two centuries of development in Virginia, the most valuable form of property was men.

In the beginning, and for a long time afterward, these men were white. Drawn from the reservoir of human misery at the bottom of English society, they were hardly freer than slaves to choose their passage. For many years after the 1622 massacre, "the danger and scarcity of the Inhabitants [of the Colony] was so famed through *England*," explained Berkeley, "that none but such as were forced could be induced to plant or defend the place." The destitute, the criminal, the fugitive, provided the labor force for the Virginia plantations. Contracted for years of servitude, they constituted three quarters of the immigrants during the first half-century of the colony's existence.

Sometime during the 1640s, the rate of mortality began to decline. In previous years, five of every six settlers coming to the Tidewater had been expected to die in "seasoning." By mid-century, the figure had dropped to one in nine. The population, which had grown to eight thousand by 1644, increased three times during the next two decades. Fortunes were stabilized, dynasties born. Byrds and Carters, Lees and Randolphs came to settle, acquire plantations, and establish a political and economic estate that would dominate Virginia society for more than two hundred years.

In 1642, the aristocratic William Berkeley, a member of the King's Privy Chamber, was appointed Governor. Like the majority of the colony's planters, he was a Royalist and Cavalier. Under Berkeley's rule, Virginia became "the only city of refuge" in the King's dominions for his distressed loyalists during England's Civil War. When the King was beheaded in 1649, the Virginia Assembly declared it a crime contrary to the laws of nature, of nations, and of God.

A year later, Cromwell's revolutionaries took a step toward securing the monopoly of tobacco that had previously eluded the Crown. The Puritan Parliament forbade Virginia and the other British dominions from trading directly with the Dutch, and benefiting from the competition. The colonies were reminded that they owed their existence to English money, enterprise and protection, and were warned that in ignoring English authority they were rebels and traitors to the state.

"We are forsooth their worships slaves," Berkeley exclaimed as he answered the challenge before the Virginia Assembly. "Surely Gentlemen, we are more slaves by nature, than their power can make us." Berkeley contrasted revolutionary England with conservative America: "Consider yourselves how happy you are, and have been, how the Gates of Wealth and Honour are shut on no man, and that there is not here an Arbitrary hand, that dares to touch the substance of either poore or rich." What could Virginians hope for in a change of government in England that they did not already have in America? "Is it liberty? The sun looks not on a people more free than we are from all oppression." Is it wealth, or security for wealth? Virginians had the opportunity for the one and assurance for the other. "Is it peace? The Indians, God be blessed, round about us are subdued: we can only feare the Londoners, who would faine bring us to . . . poverty . . . would take away the liberty of our consciences, and tongues, and our right of giving and selling our goods to whom we please."

Three years later, Cromwell's emissaries landed in Virginia. The colonists submitted to the Puritan authority without a struggle, yet the consequences were small. Geography again ensured a certain independence. The first article of their submission guaranteed Virginians the rights and privileges of freeborn Englishmen, and the commitment was kept. Cromwell's military forces, already arrayed against Ireland, Scotland and the West Indies, were never dispatched to the Chesapeake. Although Berkeley was relieved of his office, authority continued to rest in the Assembly, which ruled without interference from Westminster until 1660. When the Restoration brought the end of the Puritan Protectorate and the ascension of Charles II to the English throne, Berkeley was returned to the Governor's office.

But Restoration proved no boon for the Royalist colony. Shortly after the King's return, a new Navigation Act tightened London's control of the Virginia trade and extended its tax on tobacco. The tax was calculated by the weight of the leaves, rather than the price, which London's monopoly continued to depress. Soon Virginians were complaining that the Crown received more for tobacco than the producers themselves. "The Merchant buyes it for one penny the pound," observed Berkeley on a special embassy to London, "and we pay two pence for the custom of that which they are not pleased to take from us." As a result, Virginia's planters had been reduced "to that extremity, that they can neither handsomely subsist with [tobacco], nor without it."

Conditions that were burdensome for the planters were catastrophic for those beneath them on the social ladder. Worst hit by the economic crisis was the class of freedmen that had come into existence as the mortality rate fell and servants began to survive their terms of servitude. Poor immigrants to Virginia had always been offered the prospect of being "master and owner of [their] owne labour and land" when they completed their service. By the time they had begun to survive long enough to take advantage of the offer, the opportunity to do so had all but disappeared. Most of Virginia's fertile river lands had already been claimed by a relative handful of wealthy planters. Freedmen seeking access to planting land had the choice of establishing a precarious foothold on the rim of the Indian frontier, or of renting acreage from their former masters. The only alternative was to join the growing ranks of the landless poor, who worked when there was work, and subsisted as a vagrant "rabble" when there was none. As Virginia entered its eighth decade, the prospect was more likely that there would be none.

For years, overproduction had depressed tobacco prices and reduced the demand for labor. Efforts which Berkeley and others had made to diversify the economy and control production at the source had failed. In the decade between 1664 and 1674, England warred twice with Holland in an effort to stifle its commerce with the colonies. This further depressed the price of Virginia's tobacco, while converting a beneficial (if illegal) trading partner into a military enemy. To the hardships of depression and war was added the havoc of natural disaster. An epidemic killed 50,000 cattle one year, a hailstorm wiped out the spring crops another, and a drought ruined the harvest a third.

These trials, which bore most heavily on the marginal poor, resulted in growing tension in the colony and increasing apprehension among its planter rulers. Their anxiety was compounded by the presence of a factor that distinguished the lower classes in America from their English counterparts. The freedmen were armed. "There is no Custom more generally to be observed among the Young Virginians," an English visitor was later to note, "than that they all learn to keep and use a gun with a Marvelous dexterity as soon as ever they have strength enough to lift it to their hands." An instrument of frontier survival introduced an unforeseen element into the relations between ruler and ruled. "How miserable that man is," Berkeley was soon to lament, "that Governes a People wher six parts of seaven at least are Poore Endebted Discontented and Armed."

To contain the pressures within the colony, the House of Burgesses enacted measures extending the terms of servitude for indentured labor. In 1670, the suffrage was restricted and the burgesses for the first time instituted a property qualification for voting. Propertyless freedmen, they argued, "haveing little interest in the country, doe oftner make tumults at the election to the disturbance of his majesties peace, then by their discretions in their votes provide for the conservasion thereof."

But tightening controls in the midst of deteriorating conditions only increased the tensions. In the spring of 1675, incidents on the Indian frontier set in motion forces that were to overwhelm the bulwarks of the Chesapeake peace.

Within months, the colony was torn by civil war, its governor in flight and capital in flames, in the first revolt against the English authority in the New World.

2

Bacon's Rebellion

THE year 1675 began in Virginia with three prodigies, later seen as portents of the calamities to come. The first was a comet that appeared every evening for a week, "streaming like a horse taile westwards," and then sinking on the rim of the northern sky. The second was flights of pigeons nearly a quarter of the sky in breadth. Their weight was said to have broken down the limbs of large trees where they rested at night, and their sight was fearful to the older planters, who said it was the same as had appeared "when th' Indians committed the last massacre, but not after, untill that present year 1675." A third sign was swarms of flies about an inch long and a quarter-inch thick that rose out of spigot holes in the earth and ate the newly sprouted leaves from the tops of the trees, and then in a month were gone.

The events began with an incident in the Northern Neck, the last settled region of the Tidewater. It took place on a sabbath morning in July, about the time that King Philip was first joining forces with Weetamoo in the Pocasset swamp in their war against New England. A group of parishioners was crossing Thomas Mathew's plantation in the Potomac River Valley on their way to church. Passing the house of Mathew's overseer, they saw him bleeding on his threshold. On the ground in front lay the hacked remains of an Indian servant. As they approached, the overseer gasped, "Doegs, Doegs," and died.

The Doegs were Maryland natives. Their raid, they claimed later, was revenge against Mathew, who had failed to pay for goods he had received from them. A war party had been sent across the river to steal some of his hogs, but was discovered, and several Doegs were killed. When the survivors reported what had happened, another war party went to avenge them and killed the overseer.

The local militia now gathered a force of thirty settlers and started up the Potomac to search for the Doegs. At dawn, they crossed the river into Maryland and, coming on a fork in the path, divided their forces. One of the companies was led by a Captain Brent, the other by a Colonel Mason. Within a short distance of the fork, each arrived at an Indian cabin and surrounded it. Captain Brent was first to call on the occupants to come out. When a chief emerged, Brent seized him by his lock of hair, saying they had come for the murderer of Mathew's overseer. The Indian protested his ignorance, but slipped free of Brent's grip, and the Captain shot him dead with his pistol. Seeing their chief fallen, the Indians inside fired two or three times at the militia and attempted to escape. As the natives crowded through the cabin door, the soldiers fired back, killing ten and capturing the rest, including a boy of about eight, who was the son of the dead chief.

Meanwhile, the Indians trapped by Mason's party at the other cabin heard the shots and fled toward the brush through a hail of bullets. Fourteen had fallen by the time one grabbed Mason by the arm and was able to blurt out, *"Susquehanoughs netoughs!"* Mason turned and ran among his men shouting, "For the Lords sake shoot no more, these are our friends the Susquehanoughs."

The Susquehannock Indians had seemed "like Giants" to John Smith and the early Virginians when they encountered them, "the most strange people of all those Countries" of the Chesapeake. "For their language ... may well beseeme their proportions, sounding from them, as it were a great voice in a vault, or cave, as an Eccho," while their dress was "Cassacks made of Beares heades and skinnes that a man's necke goes through." They were Iroquois who had been decimated by plague and driven from their former habitations in the north by hostile Senecas. When Smith met them half a century earlier, they had been a formidable tribe among the Tidewater natives, capable of sending nearly six hundred men into the field of battle. But war and disease had reduced them to a remnant. Only about a hundred warriors survived.

But weakness had not made the Susquehannocks submissive. After the ambush, they launched sharp reprisal raids against the Maryland and Virginia frontiers, and built a palisaded fortress on the Potomac. On August 31, Governor Berkeley ordered a military force to investigate. Commanded by John Washington and Isaac Allerton, the force sailed up the Potomac, where it was joined by 250 Marylanders, an army of 1000 men.

The Susquehannock fortress was laid out in a square with high embankments on four sides, and enclosed by a ditch. A bulwark of trees, their trunks buried in the earth and their tops twisted together to make a wall half a foot thick, was formed around it. On one side, an open space extended several hundred feet to a point where the river was joined by Piscataway Creek. The settler armies pitched their camp on a hillside facing the fortress, their cavalry horses dispersed among the tents. Below, the broad Potomac flowed down from the Virginia highlands past Mockley Point toward Chesapeake Bay and the sea.

The first to reach the fortress were the Marylanders. Their commander immediately requested a meeting with the Indians, who sent out five of their chiefs under a flag of truce. They were told that the colonists had come to revenge the outrages committed against their settlements. The chiefs answered that they were not responsible for the raids, and laid blame on the Senecas. But the Maryland commander did not accept their answer and placed them under guard.

The following day, the Virginia commanders, Washington and Allerton, marched to the north bank of the creek to join the negotiations. The five chiefs were brought before them and again charged, this time with the murder of Mathew's overseer as well. Again they protested their innocence, but the colonists refused to believe them and ordered them bound.

One of the chiefs showed a medal he had been given by a former Maryland governor who had promised him protection and friendship for as long as the sun and moon would endure. But the Maryland commander disregarded the medal, and the chiefs were led off. Before they had been taken five hundred yards, their guards struck them from behind, smashing their heads.

When the five chiefs failed to return, the Susquehannocks inside the fort began firing at the militias. During the battle, the colonists called on the Indians several times to come out and negotiate. Each time the Indians responded, "Where are our . . . Great Men?"

The siege of the Susquehannock fortress lasted six weeks. During the struggle, small groups of Indians slipped away at night, killing militia guards as they passed through the encircling forces. Finally, the last of those still able to leave bolted the enclosure together. Shouting and firing their weapons, seventy-five men, women and children broke to the safety of the woods. When they were inside the boundaries of the Virginia Colony, the survivors regrouped and prepared their revenge.

In late January, the solitude of Virginia's western wilderness was shattered by a human firestorm. It raged all night through the plantations of Sittenburne Parish above the falls of the Rappahannock, igniting crops and buildings, and sweeping the settlers and families caught in its path to a fiery doom. Thirty-six men, women and children were killed before its violence was spent, some dying immediately, others spared only to be flayed by their captors and then burned alive.

News of the Susquehannock fury spread through the colony as settlers abandoned their homesteads and families fled. Within a fortnight, the plantations in the upper part of the parish had been reduced from seventy-one to eleven. Meanwhile, the Susquehannocks had shifted the storm center south, from the Rappahannock to the James, killing the overseer at the plantation of Nathaniel Bacon, destroying cattle and crops, and then extending the destruction to William Byrd's estate nearby.

After these attacks, the Susquehannocks paused in the path of their revenge to send a message to Governor Berkeley. They were sorry, they said, to see the Virginians who had been their friends become their enemies. Yet, their own emissaries of peace had been murdered, leaving them no recourse but what they had chosen. For each of their dead, ten settlers had been killed, to make up the disproportion between their great men who had been murdered and those whom they had slain. Yet, if they could have peace now and an indemnity for what they had lost, they were prepared to renew their league of amity with Virginia. Otherwise they would fight to the last.

When Governor Berkeley received the peace message from the Susquehannocks, he revoked his previous orders to send a force against them. Disbanding the army already formed, he sent word to the settlers in frontier areas to draw together for their own protection. He also called a session of the Burgesses to discuss his plans for the colony's defense.

It was a conservative strategy, designed to avoid further incidents at the frontier. The Susquehannocks seemed content with the revenge they had taken, and further escalation of the conflict would disrupt the fur trade and endanger the downriver plantations. Moreover, Berkeley feared that Virginia would invite the fate of New England, at that moment "ingaged in a warr with their Indians" which "wil end in their utter ruine." He was convinced that there was a connection between Philip's campaign against Plymouth and Massachusetts, and Virginia's troubles with the Susquehannocks. "The infection of the Indians in New-England has dilated it selfe to the Merilanders and the Northern parts of Virginia," he wrote to the colony's secretary. Above all, Berkeley wanted to avoid antagonizing the friendly and tributary tribes within the colony. "Our neighbour Indians are pretty well secured," he wrote, "for it is no doubt but they alsoe would be rid of us if they Could but I thanke god they have not dard to shew themselves our Enemies yet."

When the Assembly met, the tributary tribes were designated for recruitment as scouts and allies for the colony's defense. To prevent repetition of the recent frontier incidents and the unauthorized sales of guns to the natives, Berkeley suspended the Indian trade, putting its control in the hands of himself and his associates. Local commanders were forbidden to launch attacks on the enemy without the Governor's orders.

The centerpiece of Berkeley's strategy was the construction of a series of forts at the heads of the Chesapeake rivers, each to be manned by a levy of five hundred soldiers drawn from the lower counties. Such forts had proven effective during the Indian rising thirty years earlier, and since that time, the settler population had steadily increased while the native population had waned. The settlers now outnumbered the Indians thirteen to one.

But whatever its prospects for long-term success, Berkeley's strategy failed to allay the fears of the frontier settlers or to satisfy their growing demands for action against the Indians. These demands had beeen urgently pressed after the disbanding of the armed force. They now surfaced in a way that began to threaten the stability of the regime itself. As the Governor temporized and laid his plans for the new forts, his delay in dealing with the Indian menace began to be ascribed to avarice rather than policy. He, himself, became the focus of the discontent.

Berkeley's prosperity had flourished with Virginia's. His estate at Green Spring was one of the largest in the colony and his brick manor house its most stately residence. A speculator and trader, he had promoted explorations beyond the Alleghenies, extending the colony's commerce with the Indians. When the Crown granted proprietaries in neighboring Carolina, he was made a principal, appointing himself both Governor and Captain-General of the new colony. He was the King's deputy in granting land and appointing officials, in calling the Assembly and approving its acts. He was Commander in Chief of the military forces, Vice-Admiral, Lord Treasurer, Lord Keeper of the Seal, Chief Judge in all courts, President of the Council and Acting Bishop of the Anglican Church. All the hierarchies of Virginia's society ascended to his eminence.

Berkeley's order to the frontier to look after itself was assailed by his opponents as providing the Indians with both the opportunity and the encouragement to commit their outrages. His suspension of the fur trade was denounced as a bid to extend his personal monopoly, and it was said that for the profits of beaver he was ready to protect the Indians rather than the colonists.

But the thrust of the popular attack on Berkeley was directed against the proposal for the construction of the five forts. These were decried as expensive "mousetraps," ineffective against the enemy and costly to the taxpayers, but lucrative to the rich men on whose lands they were to be built, and so a "new device to draw money out of the poor man's pockets!"

"It rent the hearts of many that they should be compeld to work all day, nay all the year, for to reward those mole catchers at the forts . . . and at night could not find a place of safety to lie downe in, to rest their wery bones, for feare they should be shattered all to pieces by the Indians."

The discontent was centered in New Kent and the Southside counties below the James. Here the freedmen, denied access to the rich plantation lands of the Tidewater, lived at subsistence levels and coped with the burdens of heavy taxation and unemployment caused by the tobacco depression. The colony's tributary Indians were also concentrated in these areas, having also been pushed onto the marginal lands adjacent to the Southside and New Kent settlements. Many of the freedmen, rather than be tenants, seized the "remote barren Lands of the Indians," observed a supporter of Governor Berkeley. Although boundaries had been marked between them, by treaties, the freedmen let their cattle and hogs graze on the Indians' lands, "and if by Vermin or otherwise any be lost, then they exclame against the Indians, beate and abuse them (notwithstanding the Governors endeavour to the contrary). And this by the most moderate people is looked upon as one of the great causes of the Indians breach of peace, for itt is the opinion of too many there . . . that faith is not to be kept with the heathens."

The freedmen of the frontier did not share Berkeley's distinction between friendly and hostile tribes. "How shall wee know our enemyes from our Friends," they asked. "Are not the Indians all of a colour?" They called for war against all Indians who did not surrender their arms, provide hostages as proof of their fidelity, and aid in the war effort. "[If] wee must bee hang'd for Rebells for killing those that will destroy us, let them hang us, wee will venture that rather than lye at the mercy of a Barbarous Enemy, and be murdered as we are."

Following the March Assembly, complaints among the freedmen began to assume the dimensions of a more serious revolt.
In April, a force of armed Southsiders came to Berkeley seeking
a commission to go out against the Indians, who were rumored to
be coming down the heads of the James, fifty or sixty miles
away. When the Governor rejected their request, dismissing
them as a rabble, the volunteers withdrew to an encampment at
Jordan's Point, near Merchant's Hope in Henrico County, along
the southern bank of the James.

About the same time, across the river from their camp, four
of the largest planters of the frontier region were meeting to
discuss the situation. Among them was one of the Governor's
three councilors, Nathaniel Bacon, whose plantation had been
among those attacked by the Indians. Another was William
Byrd, Bacon's partner in the beaver trade before it was suspended by the Governor's order. As their talk progressed, the
other three tried to persuade Bacon to go see the volunteer
army that had gathered on the far side of the river.

Bacon had come to Virginia two years earlier, an "indifferent
tall but slender" man, "blackhair'd and of an ominous, pensive,
melancholly Aspect," which, one detractor said, shielded "a most
imperious dangerous hidden Pride of heart." The son of an
English squire and a cousin of the Governor's wife, he had arrived on a tobacco ship and had been welcomed by Berkeley,
who had made him a councilor. "Gentlemen of your quality
come very rarely into this country," the Governor wrote, "and
therefore when they do come are used by me with all respect."
Berkeley then assisted him in establishing a plantation on the
Henrico frontier, and in acquiring a license in the beaver trade.
With the other large landowners of the frontier, he shared an
antipathy for the Indians and a resentment of the downriver
planters.

Bacon consented to cross the James to see the soldiers at
Jordan's Point. They had been notified in advance of his coming, and when he arrived a shout went up: "A Bacon! a Bacon!
a Bacon!" He agreed to lead them, his resolve strengthened by
the assurance of his friends "that they would also goe along
with him to take Revenge upon the Indians, and drink Damna-

tion to their Soules to be true to him, and if hee could not obtain a Comission they would assist him as well and as much as if he had one."

Six months earlier, during the first incident with the Susquehannocks, Bacon had seized some friendly Appomattocs Indians and charged them with stealing corn. Berkeley had rebuked him for his "rash heady actions," which could produce "a Generall Combination of all the Indians against us." Now, as Bacon put himself at the head of the Jordan's Point army, Berkeley again rejected his request for a commission and warned him against becoming a rebel.

Bacon replied that his readiness to lead an Indian campaign had already had a salutary effect. "Since my being with the volunteers," he wrote, "the Exclaiming concerning the forts and Leavys had been suppressed and the discourse and earnestnesse of the people is against the Indians."

Berkeley adamantly repeated his refusal and summoned Bacon, who instead proceeded with his army to New Kent. When Berkeley was so informed, he issued a proclamation removing Bacon from the Governor's Council and declaring him a rebel. At the same time, he offered to resign as Governor to show that it was a question of authority and not his own record, and he announced new elections broadening the suffrage. All freedmen and not merely freeholders would be allowed to vote.

Following the proclamation, Berkeley led a company of three hundred men to the western plantations of the James, where he intended to arrest the insurgent. But Bacon had taken his army south in pursuit of the Susquehannocks, and when the Governor arrived at Curles Neck, he found only Bacon's wife. Berkeley informed her that he would most certainly hang her husband when he returned, and headed for Jamestown.

Bacon had made his way to a fort along the Roanoke River on the border of Carolina, inhabited by the friendly Occaneechee Indians. The Occaneechees offered to attack the Susquehannocks themselves, and did so, killing most and taking the rest as prisoners. No sooner had this been accomplished than Bacon and his troops became engaged in a battle with the Occaneechees. They fired at the Indian fort in volleys so thick, one recalled, "that the groans of men, woemen and children were soe loud that all their howling and singing could not hinder them from being heard." Taking the refuge by storm, they "disarmed and destroid them all, and the King's Forts where all his Treasure his wife children and ammunition were." Setting fire to the structure, they killed the rest, who "all burnt except 3 or 4 men who happening to escape brok out and had a Welcome by a liberall volley of shott from our men who lay close upon them."

Some of Bacon's opponents charged afterward that he had provoked the battle because he coveted the Occaneechees' valuable store of furs—"for itt is most true, that the great designe (which is confessed by some that was with him) was to gett the beaver." Bacon and his men denied the accusation, insisting that their action was defensive and that they did not take any plunder, "but burn't and destroid all. . . . Wee have left all nations of Indians (where wee have bin) ingaged in a civill warre amongst themselves," they reported, "soe that with great ease wee hope to manadge this advantage to their utter Ruine and destruction."

To the frontiersmen of Virginia, Bacon's campaign against the Indians was a great victory, and he returned to Henrico in triumph. "The country does so really love him," his wife Elizabeth wrote to her sister-in-law, "that they would not leave him alone anywhere." Nobody was against him, "but the governor and a few of his great men which have got their estates by the governor."

After missing Bacon at Curles Neck, Berkeley had returned to Jamestown to prepare for the next Assembly. Once again he invited Bacon to submit, indicated he would pardon him and offered to let him state his case before the King. Bacon declined, refusing to apologize for what he had done in the country's defense or to give up the campaign against "all Indians in general, for that they were all Enemies." Once again he asked for a commission.

Berkeley responded with a "Declaration and Remonstrance" indicting Bacon and all his followers as rebels and traitors. Bacon's victory over the Occaneechees, "wherein he so much boasted," Berkeley declared, "was fully foolishly and as I am informed Treacherously carried to the dishonor of the English nation." But the issue between them remained one of duly constituted authority. If England itself should be invaded by enemies, Berkeley argued, any officer of the King might raise a force to protect the King's subjects. But if, after the King knew of the invasion, the greatest peer of the realm should raise forces against the King's prohibition, "this would be now and was ever in al Ages and nations accounted Treason."

The Declaration was to be read in every county court and a copy was sent to London. When these orders were given, the sixty-eight-year-old Governor returned to his estate in Green Spring and put his wife aboard a ship for England with a letter asking to be replaced. ("Sir I am so over weaned with riding into al parts of the Country to stop this violent Rebellion that I am not able to support my selfe at this Age six months longer and therefore on my knees I beg his sacred majesty would send a more Vigorous Governor.")

In the last days of May, elections were held and on June 5, 1676, the new Assembly met in Jamestown. Its composition reflected the rising discontent in the colony and the broadening of the electorate that Berkeley's compromise had sanctioned. Some of the new burgesses, it was observed, were from the ranks of society, not freeholders of property, as they had been, but "Free men that had but lately crept out of the condition of Servants." Most were sympathetic to Bacon and his Indian crusade. Though under a charge of treason, Bacon was chosen by the electorate to represent Henrico County in the new Assembly.

On June 6, after some hesitation, Bacon sailed downriver, accompanied by forty armed followers, and anchored below Swann's Point near Jamestown, where the House was already in session. From the sloop, he sent word to Berkeley, asking him permission to come ashore in safety and take his seat in the Assembly. Berkeley's answer was given shortly in the form of a fusillade from the great guns of the Town Fort. Retreating to a point out of range, Bacon waited until nightfall and then slipped ashore to consult with his confederates in the town. Afterward, he returned to the sloop, and the following morning he attempted to sail upstream. But before he could get free, he was cut off and captured by the ship *Adam and Eve*, which

Berkeley had sent to take him. As the news spread, hundreds of Bacon's supporters gathered in Jamestown, a fact which his captors carefully kept from him.

When Bacon was brought before the Governor, Berkeley lifted his hands and eyes in triumph and remarked, "Now I behold the greatest Rebell that ever was in Virginia." The dejected Bacon remained silent.

The next morning, after the Assembly had met in a chamber over the general court and chosen its speaker, the Governor called the burgesses down. He then made a brief speech, in which he referred to the origins of the present troubles as a result of the unwarranted deaths of the five Susquehannock chiefs, who had gone out of their fort to negotiate under a flag of truce. "If they had killed my Grandfather and Grandmother, my father and Mother and all my friends," the Governor said, "yet if they had come to treat of Peace, they ought to have gone in Peace." The two commanders of the Potomac siege, Isaac Allerton and John Washington, were present as he spoke.

Then Berkeley rose again. "If there be joy in the presence of the angels over one sinner that repenteth," he said, "there is joy now, for we have a penitent sinner come before us. . . . Call Mr. Bacon."

Bacon came forward, sank to one knee and handed the Governor a letter of submission:

> I Nathaniel Bacon Jr. of Henrico County in Virginia doe hereby most Readily freely and most Willingly Acknowledge that I have been Guilty of diverse late unlawfull mutinous and Rebellious Practices Contrary to my duty to his most Sacred Majesties Governor and this Country by beating up of drums raiseing of men in Armes marching with them into Severall parts of his most Sacred Majesties Colony not only without Order and Comission but contrary to the Expresse Orders and Comands of the Right Honorable Sir William Berkeley Knight his Majesties Most Worthy Governor and Captain General of Virginia.

Bacon also acknowledged that the Governor had made him "severall Reiterated Gracious offers of Pardon," and promised that he would honor a new offer with "true faith and allegiance."

Berkeley said, "God forgive you, I forgive you." He repeated it three times.

Then Berkeley stood once more. "Mr. Bacon! if you will live Civilly but till next Quarter Court [he repeated the words twice] Ile promise to restore you againe to your Place There," and he pointed to Bacon's former seat on the Council. Berkeley didn't wait for the next quarter to keep his promise, however, but did so that very afternoon, and also offered Bacon the long-sought commission for his army.

"We al thought we had Gained a great Poynt," Berkeley later wrote, explaining his leniency, "in making him acknowledge his fault on his knees before the Grand Assembly whilse he was Ignorant of the Numbers that were Armed and resolved to rescue him out of our hands." These apprehensions were shared by Berkeley's Secretary of State, Philip Ludwell, who wrote England that Bacon's followers "continue soe Insolent, that wee have all the reason in the world to suspect, their Designes are Ruinouse beyond what they yet pretend." And he spoke of his fear of an "approaching Conflagration."

The Acts of the June Assembly reflected the mood of support for Bacon, which Berkeley for the moment had to accommodate. The forts were abandoned, and the army doubled. Bacon was named General and Commander in Chief, although the Governor continued to delay the signing of his commission. Pay for the force was to be provided in part by a license to the militia to keep all plunder of the defeated Indians. To increase the potential spoils, a new law allowed that Indian prisoners be held and accounted slaves for life. Berkeley's distinction between friendly and hostile natives was maintained, but Bacon's recent campaigns had already reduced this to a fine point. There were virtually no friendly Indians any more, wrote Ludwell to a correspondent, "but at least 1500 enemies more than wee needed to have had."

The June Acts had restored the right to vote to freedmen. They also provided that councilors and ministers would no longer be exempt from levies, and forbade all lower officials from taking fees, except for services rendered. Finally, they pardoned all "treasons . . . murders, fellonies, offences, crimes, contempts and misdemeanors" committed between March 1 and June 25.

While these matters were being settled, the central figure in the drama disappeared. Frustrated by Berkeley's refusal to sign the commission promised him and fearful for his safety, Bacon went back to Henrico.

On reaching the upper parts of the James, he was met by frontiersmen who were eager to know if he had received the promised commission. When they found that he had not, it was reported, "they began to sett up their throats in one comon kry of othes and curses," saying that they would either have a commission and serve under him, or they "would pull downe the Towne."

Three or four days later, Jamestown received word that Bacon was thirty miles up river with a troop of five hundred men. Berkeley sent for the militia, but so few responded that he was compelled to dismiss them. The troops led by Bacon— 400 on foot and 120 on horseback—arrived first at Sandy Bay, half a mile above Jamestown. Entering the town, they formed a body on the green "not a flight shot from the End of the Statehouse." They took possession of the river, the fort and all the avenues, disarmed everyone in sight, and then beat the drum for the Assembly to convene.

Less than an hour later, Bacon appeared at the corner of the State House with a file of riflemen on either side. As the Assembly watched from the windows, the aged Governor and his handful of councilors went out to meet them. Both Berkeley and Bacon were agitated, "like men Distracted." Bacon strutted "betwixt his Two files of Men with his Left Arm on Kenbow [akimbo] flinging his Right Arm every way." He repeated his demand for a commission while the crowd around them chanted, "Noe Levies, Noe Levies." Again Berkeley refused, saying he would rather have both his hands cut off than grant the commission that Bacon wanted. Then, suddenly baring his breast, he cried at Bacon, "Here! Shoot me, foregod, fair Mark, Shoot," and started to draw his sword, saying, "Lett us first try and end the difference singly between ourselves."

Bacon answered that he had not come to hurt the Governor

or anyone else. "We are Come for a Comission to save our Lives from th' Indians, which you have so often promised, and now We will have it before we go."

But the Governor abruptly turned toward his private apartment at the other end of the State House, ending the conversation. The gentlemen of his council trailed behind him, and behind them Bacon, by now in a frenzy, "with outragious Postures of his Head, Arms, Body, and Leggs, often tossing his hand from his Sword to his Hat." Following all was a detachment of Bacon's fusiliers. Pointing their cocked weapons at a window filled with the heads of terrified burgesses, they chanted, "We will have it, we will have it" (meaning the commission), until one of those inside, waving his handkerchief, cried back, "You shall have it, you shall have it," three or four times. The soldiers then set down their weapons. At the same time, the Governor strode into his quarters, with the frantic Bacon shouting after him, "I'le Kill Governor, Council, Assembly and all, and then Ile Sheath my Sword in my own heart's bloud."

An hour later Bacon was in the State House haranguing the burgesses for his commission. But after hearing him out, they told him that the granting of the commission was not in their power "nor of any other, save the Kings Viceregent our Governor." Now it was Berkeley's turn to yield under duress. With Bacon in absolute control of Jamestown, he signed the commission, making Bacon the General of all the volunteers of Virginia against the Indians.

In the midst of these proceedings, word came that the Indians had killed eight settlers in the heart of the country. Seizing the opportunity, Berkeley urged Bacon to hurry to the Indian frontier and requested that the members of the Assembly be allowed to return home to protect their families. He then withdrew to Green Spring, while Bacon took his army westward, to the falls of the James.

Though many of his followers came from the poorer classes, and some talked openly "of shareing men's estates among themselves," Bacon was himself a conservative. "No man could perceive in my manner, estate, or manner of living," he wrote in a letter defending himself, "how any indirect end, as levelling or rebellion, could make me desirous to exchange my fortune for worse." In his own view, he had limited himself to actions which protected the colony against its external enemy. Events now conspired to push Bacon beyond his limit.

Just as he was preparing to leave the encampment, news came that Berkeley had left Green Spring and gone to Gloucester County to raise a force against him. Once again Berkeley had declared him a rebel and a traitor. Bacon changed his plans, returning to the Tidewater to meet Berkeley's challenge. With this decision, he had crossed the boundary into civil war.

In Gloucester, however, Berkeley had failed to assemble an army. A thousand men had responded to his call to arms. But when they found that it was Bacon and not the Indians they had been summoned to fight, they left. Berkeley was powerless, but it was too late for Bacon to turn back.

On July 29, Bacon entered the Middle Plantation, and the next day issued a "Declaration of the People," indicting Berkeley and his supporters. It attacked the government for having raised "great unjust taxes upon the Commonalty" on "specious pretences of publique works," which were in fact "for the advancement of private favorites and other sinister ends." It accused the Governor of "advanceing to places of Judicature scandalous and Ignorant favorites," of having "wronged his Majesty's prerogative and interest by assumeing Monopoly of the Beaver trade," and of having "protected, favoured, and Imboldned the Indians against his Majesties loyall subjects."

The declaration demanded that the Governor and his supporters surrender within four days to Bacon and his army. Otherwise they would be condemned as traitors to king and country, and their estates confiscated. It was signed "Nath. Bacon, Generall by Consent of the People."

Simultaneously, Bacon issued a manifesto mocking the authority that had marked him for a traitor: "If Vertue be sin, if Piety be guilt, all the Principles of morality goodness and Justice be perverted, Wee must confesse That those who are now called Rebells may be in danger of those high imputations." The real guilt of the rebels, he declared, was "our open and

manifest aversion of all, not onely the Foreign but the protected and Darling Indians ... our Design not only to ruine
and extirpate all Indians in Generall but all Manner of Trade
and Commerce with them."

As he composed these documents, Bacon summoned the
"prime gentlemen" of the region to his quarters. When they
were assembled, he asked them to sign an oath promising not to
aid the Governor against him while he prosecuted the Indian
war. The planters agreed to the oath, but balked when Bacon
added two clauses which pledged them to oppose the Governor
if he attacked Bacon, and also any troops that might be sent
from England, before the King could be informed of the situation.

These provisions "did marvellously startle" those present, and
they refused to sign. But Bacon could not afford their neutrality.
After locking the doors of the house, he continued his case.
From noon to midnight he persuaded and cajoled them. They
must swear to all parts of the oath, he insisted, or there would
be no security, either for the country, the army or himself.
The Governor had already proclaimed him a rebel, and knew
that he would charge the Governor with no less than treason.
Since the Governor would suspect anyone who subscribed to
the least part of the agreement, they had no reason not to agree
to it all.

In the midst of these arguments, a gunner from the fort on the
York River appeared at Thorpe's house, begging aid for the
"poore people fled into it for protection" from Indian attack.
When asked how the strongest fortress in the country could
be in such danger, he replied that Berkeley had come in his ship
and seized its ammunition and arms. This news provided Bacon
with the argument he needed to sway even the most skeptical.
One by one they signed the oath.

Bacon was now ready to take the offensive. He dispatched
Giles Bland and William Carver to assemble a sea force and
invade Berkeley's sanctuary in Accomack. With three hundred
men they set sail for the Chesapeake's eastern shore. At the
same time, Bacon himself set out on his long-planned Indian
march.

At first, his party proceeded westward to the falls of the

James, where the hostile Susquehannocks had struck last. But the Indians had long since retreated to the forest uplands, beyond the reach of Bacon's force and supplies. After crossing the fall line, he switched his course northward, taking his men to the freshes of the York, which was the territory of the Pamunkeys, one of the tributary tribes most friendly to the colony.

After stopping a day because of rain—the summer was excessively wet—Bacon and his men pushed on when they could, "hunting and beating the Swamps up and down" in the August heat, until at last they reached a high ground. Bacon called a halt and addressed his troops: "I had rather my carcase should lye rotting in the woodes, and never see English mans face againe in Virginia," he said, "than misse of doing that service the country expects from me, and I vowed to performe against these heathen." Not to return successful would inspire the enemy as much as it would discourage the English. It would cause his adversaries "to insult and reflect on mee; that my Defence of the country is but Pretended and not Reall and (as they already say) I have other Designs and make this but my Pretense and cloke." Therefore he was resolved to go ahead at all costs, and any who wished to accompany him should also resolve "to undergoe all the hardshipps this wilde can afford." The others he gave leave to return to the plantations.

The next morning Bacon's men entered the Dragon Swamp and came upon the friendly Pamunkeys as they lay encamped by a small run of water. The Indians made no effort to resist but fled, with Bacon's forces pursuing. Several were killed and nearly fifty taken prisoner. Afterward, Bacon's men plundered the Pamunkey camp of its furs, cloths and other marketable possessions.

In the meantime, the naval invasion of Accomack had miscarried. Bland and Carver were captured, along with their entire fleet. Since Bacon was still away in the fevered thickets above the fall line, Berkeley decided to counterattack. Recruiting an army of three hundred men, he boarded five ships and ten sloops and set sail for Jamestown.

Berkeley's success in recruiting his army was the result of

a device which previously would have been inconceivable. Before, fear of the freedmen had played an important role in his attitude toward Bacon. How far was the ambitious rebel prepared to exploit the general discontent? Now, backed to the wall by his more popular adversary, Berkeley himself offered supporters the prospect of an improvement of their fortunes. To those who would join him, he promised new frontiers of liberty and new opportunities for material gain. For those servants whose masters had taken Bacon's oath—immediate release from servitude. For everyone, exemption from taxes (excepting church dues) and the opportunity to plunder the rebels' estates.

When word of the Governor's approach reached Bacon's supporters in Jamestown, they were thrown into a panic:

> All lookeing upon them selves as a people utterly undon[e], being equally exposed to the Governours displeasure, and the Indians bloody cruillties; Som[e] cursing the cause of there approcheing destruction, lookeing upo[n] the Oath to be no small ingredient, helping to fill up the measure of there Miserys: Others wishing [Bacon's] presence, as there onely Rock of safety, while other[s] look'd upon him as the onely quick sands ordained to swollow up and sinke the ship that should set them on shore, or keep them from drownding in the whirle poole of confuseion.

Arriving before the town with his flotilla, Berkeley summoned the inhabitants to surrender, promising a pardon to all except Bacon and his chief advisers. This proclamation was acceptable to many in the town, but some didn't trust it. Finally, they resolved to desert the citadel altogether, a plan which was put into action that night, "every one shifting for him selfe . . . in the gratest hast posible, for fere of being sent after."

With the town abandoned, Berkeley entered the next day at noon, kneeling first on the shore to thank God for his success. But no sooner had the Governor occupied the town with his forces than Bacon returned from the march against the Indians and put the capital under siege.

Bacon too, of late, had been hard pressed to raise an adequate force. During the rigors of his campaign against the Pamunkeys, his army had dwindled to little more than a hundred weary troops. In recruiting new soldiers for the siege, he resorted to Berkeley's frontier promise: liberty for any servant who would fight for him and (in a move outbidding Berkeley) for any Negro slave as well. When he arrived in Jamestown two days after the Governor, the three hundred men who came armed in his support were predominantly servants and slaves, to whom he had promised freedom.

Bacon also showed his shrewdness in placing the hapless Pamunkeys at the head of his columns. "As hee marcheth the People on the high wayes com[e] forth Praying for his happiness and railing ag't the Governour and his party, and seeing the Indian captives which they led along as in a shew of Tryumph, gave him many thanks for his care and endeavours for their Preservation bringing forth Frutis and Victualls for his Soldiers, the women telling him if hee wanted assistance they would come themselves after him."

Upon his arrival at Jamestown, Bacon had ridden onto Sandy Beach and fired his rifle at the palisade. Then, having surveyed the site, he had decided to dig a "French work" for a siege of the capital. To protect his positions from the great guns of the fort while the work was in progress, he rounded up the wives of the "prime gentlemen" in the town, and placed them on the ramparts of his trenchwork. As the work neared completion, he removed the "white aprons" and replaced them with the captured Pamunkeys.

Berkeley now gave the command to engage the rebels, but when his soldiers went to battle many mutinied and their officers "did not doe their whole Duty to suppresse them." Despite their superior numbers, they were badly beaten and Berkeley was forced to abandon the citadel. On September 19, Bacon entered Jamestown. Waiting until nightfall, so that the flames would appear more dreadful against the night sky, he set fire to Virginia's capital, burning every building within its walls, State House and all, not sparing even the church, which he torched himself.

After this act, which awed and frightened the Virginians, Bacon marched to Green Spring, where for several days he

feasted his men at the Governor's table. Accompanied by
William Byrd, he then took his army to Gloucester County to
plunder the loyalist estates. At Warner Hall, which was seized
as a temporary headquarters, Byrd was seen wandering through
the house, taking whatever precious goods he found, such as
"silks, fine Hollands, or other fine Linnings, silke stockings,
Ribbond, or the like," and sending them to Bacon's room.
Finally he passed out from too much wine, with Colonel
Warner's keys fastened firmly to his body, so "the soldiers
with him, lifted him up, and removed him . . . asleep from place
to place, and from chest to chest and tooke such goods as best
liked them."

Plundering became so much the preoccupation of Bacon's
troops that he was soon forced to seek measures to control it.
At the same time, he laid plans to invade the eastern shore,
where Berkeley had taken refuge once again.

The plans were not realized. The long swamp marches in the
wet and hot Virginia summer had taken their toll. For weeks
Bacon had been afflicted with lice and dysentery; the "swarms
of Vermyn," it was said, bred so intensely in his body that he
could not destroy them, and on October 26, 1676, he died.

The manner of his dying suggested an irony to his enemy:
"His usual oath . . . which he swore at least a Thousand times
a day was 'God damme my Blood!' " wrote Berkeley, "and God
so infected his blood, that it bred lice in an incredible number
so that for twenty dayes he never washt his shirts but burned
them. To this God added the bloody flux and an honest minister
wrote this epitaph upon him: 'Bacon's dead. I am sorry at my
heart/That lice and flux should act the hangman's part.' "

When troops from England arrived three months later, they
found the country desolate, its capital burned and its great
estates plundered. But they also found the Governor again in
control. Pockets of rebel soldiers had survived the death of
their leader, but they were now occupied almost exclusively in
plundering. The naval forces of the Governor dispersed and
subdued them easily.

As Berkeley vanquished his foes, he delivered them to the
hangman's noose, confiscating their estates and worldly goods

to replenish his plundered stores and those of the loyalist faction. About the middle of November, Captain Thomas Hansford, one of Bacon's chief officers, was taken prisoner. At his court martial, he requested only "that he might be shot like a Soulder and not . . . hang'd like a Dog." He was told by the court that he must be hanged as a rebel taken in arms against the King. This he denied up to the very end. On the scaffold designated for his crime, he declared that he "dyed a Loyall Subject, and a lover of his Countrey; and that he had never taken up arms, but for the destruction of the Indians, who had murthered so many Christians."

Hansford was the first settler born in Virginia to die upon a gallows. Later generations would memorialize him as "the first Native Martyr to American Liberty," and his leader, Bacon, would himself be called the "Torchbearer of the Revolution."

The Green Spring loyalists had no sooner won their struggle than they too were caught up in a conflict with the King. When the English troops arrived in January, they came with a royal commission to investigate the causes of the rebellion and restore order to the Crown's most valuable colony. Informed beforehand of the many grievances against Berkeley's administration— its arbitrary taxes, excessive salaries and unwarranted gifts—they came armed with a pardon for all the rebels, except Bacon, and a letter from the King accepting Berkeley's request for recall. They also had instructions to make "a good and just peace with the Neighbour Indians."

Shortly after their arrival, the commissioners sent a formal letter to the Virginia Assembly urging the conclusion of such a peace. The letter included a sharp attack on the attitudes toward the natives exemplified by Bacon and the rebel frontiersmen, "who soe rashly and causelessly cry up a warr, and seem to wish and aime at an utter extirpation of the Indians, (and are yett still the first that Complaine and murmer at the charge and taxes that on any just occasion attends such a warr)."

It was "a base ingratitude," they added, and "mere madness" for the colonists "to strive to destroy and extirpate those amicable Indians, who are soe farr from hurting them or us, that we must confess they are our best guards to secure us on the Frontiers from the incursions and suddaine assaults of those other Barbarous Indians of the Continent." The frontiersmen who wished the Indians' destruction did not understand their own security and interest, which was to be "satisfyed that they can quietlie enjoye soe large and faire a portion of their possessions as nowe they doe," and "not still Covett and seek to deprive [the Indians] of more, out of meer Itch of Luxurie rather than any reall lack of it." Such grasping "shames us and makes us a Reproach and byword to those more Morall heathens."

But while rebuking the rebels, the royal commissioners also discovered that the supporters of Bacon included almost the entire colony; the victorious Green Spring loyalists were isolated. All reports, including the Governor's, agreed "that of above fifteen Thousand, there are not above five hundred persons untainted in this rebellion." Under the scourge of Berkeley's revenge, this majority had become "of soe sullen and obstinate an humour," the commissioners warned the King, that if not treated with mercy and grace, " 'tis to be more than fear'd (as the common Rumour indicates) that they will either abandon their Plantations, putt off their servants and dispose of their stocks and away to other parts, or else . . . will only make Corne, instead of Tobacco, and soe sullenly sitt downe—carelesse of what becomes of their owne Estates or the Kings Customes."

Faced with the prospect of such a planter rebellion, the commissioners attempted to stop the confiscations of rebel estates and the executions of their masters. They admonished Berkeley, urging him to respect the King's pardon and written intent. But the Governor was firm in his course. For three months Berkeley and his faction continued to hang men and garner their possessions, while the King's representatives tried in vain to persuade him to return to England. When Berkeley finally left Virginia, on May 5, 1677, he left behind an Assembly of his peers determined to defend the fruits of the civil war they had won and the rights of the colony they ruled, even to the point of opposing the Crown and its royal governors.

When Berkeley reached London, he was a sick man, worn

down by the long struggle with Bacon, and already too ill for his audience with the King. A man who was with the Governor during his last days reported that the King had said of Berkeley, " 'That old fool has hang'd more men in that naked Country, than he had done for the Murther of his Father,' " and that hearing it, this royalist and American "dyed soon after without having seen his Majesty."

3

Durante Vita

THE waning of mortality in Virginia had created a class of freedmen, and a source of instability for its plantation society. Sometime after mid-century, the increasing opportunity for survival introduced a new factor into the colonial balance. As field laborers began to live longer than their terms of indenture, it began to be profitable for planters to think of their servitude in terms of life.

In 1650, the price of a black slave imported from Barbados to Virginia had been double that of a white servant whose passage was paid from the mother country. Neither was expected to last five years in the Tidewater fevers. As a result, there were only about three hundred slaves in the entire colony. Then the mortality began to subside. Within fifty years, black slaves constituted half the labor force and were being imported at the rate of more than five hundred a year. By that time, Virginia had become an important port of call in an international commerce which affected the course of empires.

The Atlantic slave trade had been conceived, improbably, two centuries earlier as an act of mercy. When Bartolomé de Las Casas beheld the suffering of the Indians of Hispaniola, he was overcome with pity. In the fifteen years since Christopher Columbus had discovered the Indies and staked his claim to a new world, Las Casas calculated, three million of its inhabitants had perished under the Spanish regime. Hundreds of thousands of Hispaniola's natives had been slain by Columbus and his conquistadores; others were shipped to Castile as slaves; still others were consumed in the mines to which they were driven to dig and labor for gold.

"Who of those born in future centuries will believe this?" Las Casas lamented. "I myself who am writing this and saw it and know most about it can hardly believe that such was possible."

In an effort to protect the remaining Indians from extinction, Las Casas appealed to the Spanish Crown. He asked the King to permit the import of stronger and more durable blacks from Africa to work in the Spanish mines. Las Casas' petition was supported by other courtiers with a greater influence and a less charitable interest in an African slave trade, and in 1517 the King consented.

For more than two centuries the slave trade was the pivot of European world empires, as Portuguese, Dutch, French and English sovereigns warred for the Spanish *asiento*—the right to transport slaves to the Spanish colonies in the New World. (Spain itself was excluded from the trade by a Papal Bull of 1493, which had divided the world and set the limits of empire. In the Pope's division, Africa was awarded to the Portuguese, the West Indies and most of the Americas to Spain.)

The struggle for a slaving empire was as transoceanic as the trade itself. Along the Gulf of Guinea and the western coasts of Africa, through the bights of Benin and Biafra, the slavers vied for Ashantis and Yorubas, Mandingos and Ibos to sell in the American Indies. Warfare spread through the African continent as tribal chiefs hunted captives for the trade. "Whenever the king of Barsally wants Goods or Brandy," an English slaver reported, "the king [plunders] some of his enemy Towns, seizing the People and selling them for such Commodities as he is in want of, which commonly is Brandy, or Rum, Gunpowder, Ball, Guns, Pistols and Cutlasses. In case he is not at War with any neighboring King, he falls on one of his own Towns, which are numerous, and uses them in the very same Manner."

In 1564, John Hawkins raided the Guinea coast, taking

three hundred Africans to Hispaniola, thus becoming the first Englishman to break the monopoly held by the Portuguese. More than a hundred years later, after a victory over the French, Britain acquired the coveted *asiento* and became the dominant slaving power.

It was the beginning of an era of boom in the slave trade that lasted for almost a century. Every year tens of thousands of Africans were transported in closely packed vessels across the Atlantic to destinations in the New World. "No one who has never seen a slave deck can form an idea of its horror," wrote a contemporary. On a lower level, only five feet high, twenty feet wide and a hundred and twenty feet long, more than seven hundred Africans would be laid side by side during the stifling nights of the ocean passage, so cramped they could not move. In the morning, they would be brought once again onto the main deck, weak and sick from their ordeal. "The stench, the suffocation, the confinement, oftentimes the violence of a neighbor, brought to every dawn its tale of corpses, and with scant gentleness, all were brought up and thrown over the side to the waiting sharks."

Perhaps a fifth of those transported died from the rigors of the "middle passage." Others, of their own volition, leaped to graves and freedom in the sea. Of those who survived, most were bound for the sugar islands of the West Indies, but an increasing number were shipped to Britain's colonies in the north.

The North American slave trade had begun at the end of the Pequot War, when the *Desire* sailed from Salem with a cargo of Pequot captives. Six years later a ship left Boston bound for Africa, where it picked up Negroes and carried them to Barbados. It returned to Boston the following year with salt, sugar and tobacco. This was the beginning of a triangular trade which soon became the cornerstone of New England's prosperity. It also gave rise to a new industry in New England and an unrivaled source of wealth in rum.

A "hot, hellish and terrible liquor" of the West Indies, rum was distilled from sugar cane and molasses. The natives of the islands called it "coow woow," and the settlers "kill devil." By the eighteenth century, it had become the main currency of the Atlantic slave trade.

"With missionaries on deck and rum in the hold," the slavers sailed from Boston and Providence, Newport and New London, for the west coast of Africa. There they traded rum for slaves, carried their cargoes to the Indies for sugar and molasses, and returned to New England, where the ingredients were used for the manufacture of more rum. By the middle of the eighteenth century, there were a hundred and fifty distilleries in the Puritan commonwealths of New England, and the manufacture of rum had long since become its principal industry.

As the Atlantic commerce thrived, the number of chattels in Britain's North American colonies increased. In 1710 there were 40,000 slaves in the colonies. Half a century later there were ten times that figure. Forty percent of them, moreover, were concentrated in one colony, Virginia.

In the beginning, the introduction of slavery in Virginia had been imperceptible. While black Africans were still an incidental element in the colony's population, the plantation system already accommodated a servile labor force. Overseers, corporal punishments and a legal code for runaways were established institutions. It was not until 1661 that a statute passed by the Virginia Assembly marked the first legal recognition of the existence of permanent servitude. The statute provided that a white servant who escaped with a Negro would be liable for the lost labor of both, because the Negro was "incapable of makeing satisfaction by addition of time." Two years later, Maryland passed a similar law, and the following year the first categorical act stating that Negroes were to serve *durante vita* —for life.

The principal employment of black slaves was in the rice and tobacco fields of the plantation economy. Tobacco, the staple of Maryland and Virginia, was a year-round crop; the Carolinas grew rich on rice and indigo. The rice crop was cultivated in hot swampy lowlands, rife with malarial fevers; indigo was grown on the light upland soils. In the early spring, the rice fields were flooded and the slave force shifted to the highlands, where they planted the indigo, gathered pitch and cut timber for export. Afterward, the flooding was drained, the young plants weeded, and then flooded and drained twice before the cropping in the fall. Following the harvest, there was threshing, cleaning and drying, then packaging and shipping, and afterward, during the winter, the preparation of the old ground for new planting.

The slave lacked the servant's incentive of future promise as a spur to his labors; his chains bound him to the plantation, but they did not make him work. Whereas the indentured servant could be punished by the extension of his term, the slave could not. A law passed by the Virginia Assembly in 1669 sought to rectify the situation in which the life term of the slave served to limit his oppression:

> *An act about the casuall killing of slaves.*
>
> Whereas the only law in force for the punishment of re-fractory servants resisting their master, mistris or overseer cannot be inflicted upon negroes [because it provided for an extension of their term of service], nor the obstinacy of many of them by other than violent meanes supprest, *Be it enacted and declared by this grand assembly,* if any slave resist his master... and by the extremity of the cor-rection should chance to die, that his death shall not be accompted Felony, but the master ... be acquit from moles-tation, since it cannot be presumed that prepensed malice (which alone makes murther Felony) should induce any man to destroy his own estate.

By this act, the power of master over slave was made absolute.

In order to justify the power, it became necessary to draw a further juridical line between servant and slave, between white and black. In 1670, free Negroes and Indians were pro-hibited from having Christian (i.e., white) servants, and ten years later the Assembly prescribed thirty lashes "if any negroe or other slave [i.e., Indian] shall presume to lift up his hand in opposition against *any* christian," whether master or servant. Indian and black were thus legally and morally diminished to a status below the status of the white.

The joining of Indian and black in the slave statutes was not incidental to white dominion on the Virginia frontier but an integral element of its design. A legal basis for Indian slavery had been established during Bacon's Rebellion, when the June

Assembly granted militiamen the right to sell their Indian captives. Following Bacon's defeat, the provision was confirmed and soldiers were ordered to "retayne and keepe all such Indian slaves or other Indian goods as they either have taken or hereafter shall take."

Enslaved as enemies or anathematized as slaves, Indians and blacks were to whites an untamed, alien presence, an abiding threat to the stability and order of their New World communities. On the one hand, slaves were considered a necessity. "The plantations and estates of this Province cannot be ... brought into use without the labor and service of negroes and other slaves," proclaimed the preamble to the slave code of South Carolina.

On the other hand, the peoples enslaved derived from fundamentally different origins and possessed special natures, requiring special laws of control: "The said negroes and other slaves brought unto the people of the Province for that purpose, are of barbarous, wild, savage natures, and such as renders them wholly unqualified to be governed by the laws, customs, and practices of this Province."

It was therefore necessary to make laws to "restrain the disorders, rapines and inhumanity to which they are naturally prone and inclined; and may also tend to the safety and security of the people of this Province and their estates."

Even as the wilderness was being conquered at the edges of colonial society, and its spaces opened for white settlement and civilization, a savage, hostile element was being incorporated into the very heart of the colonial order: an area of darkness, wild and unfathomable, an internal frontier.

The new frontier in many ways resembled the old. Conspiracies which the colonists had feared from the wilderness natives were now felt as the daily menace of their African labor force. "I Would Willingly Whisper to You The Strength of Your Country and The State of Your Militia," the Governor of Virginia confided to the Assembly in 1710, "Which on the Foot it Now Stands is so Imaginary A Defence, That we Cannot too Cautiously Conceal it from our Neighbors and our Slaves." Nor could the Assembly "too Earnestly Pray that Neither the

Lust of Dominion, nor the Desire of freedom May Stir those people to Any Attempts" against the colonial order. As between hostile neighbors and rebellious slaves, the Negroes were "The More Dangerous," because of "Their Dayly Encrease." White Virginia could depend neither on their "Stupidity" nor their "Babel of Languages" in protecting itself, for "freedom Wears a Cap which Can Without a Tongue, Call Togather all Those Who Long to Shake of[f] the fetters of Slavery."

Slaves were concentrated in the southern plantation colonies. Above the Delaware, only a small fraction of the total population were chattels, usually less than 5 percent. New York was an exception. In 1664, the Duke of York had seized New Netherland from the Dutch and the grant had been divided into four "middle colonies": Delaware, New Jersey, Pennsylvania and New York, whose sponsors were principals in the slave trade. Partly as a result of this sponsorship, chattels in the colony constituted almost 15 percent of the inhabitants.

As the slave population varied in density, so did the severity of the codes which measured white anxiety over the internal frontier. A slave found abroad after curfew in New England was punished by ten or fifteen stripes of the lash. For the same offense in Virginia, he could be dismembered. In Connecticut, a penalty of thirty lashes was sufficient to chastise the slave who struck a white. In South Carolina, it was sufficient only for the first offense. For the second, the slave was to have his nose slit and be branded in the face. For the third, he was to be put to death.

When slave rebellions occurred, retribution was swift and irrevocable. The bodies of rebels were often hanged in chains, their severed heads impaled on poles. They were then publicly displayed as a warning to others, even as the heads of Wituwamat, Philip and other natives had been displayed along the shore of settlement before them.

The colonists feared that, like the wilderness natives, blacks intended the "utter Extirpation" of white people from the New World. It was an anxiety intensified by the geography of the slave frontier: every black was a potential conspirator within the bosom of white society; every white was an accomplice in the injuries inflicted by the slave order. Those colonists who did not perpetrate brutalities directly, witnessed them daily and acquiesced.

No colony, north or south, was free from the specter of revolt. In the year 1712, twenty-seven slaves on the island of Manhattan armed themselves with guns, knives and hatchets and set fire to an outhouse near the center of town. As whites hurried to the burning structure, the blacks shot them from ambush. Nine were killed and five or six wounded. The militia was summoned and the blacks fled to the woods. When their escape was cut off, six of them committed suicide rather than be captured. The others were executed by hanging and burning; one was suspended in chains and starved, another broken on the wheel.

Tremors of the insurrection were felt up and down the seaboard settlements. In their fear, following the event, New Yorkers sought protection in more stringent laws. Slave crimes punishable by death were extended to include the willful burning of outhouses, barns, residences and corn, and conspiring to kill free subjects of the Queen.

Though rebellions were rare, individual revolt was not. The killing of masters, mistresses, overseers and whole families terrorized the plantation manor houses. Less violent forms of resistance, ranging from "laziness" to flight, cost the planters dearly. When discovered, these acts of defiance were severely revenged. Punishment for minor infringements was exacted under the lash, for more serious offenses under the knife.

The fear which ran along the internal frontier line was Biblical: what had been done to the slave would be returned to the master, an eye for an eye, and measure for measure. Guilt had a religious ground too. A Quaker meeting in Germantown expressed its opposition to slavery in these terms:

> There is a saying that we should do to all men like as we will be done ourselves; making no difference of what generation, descent, or colour they are. And those who steal or rob men, and those who buy or purchase them, are they not all alike? ... Pray, what thing in the world can be done worse towards us, than if men should rob or steal us away, and sell us for slaves to strange countries; separating husbands from their wives and children.

The argument of the opponents of slavery was a moral inversion of the law of revenge, the Christian conscience with which every colonist, freedman and master alike, had to make a final peace.

In 1732, a charter was granted for the colony of Georgia, to be located between the Savannah and Altamaha rivers, and then west to the "South Sea." The colony was to serve as a buffer between South Carolina and New Spain in Florida. Three years later, Georgia's trustees excluded slavery and liquor from its bounds, in order to render it "more Defencible" against the Spaniards, who, it was feared, would exploit both to stimulate a revolt and undermine the new regime.

Opposition to Georgia's statute against slavery brought about the first public clashes over the institution in America. In 1738, Scottish settlers in Darien defended the law in a petition to the trustees. "It's shocking to human Nature," it declared, "that any Race of Mankind, and their Posterity, should be sentenced to perpetual Slavery." It was an institution conceivable only as an instrument of retribution. The slaves had been "thrown amongst us to be our Scourge one Day or another for our Sins ... as Freedom to them must be as dear as to us, what a Scene of Horror must it bring about! And the longer it is un-executed, the bloody Scene must be the greater."

Georgia's edict was also praised by the Virginian William Byrd, whose father had survived Bacon's Rebellion to prosper in the slave trade, and who himself was a leading slaveowner and planter. In a letter to the Earl of Egmont, co-founder of Georgia, he suggested that Parliament should "put an end to this unchristian Traffick, of makeing Merchandise of our Fellow Creatures." For he viewed with apprehension the increasing numbers of black slaves in Virginia, and was burdened with the vision of another Bacon arising to ignite the fires of revolt:

> We have already at least 10,000 men of these descendants of Ham, fit to bear Arms, & these numbers increase every day, as well by birth, as by Importation. And in case there would arise a Man of desperate courage amongst us, exas-perated by a desperate fortune, he might with more advan-tage than Cataline kindle a Servile War. Such a man

might be dreadfully mischeivous before any opposition
could be formed against him, & tinge our Rivers as wide
as they are with blood.

If slavery was a source of internal division among whites,
causing them to examine their consciences and confront their
fears, it was also a powerful unifying force. As slavery made
white men masters over black, it made them more equal among
themselves. In part this was a consequence of the anxiety itself.
Just as the Indian menace on the New England frontier muted
conflicts among the settlers and created tolerance for heretics,
so the frontier of slavery created a common bond of survival
among the free. Men who were needed to suppress a rebellion
or defend a township were owed a share of social recognition
and respect.

In 1705, the Virginia Assembly took steps to enfranchise its
white freedmen and give them a stake in the colony's status quo.
It required masters to provide ten bushels of corn, thirty
shillings and a musket to servants who had completed their
terms of indenture. In addition, the Crown granted them fifty
acres of land, enabling them to join the ranks of the small
freeholders who already composed a majority of the voting
population.

The political power of the electorate had grown significantly
in the colonies following the English Revolution of 1688. In
transferring the line of royal succession from the House of
Stuart to the House of Hanover in 1701, Parliament had formally
established the principle of its supremacy over the Crown.
Political philosophers like John Locke and Algernon Sidney
elaborated theories based on natural rights to justify legislative
supremacy and government by consent, and these doctrines
found a hospitable soil in the American settlements. "Liberty
and Property" became the watchwords of an emerging republican spirit. In Virginia, the class of small property holders
was increasingly the fulcrum of its political struggles, whether
between factions of big planters, or between Assembly and
Crown.

Not all Virginians were pleased with these democratic developments. Governor Alexander Spotswood, for one, complained of "the misfortune of this Country that the bulk of the Ellectors of Assembly Men concists of the meaner sort of People." Such people favored "men of their own Stamp," and were "more easily impos'd upon by persons who are not restrain'd by any Principles of Truth or Hon'r." But the trend continued.

As a consequence of their new importance in the colonial balance and the efforts of politicians to win their favor, the freeholders gradually saw their taxes reduced to half their former rates, while their status vis-à-vis men of color continued to rise.

In 1705, the year the Assembly voted new privileges for freed servants, it also prescribed penalties of dismemberment for unruly slaves and ordered that all slave property be seized and sold by local churchwardens for the benefit of local parishes. Free blacks were prohibited from holding public office. In 1723, following a slave conspiracy, the Assembly denied free blacks the right to vote at all. It was necessary, the Governor explained, "to fix a perpetual Brand upon Free Negroes and Mulattos by excluding them from that great Privilege of a Freeman, well knowing they always did, and ever will, adhere to and favor the Slaves." It was an act of wisdom, he added, to make a distinction between the descendants of Englishmen and the offspring of blacks, "with whom they never were to be Accounted Equal."

The effort to subordinate black to white did not stop with the political sphere but reached inexorably into the private realm of family and generation. As early as 1662, Virginia had prescribed a double penalty "if any christian shall commit Fornication with a negro man or woman." Subsequent laws prohibited interracial marriages ("a disgrace of our Nation") and prescribed death or castration for any black rape of a white woman. Laws attempting to preserve a white purity extended to progeny as well. Any offspring of a mixed couple was declared legally black through three generations.

The line between the races, which was made to run as deep as blood, established a bond between all classes of white colonists. Its effect where slavery prevailed was to create an unusual space for the flourishing of a democratic spirit. The class of laborers, whose power was normally regarded as a threat to established order, was outside society altogether. This created a political ground for equality among whites. Another ground was psychological: "There is ... a circumstance attending these [southern] colonies," observed Edmund Burke, "which ... makes the spirit of liberty still more high and haughty than in those to the northward. It is, that in Virginia and the Carolinas they have a vast multitude of slaves. Where this is the case in any part of the world, those who are free, are by far the most proud and jealous of their freedom. Freedom is to them not only an enjoyment, but a kind of rank and privilege."

The American mission had become secularized since the days of the early Puritan settlements. But the spirit that informed it had not changed. Just as the freedom enjoyed by whites in the southern colonies conferred status and privilege, so Godliness was a sign of election for the Puritan settlers, ratifying their rights to the bounties of the New World. An indivisible bond linked power and virtue on the American frontier: the liberty of possession and the liberty of self. It was characteristic of America's political philosophers that this should be accepted as a practical truth, and cast in a universal light: "Man has certainly an exalted soul," observed John Adams, "and the same principle in human nature,—that aspiring, noble principle founded in benevolence, and cherished by knowledge; I mean the love of power, which has been so often the cause of slavery, —has, whenever freedom has existed, been the cause of freedom."

PART III

THE CAUSE
OF
FREEDOM

1

Forest Wars

IN the years intervening since the first settlements at James-town and Plymouth, the displacement and extirpation of the Indians of the coastal plain had been steady and unrelenting. The tide of colonization flowed inland from the bays, following the rivers and the river valleys, and inundating the native peoples in its path. But its progress was not everywhere the same. In New England and the Chesapeake, Wampanoags and Pequots, Powhatans and Susquehannocks first opposed and then resisted its course. Now their survivors were but a scattered flotsam on the surface of the colonial stream.

Elsewhere, tribes attempted to avoid their fate. Across the rolling woodlands of Pennsylvania and the lands stretching north to the Great Lakes, Delawares, Shawnees, Eries and Hurons did not resist but adapted to the current and tested it for a foothold to survive. In the end, their efforts were also in vain, and the flood of settlement submerged them. But the thunder gods of their deluge were native rather than European, their conquerors were the Iroquois—the most feared and inde-pendent of the wilderness tribes.

At the time of the first European settlements, the Iroquoian peoples occupied a territory extending from the Great Lakes in Canada to the border of New England. Hurons and Eries made their homes in the north on the banks of the Canadian water-ways; Tuscaroras and Cherokees had migrated down the Appalachian system as far south as Georgia and the Carolinas. Along the Niagara lived the parent tribe of all the Iroquois, and in one of its villages dwelled a woman named Ji-gon-sa-seh— "the Mother of Nations," who was thought to be a lineal descendant of the first woman on earth.

The Huron-Iroquois lived in peace with the Algonquin natives who were the predominant peoples of the Canadian woodlands. But both were at war with the league of Iroquois tribes, which had been formed in the region to the south. The "Five Nations" lived along the plain of Lake Ontario and the green valley of the Mohawk River. Their league was called *Ganonsyoni*, which meant "The Lodge Extended Lengthwise," and all the tribes were considered to be a family dwelling in the lodge. Mohawks were Keepers of the Eastern Door, Senecas of the Western; Onondagas, who lived in the center, were Keepers of the Fire; Oneidas and Cayugas were Younger Brothers. At the grand councils, which were held in Onondaga, younger and elder brothers sat on opposite sides of the lodge across the fire; the Onondagas sat in the middle and kept the balance. The League of Five Nations was a powerful wilderness force. Its members called themselves *Ongue-honwe*—"Men Surpassing All Others."

Before the English built their first settlements on the lands of Powhatan and Massasoit, other Europeans had made contact with the tribes of the far north. In 1534, the Frenchman Jacques Cartier sailed into the mouth of the Saint Lawrence River, which linked the Great Lakes to the sea, and was greeted by natives who offered him walrus, bear and fox pelts for axes, knives and other iron implements not found in the New World. The following winter he returned with more iron goods and was feted by a thousand Indians gathered on a slope which he named Mont Réal, overlooking the juncture of the Saint Lawrence with the Ottawa River.

Regular trading was established between the French and the Canadian natives. Following subsequent voyages by Samuel de Champlain, the French established trading posts at Montreal, Trois Rivières and Quebec along the Saint Lawrence. Native competition for a share in the commerce was great. Long-standing rivalries between the Iroquois League and the Laurentian tribes erupted in open warfare. In the summer of 1609, Champlain sailed south with a war party of Hurons and Algonquins to the Lake of the Iroquois. At nightfall, he set up camp on the shore of the lake, which he renamed Champlain.

The following morning, two hundred Mohawks approached his forces. They were "stout and robust in appearance," he recalled, and "they came at a slow pace towards us, with a dignity and assurance which greatly pleased me, having three chiefs at their head."

Champlain was wearing a plumed helmet and a plate corselet, and he carried an arquebus, which he had loaded with four balls. When the antagonists were thirty paces from each other, the French Captain raised his musket to his cheek and fired, instantly killing two chiefs and mortally wounding the third. Another blast from one of the French muskets broke the Mohawk ranks, and they fled in disorder.

Even while these shots were crackling in the primeval stillness of Lake Champlain, a Dutch vessel was following the expansive current that flowed north from the sea to its headwaters in the Mohawk Valley. Henry Hudson was searching for a northwest passage to the Orient when he discovered the river that came to bear his name. Encountering natives (the Dutch called them *Wilden* or *wilde Menschen*), he traded knives, hatchets and brandy for otter and beaver skins. The Dutch built two posts, one on the island of Manhattan in the sea harbor of New Amsterdam, and the other just below the juncture of the Mohawk and Hudson rivers, which became known as Beverwyck, signifying its place as the center of the fur trade.

The natives who met Hudson were Mohicans, an Algonquin tribe dwelling on the east bank of the river. About ten years after the Dutch established their trading posts, war broke out between the Mohicans and the Mohawk Iroquois of the west bank. The Mohicans were defeated and driven into the Connecticut Valley, where they split into two branches under the sachems Uncas and Sassacus, the one forming an alliance with the nascent Massachusetts Bay Colony, the other resisting the English advance, and taking the name Pequot for his tribe.

From the moment of the Mohawk victory on the Hudson,

the Five Nations became the chief trading partners of the Dutch. In 1626, seven thousand beaver and nearly a thousand otter skins were shipped from New Amsterdam to Holland; by 1633, the number had increased to nearly thirty thousand.

Long before the appearance of the Europeans, the peoples of the New World had conducted an extensive trade with one another. Grain surpluses were exchanged for meat and fish, tobacco for foodstuffs; copper mined in the northern Great Lakes found its way as far south as the Chesapeake, while obsidian for making arrowheads traveled more than a thousand miles from its sources in the west.

But the trade with the newcomers was different. The Indians of the New World were living in the Stone Age when Europeans first encountered them. Their trade was the exchange of simple surpluses. The new commerce transformed the very structure of native life. The wooden and clay vessels in which meals were cooked on laboriously heated rocks were replaced with iron kettles. The trees previously toppled by a painstaking effort of burning and girdling were now swiftly cut with metal axes. The game animals arduously stalked with flinthead spears and arrows were now pursued with powder and shot. The stone club and bow gave way to the steel tomahawk and gun. Firearms became the principal instruments of war; bowmen became scarce, combat more deadly.

To repair and supply the new weaponry, the Indians had to return continually to the colonial source. In war and peace, the native became dependent on the European trader. Since the demand for fur hats and coats in the capitals of Europe was unrelated to the forest cycles, the hunt came to embrace all seasons and spread across limitless stretches of the interior. Once part of the rhythm of wilderness life, the quest for fur-bearing animals became an encompassing occupation. Tribal boundaries were invaded; communal blood was spilled.

In 1640, the beaver vanished from the Mohawk and Hudson valleys. The supply had been exhausted by the hunt. The disappearance of the principal fur-bearing animal of the Iroquois threatened the League with extinction. Without pelts they had nothing to exchange for the guns and powder that had become the very means of tribal sustenance and defense. To avert disaster, the Iroquois donned their ceremonial paint and took to the warpath along the northern trails. Their objective: the conquest of the Huron-Iroquois and control of the Ottawa and Saint Lawrence furs.

The Hurons had long acted as middlemen for the fur commerce in the Great Lakes regions, taking the skins of the Petuns and Georgian Bay Ottawas over the river routes to the French posts on the Saint Lawrence. Until recently, they had greatly outnumbered the Iroquois of the Five Nations. But in the winter of 1637, an epidemic of smallpox had swept through the Huron communities, taking half the population in its wake. Reduced by disease and lacking firearms, the Huron survivors were no match for the war parties that descended on them in unprecedented strength beginning in the year 1641. Senecas, Cayugas, and Onondagas of the League laid siege to the frontier villages of Huronia, while the trade convoys along the Ottawa and Saint Lawrence rivers were under constant attack by Mohawks and Oneidas.

"The scourges of God have fallen, one after another on this poor Barbarous People," lamented a Jesuit missionary; "the terror and dread of War have followed the fatal diseases which in previous Years caused mourning and desolation everywhere." Under cover of night and hidden by the forest shadows, parties of the enemy had crept into the Huron country to strike without mercy. "Even women, and children at the breast, are not in security within sight of the palisades of their own villages," the Jesuit reported.

When the Huron men took their beaver-laden canoes down the waterways to Trois Rivières or Quebec, the Iroquois lay in wait for them, ready to ambush their convoys and wreak terrible torments on those taken alive. The Hurons were virtually defenseless against these attacks, because of the Iroquois firearms, acquired from the Dutch. "A single discharge of fifty or sixty arquebuses," reported a Jesuit missionary, "would be sufficient to cause terror to a thousand Hurons who might be going down in company, and make them prey of a hostile Army lying in wait for them as they pass."

The Iroquois had raided the Huron trading routes before, but the attacks had been seasonal and sporadic. Now they were conducted with a thoroughness that brought the fur traffic to a halt. Where previously the attacks had been launched during the summer months at isolated points along the rivers and the river portages, they were mounted now the length of the routes, all year round. Whereas in the past the Iroquois had attacked villages in occasional raids for purposes of revenge, the attacks now lasted all summer and were waged without quarter. Entire communities were destroyed.

Other tribes of the trading empire the Hurons had built were drawn into the vortex of destruction. The Algonquins of Iroquet were dispersed into the interior, and the Allumettes of the Ottawa region, having first been decimated by disease, were scattered by the Iroquois assaults and "reduced to nothing."

The newly acquired weapons of the Iroquois accounted in part for the levels of destruction, but the objectives of warfare had also changed. Previously, the wars of the forest had been conducted for limited purposes: to establish a superiority or redress a grievance. Their range was restricted, their torments circumscribed. The strongest members of the community bore the burdens of victory and defeat. Tribute payments compensated losses and established tribal primacy. But the wars in which the Iroquois were now engaged were different. They were less to humble the opponent than to eliminate him from the competition.

Four years after the Iroquois attacks began, negotiations between the French and the warring tribes established peace along the northern trade routes. During the interlude, the Mohawk Iroquois made efforts to divert the Huron fur trade through their territory in order to collect a tribute. They also proposed "that the chase be everywhere free; that the landmarks and the boundaries of all these great countries be raised; and that each one should find himself everywhere in his own country." These demands were not met: the Iroquois remained excluded from the Canadian fur trade and the economy it supported. The attacks resumed.

In March 1649, a series of disasters struck Huronia. At dawn on the 16th, with the winter snow still blanketing the forest floor, a thousand Iroquois of the Seneca and Mohawk nations entered the unsuspecting village of St. Ignace and massacred the population. Only three of the inhabitants escaped to the town of St. Louis, a few miles away, where the Iroquois began a second devastating assault. Of 150 defending warriors, only a score survived. The Iroquois themselves suffered severe losses and retreated from the town, pursued by several hundred neighboring Petuns, who now joined the Huron cause.

But the blow to Huronia had been mortal. Never had its villages been attacked in winter; never had the attackers appeared in such force or been so wanton in their destruction. Panic seized the survivors, who set fire to their own villages and fled. Some escaped to the Petuns and Eries, some to the Ottawas in the west. But most made their way to the Jesuit mission on Christian Island in Lake Huron. This was to be the graveyard of the Huron Nation.

Throughout the summer, the Huron refugees crowded into the Jesuit sanctuary, until by autumn the number on the island reached ten thousand. Winter came and covered the ground in deep snow; the lakes and rivers froze. The Hurons, who had neither stored provisions nor had time to sow and harvest a crop, soon became desperate. "Then it was," one Jesuit recorded, "that we were compelled to behold dying skeletons eking out a miserable life, feeding even on the excrements and refuse of nature." The Hurons were no less horrified than Frenchmen at the idea of eating human flesh, the missionary observed, but now "necessity had no longer law; and famished teeth ceased to discern the nature of that they ate. Mothers fed upon their children; brothers on their brothers; while children recognized no longer, in a corpse, him whom, while he lived they had called their Father." By the spring, scarcely five hundred Hurons remained to attempt a final pilgrimage to the safety of Quebec.

Meanwhile, the wars of the Iroquois continued. In November, word reached the mission on Christian Island that the League was about to attack the Petuns, who had come to Huronia's aid. The information was relayed to St. Jean, a village of five hundred Petun families. The Petuns decided to send out a war party and attempt to strike the Iroquois first. But the Iroquois eluded the warriors and, circling back, surprised the undefended village. Some of the populace managed to flee, others less fortunate were slain on the spot and the village was put to the torch. All the old and young who were judged too weak to make the retreat were put to death.

Two days later, the Petun warriors of St. Jean returned. Already they suspected the misfortune that had overtaken them: "But now they beheld it with their own eyes . . . at the sight of the ashes, and the dead bodies of their relatives, their wives, and their children, they maintained for half the day a profound silence,—seated, after the manner of savages, upon the ground, without lifting their eyes, or uttering even a sigh,—like marble statues, without speech, without sight, and without motion. For it is thus that Savages mourn."

Following the disaster to the Petuns, the Iroquois attacked the Neutrals of Niagara, dispersing the survivors as they had the Hurons, Allumettes and Iroquets before them.

In 1653, the Iroquois signed a peace with the French. The following year, they defeated and dispersed the Eries, the last of their major rivals in the lower Great Lakes region. They had accomplished their main purpose—the breaking of the fur monopoly of the Huron-Algonquin tribes. "The Huron fleets no longer come down to trade," a missionary reported; "the Algonquins are depopulated; and the more distant Nations are withdrawing still farther, fearing the fire of the Iroquois."

But even as the Iroquois completed their conquests, the fruits of victory seemed to slip from their grasp. They had failed to extinguish the remnants of the nations they had destroyed, and the survivors were able to find refuge among remoter peoples. Many Hurons joined the Georgian Bay Ottawas, who had migrated to the shores of Lake Superior after the destruction of Huronia. Other migrants fled the path of the Iroquois conquests westward. Algonquin Sauks, Fox, Potawatomis and others abandoned the region of lower Michigan and fled to the security of the northern lake and Green Bay. No matter how deep into the interior wilderness the tribes retreated, however, the lure of the European market remained. As the refugee Indians regrouped, they were drawn once again to the chain of dependence and conflict; the channels of trade extended themselves farther and farther west. The powerful Ottawas now supplanted the Hurons as middlemen, organizing the traffic along the waterways and portages to the French posts at Trois Rivières and Montreal.

Meanwhile, the Iroquois had also begun to expand their quest for beaver south to the valleys of the Delaware and the Susquehanna and west across the Appalachian barrier to the Ohio and the Mississippi. A powerful impetus to the new expansion was given by the English conquest of New Netherland in 1664. As a result of the English victory, the Dutch colony became New York, Beverwyck was renamed Albany and the League of the Iroquois came to hold a crucial balance between the empires of France and England as they confronted each other across a continent.

Following the English victory, a wave of immigrants poured into the Hudson Valley, trade expanded, and by 1670 the Iroquois were bringing annually more than a million pounds of beaver skins to the Albany post for shipment to markets abroad. The Five Nations held the western gate to the English commerce from New York, and the southwestern gate of the French commerce to the interior. Continual warfare was the price they paid to maintain the advantage. Their conflicts extended from the lands of the Abnaki on the coast of Maine, to the Pennsylvania valley of the Susquehannas, and as far west as the Illinois.

But the most formidable foe of the Iroquois was the French, who faced them across the length of the northern tier. In the past, New France had made attempts to win the Iroquois from the English trade, but to no avail. Superior efficiency in industry, domination of the sea lanes, and the impassability of the Saint Lawrence during the long Canadian winters provided the English with an insurmountable advantage over the French trade. One beaver skin in Albany was worth as much in manufactured goods to the natives as four skins in Montreal.

For almost a century, the English trade alliance with the Iroquois provided a critical military shield for the English colonies against the French. The territory of the League lacked a mountain wall, and with its extensive river and lake systems was the natural gateway to the interior of the continent. It had always been the dream of the French to block this passage— drawing a military line down the Hudson Valley from the Saint Lawrence to Manhattan—and cut the English colonies in two. The small English settlements along the line of advance could not have resisted the French strength. All that stood between France and control of the valley was the League of the Iroquois, "a bulwark," as one New York governor put it, "between us & the French & all other Indians."

Unable to seize the trade directly to the south, the French sent their captains inland along the Great Lakes system and down the waterways that fed them. In 1672, Louis de Baude, Comte de Frontenac, became Governor of New France and built a fort at the entrance to Lake Ontario. Ottawas, Potawatomis and other western tribes that had previously brought their pelts over the perilous river routes to Montreal now traded them at Fort Frontenac. From this traffic, the Comte and his commander, Robert Cavelier, Sieur de La Salle, reaped handsome profits.

Six years after the construction of Fort Frontenac, La Salle built a fort at Niagara as the second of a projected chain of posts aimed at controlling all the western tribes and the Iroquois fur trade. To the Niagara post came Potawatomis, Eries, Miamis and southern Ottawas who had previously brought their furs to the Iroquois. La Salle also began the purchase of bison skins from the tribes farther west, as well as otter, marten, bear and deer skins, which he shipped across Lake Ontario and up the Saint Lawrence.

In 1682, La Salle navigated the Mississippi all the way to the Gulf of Mexico and claimed for the French King "possession of that river, of all the rivers that enter it and of all the country watered by them." To back his claims, the French continued the line of forts they had begun along the water routes west and south toward New Orleans, in the process engrossing all the English settlements in America.

As New France encroached more and more on the Iroquois trade, conflicts with the Five Nations grew more frequent and more intense. In 1687, a royal memo declared that war with the Iroquois was "absolutely necessary to avert from us a general Indian Rebellion which would bring down ruin on our trade and cause eventually even the extirpation of our Colony." Acting on this policy, the French launched a punitive assault against the Senecas, burning and destroying five of their villages. The League retaliated. In 1689, they destroyed the post at Niagara and then fell upon the village of Lachine, near Montreal, massacring the inhabitants—men, women and children.

Even as the Iroquois were inflicting the worst defeat ever suffered by New France, the French and English powers were coming to blows on the continent of Europe. Their conflict extended over the global lengths of their empires in battles that raged from the slave markets of western Africa to the fur routes of the Canadian north.

At the outset of King William's War (as the conflict was called in America), the Governor of New York sent a plea to the other colonies. Emphasizing the urgency of the Iroquois alliance to the security of the English settlements, he asked for a joint effort in defense of the Albany frontier, "the only bulwark and safe guard of all their Majestys' plantacions on the main of America. For we have nothing but that place that keeps our Indians steady to us and the loss of that must be the loss of them, and the loss of them must be the loss of all the King's interest on this Continent."

But the colonies were too divided among themselves to heed the call. Conflicting claims to wilderness territory and rivalries over shares in the fur trade frustrated the effort to form a common defense. As a result, although their conflicts with the French extended the length of the northern frontier, the burden of the warfare fell on their Indian allies. "You Sett us on dayly to fight & destroy your Enemies," a Mohawk sachem complained bitterly to the English afterward, ". . . but wee See not that you doe anything to it yourSelfs, neither doe wee See any great Strenth you have to oppose them if [the] Enemy should break out upon you."

In the eight years of King William's War, the Five Nations lost nearly a third of their warriors. The fighting had little effect, however, on the boundaries and other disputed claims between New England and New France, and when the conflict in Europe resumed over the Spanish succession a few years later, hostilities were renewed in America also. This phase of the Anglo-French struggle was known as Queen Anne's War.

In this conflict, the Iroquois did not fight as allies of the English. During the summer of 1701, they had come to an agreement with the French and French Indians to remain neutral in future wars. New York followed the Iroquois example, adopting a policy of neutrality in Queen Anne's War to protect its fur trade. As a result, New England was left to battle New France alone. Queen Anne's War was as inconclusive as its predecessor, although the French lost Acadia. The fighting was ended by the Peace of Utrecht in 1713.

In the course of the wars which the Iroquois had waged for the northern furs, they had come to exercise sovereignty over a vast territory in America: from the Kennebec River in Maine, west across the Appalachian mountain barrier to the valley of the Ohio, and then north to Lake Michigan and the Canadian Ottawa River. Many tribes came under their dominion. Some had not been vanquished but had migrated to the Iroquois regions in order to place themselves under the protection of the League. The Tuscaroras had been driven from their homes in the Carolinas in 1715 by the expanding settlers and appealed to the League for aid. They were allowed to settle in the Iroquois territory of northern Pennsylvania and were admitted to full membership in the confederacy, which became the Six Nations.

Other tribes had to content themselves with a tributary status. The Nanticokes and Conoys had migrated to the Susquehanna Valley of Pennsylvania to escape subjugation by the settlers of Maryland. Under policies laid down by its founder, William Penn, and continued under its Quaker regimes, the colony of Pennsylvania was more willing to recognize native rights than other colonial governments. "The people of Maryland do not treat the Indians as you and others do," an Iroquois spokesman told Penn, "for they make slaves of them and sell their children for money." Fear of enslavement and persecution caused the Miamis and the Tutelos to move up the Chesapeake and avail themselves of the liberality of the Pennsylvanians and the protective shield of the Iroquois League. From the south also came the Shawnees, and from the east the Delawares.

The Delawares, who had been subjugated by the League years earlier, called themselves *Lenni Lenape* or the "Original People." Dispossessed by early Dutch and Swedish settlers, and then by the English, and decimated by smallpox, they had been driven west from the Delaware basin into pastures of the Susquehanna Valley.

Under the terms of their subjugation by the Iroquois, the Delawares were confined to raising corn and subsistence hunting, and denied the power to make war. The Iroquois called this manner of subjection "making them women." "We, the Mohocks are Men," a Mohawk spokesman explained to a colonial official; "we are made so from above, but the Delawares are Women, and under our Protection, and of too low a kind to be Men."

Iroquois domination of the Delawares and the other tribes that had found refuge in Pennsylvania was encouraged by the colonial government, which derived many benefits as a result. When the Pennsylvania proprietors sought to dispossess the Indians of their land at the forks of the Delaware, it was the Iroquois who were called in to enforce the removal. The Delaware chiefs were summoned to Philadelphia to appear before their conquerors, and an Iroquois spokesman, Canesetego, addressed them: "We have seen with our Eyes a Deed sign'd by nine of your Ancestors above *Fifty* years ago for this very Land, and a Release sign'd, not many Years since, by some of yourselves and Chiefs now living," he scolded them. "But how came you to take upon you to sell . . . Land at all: We conquered you; we made Women of you; you know you are Women, and can no more sell Land than Women; nor is it fit you should have the Power of selling Lands, since you would abuse it. This Land that you claim is gone through your Guts; you have been furnish'd with Cloaths, Meat and Drink by the Goods paid you for it, and now you want it again, like Children as you are."

The warriors who came under the aegis of the Iroquois League strengthened the links of the "covenant chain" which had been forged between the colonies and the League, and which the colonial authorities hoped would block the expanding power of New France. The growth of the League was also useful to the British in advancing their own territorial claims against the French on the western frontier. At the Peace of Utrecht, the parties had agreed that the absent Iroquois were legally subjects of the English Crown. The English now used this concession to advance their claim to all the lands conquered by the Iroquois in their wars for the control of the fur trade. In particular, they invoked it to lay claim to a vast territory south of Lake Erie and west of the Alleghenies that had been emptied of its inhabitants in the course of the Iroquois conquests. In the middle of the eighteenth century, the Ohio Valley, already claimed for the French by La Salle, became the focus of a climactic struggle between the two powers for control of the American continent.

2

Battle for Empire

FROM the end of King Philip's War to the Peace of Utrecht in 1713, the line of settlement did not advance. Pioneers had long since crossed the plains of the coastal tidelands, passing beyond the fall line of the rivers to the upland valleys of the Piedmont Plateau. But for more than a century, the steep passes, dense forests and complex ranges of the Appalachian mountain barrier discouraged further advance. Traders might penetrate hundreds of miles into the continental interior; settlers still clustered along a strip of land no more than fifty miles from the shore.

Along this coastal shelf, 400,000 people engaged in farming and fishing, trade and manufacture. The territory they occupied was sparsely populated; few towns interrupted its landscape, and the scent of its uncut pine forests could be detected miles out at sea. South of the Delaware, the largest city was the port of Charleston, inhabited by scarcely 250 families. In the north, Boston and New York were the principal centers, each with less than 10,000 inhabitants, slave and free.

The Peace of Utrecht launched a new migration, which was to transform the character of the seaboard society and push its frontiers into the transmontane pastures to the west. In barely twenty years, the population of the American colonies would double, and double in twenty again. Writing at mid-century, the clerk of the Pennsylvania Legislature, Benjamin Franklin, celebrated the presence of "upwards of One Million English Souls in North-America." He found the very proportions bracing: "This million doubling, suppose but once in 25 Years, will in another Century be more than the People of England, and the greatest Number of Englishmen will be on this Side the Water. What an Accession of Power to the British Empire by Sea as well as Land! What an Increase of Trade and Navigation! . . . We have been here but little more than 100 Years, and yet the Force of our Privateers in the Late War, united, was greater, both in Men and Guns, than that of the whole British Navy in Queen Elizabeth's Time."

Although Franklin perceived the growth of the colonial power in English terms, few of those making the Atlantic crossing in these years were of English origin. Under new laws discouraging the exodus of labor, virtually the only English emigrants permitted were convicts whose sentences had been commuted to terms of indenture in the American colonies.

A quarter of the new arrivals were black slaves, shipped under the *asiento* that had been acquired by the British as a spoil of the recent peace. But the majority of the settlers who arrived after 1713 were refugees from the wars, famines and oppressions which had plagued continental Europe and Ireland for a century before. Disparate in nationality, they were divided in religion as well. Scotch Presbyterians, Irish Catholics, German Lutherans, Dutch Reformed, and a scattering of smaller sects of Mennonites, Dunkers, Moravians and Jews joined the Anglicans, Puritans and Quakers of the eastern seaboard. Their diverse presence strained at the confines of an Anglo-Saxon nationality and began to shape an identity distinctively American.

For these refugees from European disaster, the journey to the New World was almost as punishing as for the slaves dragged in chains from the African coasts. Packed in unsanitary quarters, provided with rotting food and afflicted by epidemic diseases, the new pilgrims to America suffered a staggering mortality in the middle passage. Roughly a fifth of those who sailed from Europe died at sea. Nor did landfall bring an end to the trials of the survivors. Many had traveled under "redemption agreements," whose terms provided that their passage would be paid by the purchase of their services in America. Captains of the transporting vessels locked up entire ships at the shoreline until the redemptioners were sold as indentured servants. The well and the living were often held accountable for the sick and the dead. Wives were put on the block to pay for ailing husbands, children for infirm parents. Families broken up in these transactions were often never reunited. Those who managed to depart the ships with their freedom intact were often prey to the con men and counterfeiters who plied the incoming ports with spurious currency and fraudulent land deeds. Others who escaped these misfortunes received no welcome from the Protestant English of the coast.

Finding the seaboard lands occupied, the newcomers turned their sights toward the wilderness of the western frontier. They were encouraged by colonial proprietors who had bought large tracts of wilderness land for speculation, and by officials who saw in the planting of such settlements a buffer against the Indian menace. A large number found a manageable passage west through the spacious water gaps of the central Appalachians and settled in the mountain valleys of Pennsylvania. Eventually many German and Scotch-Irish immigrants moved down the far slopes of the mountains to the great valley of Virginia and beyond.

On reaching the frontier, the immigrant poor found not only room to plant but a new sense of their place in society. "Every thing tended to regenerate them," wrote Hector St. John Crèvecoeur, who arrived a quarter of a century later, "new laws, a new mode of living, a new social system; here they are become men: in Europe they were as so many useless plants... they withered and were mowed down by want, hunger, and war: but now by the power of transplantation... they have taken root and flourished! Formerly they were not numbered in any civil list of their country, except those of the poor; here they rank as citizens." As the immigrant began to forget his former servitude and dependence, his whole attitude was transformed: "From nothing to start into being, to become a free man, invested with lands to which every municipal blessing is annexed! What a change indeed! It is in consequence of that change that he becomes an American."

The refugees staked their frontier claims with a spirit of

independence. Often they disregarded the Indian titles established by colonial governments in earlier negotiations with the
natives. Dispossessed themselves in the Old World, they defended tenaciously the ground they had won in the new. "It
was against the laws of God and nature, that so much land
should be idle while so many Christians wanted it to labor on
and to raise bread," they argued when their claims were challenged; and in so doing, they invoked an earlier rationale of
conquest.

Even as the influx of non-English immigrants began to create
the sense of an American identity, the spread of population
across an ever widening frontier weakened the bonds of colonial
authority. Relations between Indians and settlers became virtually impossible to regulate. "You must by no means pretend
to the Indians that the prices you sett are by the Governor's
appointment," a Pennsylvania official warned the traders of
Allegheny, "for you may assure yourselves that the Governor
will in no way concern himself in this point." In reply to
Iroquois complaints of unfair practices, the Governor declared,
"As to Trade, [the Iroquois] know it's the Method of all that
follow it to buy as Cheap and sell as dear as they can, and every
Man must make the best Bargain he can; the Indians cheat the
Indians & the English cheat the English, & every Man must be
on his Guard."

As the perimeter of settlement was pushed west, the Indians'
hold on the land became more tenuous and the game on which
their livelihood depended more scarce. About 1724, bands of
Shawnees and Delawares left the increasingly populous Susquehanna Valley and crossed the Alleghenies in search of a more
hospitable terrain. There, on the far side of the Appalachian
mountain barrier, lay the Ohio Valley, a territory that had been
emptied of its inhabitants by the wars of the Iroquois more
than half a century before. Descending from the escarpment
of the Allegheny Plateau, the land flowed into soft hills, and
then flattened into broad and fertile prairies. Bordered on the
north by Lake Erie and on the south by the Ohio River, which
the French called La Belle Rivière, it extended all the way to
the Wabash. Beyond lay the central lowlands of the Mississippi
and the great plains of the American west.

A ridge divided the Ohio basin from the Great Lakes, and an extensive network of rivers flowed south and north from the watershed. Their heads in the highlands were interlaced, forming a system of portages that linked the western lands of the Mississippi Valley with the fur routes of the Canadian north.

The economic and strategic advantages of the Ohio territory had long been recognized by the colonists. "The English by Setling on this side of the Cataract," argued an early petition for Ohio lands, "may without any difficulty perfectly destroy the French Comerce with the Indians and secure the Trade wholy to themselves."

Just as Virginia was the first colony to be planted on the shores of the New World, so Virginians were the first to cross the mountain barrier west. The lure of land had been a motive force in Virginia's early expansion and development. Through the headright system, every man who was not servant or slave hoped to amass his own estate. "Every one took up the Land by Patent to his Liking," observed the first history written by a native Virginian, "and not minding any thing but to be Masters of great Tracts of Land, they planted themselves separately on their several Plantations." So great was the "Liberty of taking up Land, and the Ambition each Man had of being Lord of a vast, tho' unimprov'd Territory," that a hundred years after its settlement, the colony still lacked a single place "that may reasonably bear the Name of a Town."

The profits of the fur trade provided a powerful incentive to look beyond the mountains. From the time that William Berkeley arrived in Virginia, he had taken an active interest in western explorations and the expansion of the Indian trade. In 1669, he sponsored an expedition that started from the falls of the Pamunkey, traveled upriver northwest through the Piedmont and reached the summit of the Blue Ridge. Nearly fifty years later, Governor Alexander Spotswood led an expedition over the crest of the mountains and into the Shenandoah Valley. "The Chief Aim of my Expedition over the great Mountains," he explained afterward, "was to satisfye my Self whether it was practicable to come at the [Great] Lakes."

Since the discovery of the Mississippi by La Salle, the French had moved steadily to establish their communications along the Great Lakes and down the rivers that drained and fed them. In 1699, they had begun to colonize Louisiana, and two years later Cadillac founded Detroit at the juncture of Lake Erie and Lake Huron. As a result of the French forts and their trade alliances with the natives, Spotswood warned, the British plantations were in effect surrounded.

The French, he wrote, "may not only Engross the whole Skin Trade, but may, when they please, Send out such Bodys of Indians on the back of these Plantations as may greatly distress his Majesty's Subjects here, And should they multiply their Settlements along these Lakes, so as to joyn their Dominions of Canada to their new Colony of Louisiana, they might even possess themselves of any of these Plantations they pleased." Fortunately, "Nature [had] formed a Barrier for us by that long Chain of Mountains which run from the back of South Carolina as far as New York, and which are only passable in some few places." But even this barrier could prove a menace if the French discovered the mountain passes before the English colonists were able to establish their possession. Spotswood proposed to get there first:

> ... nothing seems to me of more consequence than that now while the Nations are at peace, and while the French are yet incapable of possessing all that vast Tract w'ch lies on the back of these Plantations, we should attempt to make some Settlements on ye Lakes, and at the same time possess our selves of those passes of the great Mountains, which are necessary to preserve a Communication with such Settlements.

Spotswood's plan was premature, but following his expedition, the Virginia Assembly created the County of Spotsylvania, the first beyond Tidewater; and a decade later it was joined by Goochland (named after Spotswood's successor) and then by others. Beginning in 1730, streams of German and Scotch-Irish immigrants began to pour into the valley of Virginia. One flowed westward from the Tidewater, another down the Shenandoah Valley from the Pennsylvania highland. Within two decades, claims were laid to the entire area and the application for tracts began to extend to the region beyond the Alleghenies.

Under the terms of its 1609 charter, Virginia had no western land limit. "Virginia is Bounded by the Great Atlantic Ocean to the East," observed Thomas Lee, President of the Virginia Council, "by North Carolina to the South, by Maryland and Pennsylvania to the North, and by the South Sea to the West including California." In 1747, Lee and other prominent Virginians organized a company for the purpose of "settling the Countrys upon the Ohio and extending the British Trade beyond the Mountains in the western Confines of Virginia."

The organizers of the Ohio Company of Virginia petitioned the King for rights to half a million acres along the Ohio River, west of the mountains. The Crown responded with an immediate grant of 200,000 acres, and an additional 300,000 when the company had fulfilled the terms of the agreement by building a fort near the forks of the Ohio and settling two hundred families within seven years.

The forks of the Ohio was the strategic gateway to the coveted Ohio country. On the left, the Monongahela descended through a wooded valley. On the right, the steep-banked Allegheny flowed down from the Great Lakes. They met at the forks to form the broader current of the Ohio, which glided through rolling hillsides toward the Mississippi.

As a first step in occupying its new territory, the Ohio Company erected a storehouse at Will's Creek, along one of the favorite Indian paths over the mountains. The storehouse was set on the Allegheny divide, at the headwaters of the Potomac, and a short distance from the Youghiogheny, which descended the western slope of the mountains to the Monongahela.

The situation into which the agents and claims of the Ohio Company now intruded themselves was already complex. When the Delawares and Shawnees migrated to the valley, they had been followed by Pennsylvania traders who thus extended their commerce into the territory previously controlled by the French. Other tribes were soon attracted by the abundant game and expanding fur commerce of the Ohio, among them remnants of the vanished Huron Nation, Mingo-Iroquois and Miamis.

Already the most formidable of the western tribes, the Miamis had moved nearer to the forks to take advantage of the expanding English trade. Under their chief, Old Briton, they established a town at Pickawillany on the banks of the Miami River, which immediately became the center of British trading activity in the valley.

Three years before the founding of the Ohio Company, a third conflict had broken out between the French and British empires, known in America as King George's War. It lasted four years. During the war, a naval blockade stopped the flow of French goods to Canada, forcing up the prices at which they were sold to the valley Indians. The result was a dramatic increase in the British share of the interior fur trade.

In 1748, the Treaty of Aix-la-Chapelle brought the war to an inconclusive end. That same year, a treaty was signed in America, downriver from the forks of the Ohio at Logstown. The Logstown conference was organized in behalf of the Ohio Company by Robert Dinwiddie, Governor of Virginia, who was also a company shareholder. Its purpose was to gain from the Indians a cession of their lands south of the Ohio, confirming a similar agreement made with the Six Nations at the beginning of the war.

These developments were disturbing to the French, who saw the trade of the valley slipping irrevocably from their grasp. If the British colonists were not stopped, they could eventually reach the Mississippi basin and break the French communications with New Orleans. To prevent this, two hundred soldiers were dispatched from Fort Presque Isle on Lake Erie into the Ohio Valley. When they reached the headwaters of the Allegheny, their leader, Pierre Céleron de Blainville, buried a lead plate inscribed with the French claim. At Logstown, he addressed a gathering of Indians, chiefly Delawares, Shawnees and Mingos, and read them a warning from the French King:

> Through the love I bear you, my children, I send you Monsieur de Céleron to open your eyes to the designs of the English against your lands. The establishments they mean to make, and of which you are certainly ignorant,

tend to your complete ruin. They hide from you their plans, which are to settle here and drive you away, if I let them. As a good father who tenderly loves his children, and though far away from them bears them always in his heart, I must warn you of the danger that threatens you. The English intend to rob you of your country; and that they may succeed, they begin by corrupting your minds. As they mean to seize the Ohio, which belongs to me, I send to warn them to retire.

From Logstown, Céleron continued down the Ohio to the Miami, stopping at Pickawillany, where he urged the Indians to return to their lands in the west.

Shortly after Céleron's departure from the valley, Christopher Gist crossed the Allegheny Mountains as an agent for the Ohio Company. His purpose was to scout the company's grant, but he traveled far beyond the Monongahela to the country of the Miamis, where he succeeded in forging an alliance with the Indians.

Meanwhile, the new French Governor, the Marquis of Duquesne, viewed these continuing inroads with alarm. They indicated, he wrote, that the English intended "the destruction of the French." In 1752, New France undertook to answer the challenge in force. Aided by Ottawas and other native allies, a band of French traders attacked and destroyed Pickawillany. The Miami chief, Old Briton, was boiled and eaten before the very eyes of his people, and the tribe returned to Illinois.

Under the aggressive policy of Duquesne, a line of forts was built along French Creek and down La Belle Rivière. As the French presence extended farther and farther into the valley, the Ohio Company became apprehensive for its claim. Finally, in 1753, Virginia's Governor sent a military mission to the French ordering them to quit the lands claimed by the British Crown. To lead the mission, Governor Dinwiddie chose a fellow member of the Ohio Company, a twenty-one-year-old major in the Virginia militia named George Washington.

Washington's brothers Augustine and Lawrence were founders of the Ohio Company. Like many of the other shareholders, the Washingtons came from Virginia's Northern Neck, where the availability of cheap frontier land and slaves to clear it made the region a center of speculation and expansion. Their great-grandfather John Washington had arrived in Virginia in 1657 and acquired seven hundred acres of land through marriage, becoming a burgess and a colonel of the Virginia militia. In this capacity he was one of the commanding officers held responsible for the deaths of the five Susquehannock chiefs in the events prior to Bacon's Rebellion. Another frontier incident, in which he used a legal ruse to divest an entire Indian town of its land, earned him the name *Caunotaucarius*—"Devourer of Villages." Whenever his grandson George had occasion to address the natives in his military capacity, he signed his orders with this Indian name.

Washington and his guide, Christopher Gist, arrived at Fort Le Boeuf on December 11, 1753. They were told that the French had no intention of leaving the valley. In addition, clear indications were given that the French intended to continue their advance. By the time Washington returned to Virginia with his report, Dinwiddie had already sent a party to the forks of the Ohio to erect a fort in anticipation of the French advance. But his effort to support this force with a guard of several hundred militia had been frustrated by the Assembly, which refused the necessary funds. Many of the burgesses doubted that Virginia's claim to the Ohio was stronger than that of France, or even Pennsylvania. Others, mindful of the Governor's position as a principal of the Ohio Company, were skeptical of his intentions. Washington's report, which they now heard, was regarded by some as merely "a fiction and a scheme to promote the interests of a private company."

Even though Washington was able to convince a majority of the need for an allocation to defend the frontier, the Assembly set stringent conditions on the Governor's use of the funds, and efforts to recruit soldiers for the mission proved fruitless. Dinwiddie decided to abandon the attempt to employ the militia to guard the Ohio fort. Instead he undertook to raise a volunteer force of three hundred men. As an incentive, he set aside 200,000 acres of company land adjacent to the fort and offered each volunteer a share on completion of his service. The land was to be free of quit rents for fifteen years.

Before Washington was able to assemble his force and lead them across the mountains, however, the French struck. A thousand troops descending the Allegheny in a fleet of 360 canoes and bateaux quickly overwhelmed the work party that Dinwiddie had sent. Taking possession of their half-finished work, the French completed the structure and called it Fort Duquesne.

Informed of these developments while camped at Will's Creek, Washington immediately headed for an Ohio Company storehouse on the Monongahela, thirty-seven miles upriver from the fort. After a march covering two-thirds of the distance, he set up a camp at Great Meadows. There, friendly Delawares informed him of the presence of a party of French soldiers nearby. On the morning of May 28, 1754, Washington and his troops located the French and in fifteen minutes routed them from their position. "We killed Mr. *de Jumonville*, the Commander of the party," Washington reported, "as also nine others; we wounded one, and made twenty-one prisoners, among whom were M. *la Force*, M. *Drouillon*, and two cadets. The *Indians* scalped the dead, and took away the greater part of their Arms, after which we marched on with the prisoners under guard, to the *Indian* camp."

Thus began the "French and Indian War," the final struggle of the European powers for control of the American continent. It was a war which two years later would spread to Europe and the faraway reaches of the European empires; in its course, it would claim the lives of nearly 800,000 soldiers in lands washed by three oceans; and at its conclusion, India and Canada would pass from French control to become the far-flung wings of the British Empire.

From his camp at Great Meadows, Washington sent news of his victory to Governor Dinwiddie, while his troops erected a small palisade, which he called Fort Necessity. Meanwhile, delegates from all the colonies north of the Potomac were gathering in Albany for a crucial military conference with the Six Nations.

The conference had been called because of growing concern over the allegiance of the native allies. About a year before Washington's skirmish, colonial relations with the Iroquois had reached an impasse. An illicit commerce in arms and furs between Albany and Montreal undercut the Iroquois trade and made the Six Nations suspicious that the English and French might combine against them. Even more threatening was the colonial appetite for land, which had been whetted by the new immigration. "This hunger after Land," observed Peter Wraxall, the Secretary of Indian Affairs for New York, "is become now a kind of Epidemical Madness, every Body being eager to accumulate vast Tracts without having an intention or taking measures to settle or improve it, & Land-jobbing here is as refind an Art as Stock jobbing in Change Alley."

On June 12, 1753, seventeen Mohawks appeared at Fort George in New York for a conference with the Governor. The Mohawk spokesman was an aging sachem whom the Dutch called Hendrick. "We are come to remind you of the antient alliance agreed on between our respective Forefathers," he said. "We were united together by a Covenant Chain and it seems now likely to be broken not from our Faults but yours." The Mohawks, he said, had been faithful allies in the last war with the French and as a result stood in imminent danger from the new French advance. Yet the colonists had failed to fortify the frontiers or make other military preparations.

Another grievance concerned land: "When our Brethren the English first came among us we gave and sold them Lands, and have continued to do so ever since, but it seems now as if we had no Lands left for ourselves." In many instances of land sales the colonists claimed more land than had actually been sold to them. Hendrick cited several cases. When the meeting reconvened four days later, the Governor's reply was vague and unpromising. Some of the Mohawk land grievances, he said, were unjustified; the rest involved transactions before his tenure of office. These he intended to refer to the Commissioners of Indian Affairs in Albany.

The Mohawks were outraged by the Governor's response; none of their grievances had been answered. Nor could they expect any better from Albany: "Brother you tell us that we shall be redressed at Albany, but we know them so well, we will not trust to them, for they are no people but Devils, so we rather desire that you'l say, Nothing shall be done for us."

Hendrick concluded with a warning that the Mohawks would now send word to the other five nations that "the Covenant Chain is broken between you and us."

In London, the implications of the rupture were quickly grasped, and a letter was sent to New York: "When we consider of how great a consequence the friendship and alliance of the six Nations is to all His Majesties Colonies and Plantations in America, we cannot but be greatly concerned and surprised, that the Province of New York should have . . . given occasion to the complaints made by the Indians." Worse, the colonists had exacerbated the situation by "the dissatisfactory answer given to the Indians, [and] their being suffered to depart (tho' the Assembly was then sitting) without any measures taken to bring them to Temper or to redress their complaints."

To rectify matters, London advised that a conference with the Iroquois be convened and that New York immediately convey its interest in renewing the Covenant Chain, offering to satisfy the Indians by reasonable purchases "for such lands as have been unwarrantably taken from them." Since the uncertainty of the Iroquois alliance affected the other colonies as well, they were also advised to join in making the overture and in concluding "one general treaty in His Majesty's name" with the natives.

The proposed conference took place at Albany in June 1754. One hundred and fifty Indians gathered to meet the colonial delegates and were presented with thirty wagonloads of gifts. Hendrick and several other sachems addressed the delegates and voiced the Indian grievances.

They consisted largely of the complaints rehearsed by the Mohawks at Fort George. The frontier was undefended against the French, and the Indians—exposed to attack—were unclear as to the colonies' intentions. Their land was being taken by unscrupulous means. "We understand that there are writings for all our lands, so that we shall have none left but the very spot we live upon and hardly that," they told the Albany delegates. "We find we are very poor, we [thought we] had yet land round about us, but it is said there are writings for it all."

An additional grievance concerned the sale of liquor, the primary currency of the Indian trade: "There is an affair about which our hearts tremble and our minds are deeply concerned; this is the selling of Rum in our Castles. It destroys many both, of our old and young people. We request of all the Governments here present, that it may be forbidden to carry any of it amongst the Five Nations."

Unknown to the natives before its introduction by Europeans, alcohol quickly became a principal item in the exchange between the two cultures. "Although Drunkennesse be justly termed a vice, which the Salvages are ignorant of," wrote Thomas Morton in *The New English Canaan*, "yet the benefit is very great that comes to the planters by the sale of strong liquor to the Salvages, who are much taken with the delight of it, for they will pawne their wits, to purchase the acquaintance of it." Already rum was "the life of the trade" in the northern fur regions, Morton reported; one could have no trade at all in those parts, unless he provided the Indians with "lusty liquors."

Over the years, the rum assiduously supplied to the Indians by English and Dutch traders (the French coin was a less desired brandy) took its toll among the tribes of the coastal regions. The effects of alcohol on the natives seemed without parallel among whites. Communal drinking bouts frequently resulted in burnings, stabbings and other violent outbursts. Many tribal conflicts could be traced directly to its source. Under the influence of alcohol, native traders frequently undervalued their goods in the marketplace, and bartered their furs for spirits rather than for the necessities they had come for. Widespread drunkenness accompanied and hastened the demoralization and disintegration of tribes that had suffered displacement and defeat. "The too frequent use of [rum] with the permission or Neglect of our Colony Governments," summarized one official report, "hath destroyed more Indians than all their wars put together have done."

At the conclusion of the Albany Conference, the delegates acknowledged the justice of many of the Indians' charges: that the disunity of the colonies had prevented them from taking measures of defense; that the Iroquois alliance had been neglected; that their relations had generally suffered by being subordinated to "private gain" rather than "the public interest"; and that the Indians had been supplied with rum by traders "in vast and almost incredible quantities" and then "abused in their Trade" while under its influence. They also conceded that the granting of large tracts to private persons and companies for speculative purposes had weakened the frontiers and that it was "absolutely necessary that speedy and effectual measures be taken to secure the Colonies from the slavery they are threatened with."

To defend the colonial frontier against the French, the delegates recommended a plan with far-reaching implications: the uniting of the colonies under "one General Government . . . in America." A President General and Grand Council would manage the affairs of the United Colonies relating to matters of defense and commerce with the Indians, including the purchase of frontier lands.

The author of the plan, Benjamin Franklin, had long been convinced of the importance of uniting the colonial interest, and of securing "Room enough" on the far side of the mountains for the colonies to expand. "It would be a very strange thing," Franklin had written three years earlier, "if *Six Nations* of ignorant savages should be capable of forming a scheme for such a union [which] . . . has subsisted for ages and appears indissoluble," and yet a similar union should be impractical for a dozen English colonies "to whom it is more necessary and . . . advantageous," and who "cannot be supposed to want an equal understanding of their interests."

Yet the goal of union proved premature. Although Franklin promoted it under the dramatic slogan "Join or Die," the colonial assemblies could not overcome their parochial rivalries to ratify it. "Everyone cries a union is necessary," Franklin wrote to the Governor of Massachusetts, "but when they come to the manner and form of the union their weak noodles are perfectly distracted."

About the time that the Albany Conference was getting under way, the fort which Washington had erected in Great Meadows was attacked and destroyed by the French. A third of its defenders were killed or wounded and Washington was forced to surrender. After signing a statement of capitulation and agreeing to quit the territory belonging to France, he was allowed to return to Virginia. During the retreat, his troops, who had come with the expectation of valley land, deserted him, making any further engagements of the enemy impossible.

Washington's defeat and the withdrawal of the Virginians east of the mountains convinced London of the gravity of the French threat. Since the colonies were incapable of defending their ground in the west, it was decided to commit English regulars to the frontier struggle. The Forty-fourth and Forty-eighth regiments of foot soldiers under the command of General Edward Braddock were dispatched to the colonies. Braddock was to recruit additional troops in America and organize campaigns against the French forts at Niagara, Lake Champlain and Louisburg, as well as the forks of the Ohio. He himself was to lead the assault on Fort Duquesne.

Arriving in America, Braddock found little support in his efforts to supply or supplement his army. The assemblies of Virginia and New York voted him perfunctory funds. Wagons and horses were secured only with great difficulty and after long delays. In Pennsylvania, the general apathy was compounded by a Quaker Assembly guided by pacifist principles. "I am, Sir, almost ashamed to tell You," the Governor wrote Braddock, "that We have in this Province upward of Three Hundred Thousand Inhabitants, and besides our own Consumption raise Provisions enough to supply an Army of One Hundred Thousand Men, which is yearly exported from this City . . . And yet when their *All* is invaded they refuse to contribute to the necessary Defence of their Country, either by establishing a Militia or furnishing Men, Money, or Provisions."

After considerable delays, Braddock's army was equipped and he was able to set out with Washington and the Virginians across the Blue Ridge. For a month they marched through dense uninhabited wilderness, cutting a road over the mountains. But when they came to within ten miles of Fort Duquesne, they were ambushed by a force of three hundred French and six hundred Indians. These were Ottawas of the Great Lakes region, Chippewas, and other northern tribes. The attackers split into two streams, flanking Braddock's army and seizing the high ground on either side. Caught in the crossfire, the troops that Braddock had taken across the Blue Ridge were cut to pieces. "The dead, the dying, the groans, lamentations and cries along the road of the wounded for help," Washington recalled years later, "were enough to pierce a heart of adamant."

Nearly a thousand men were slain or wounded, including Braddock himself, who was mortally hit and died shortly after the battle. Seven years later, the Moravian missionary John Heckewelder rode past the site and found the scattered bones and skulls of Braddock's men. "The sound of our horses' hoofs continually striking against them," he wrote, "made dismal music, as, with the Monongahela full in view, we rode over this memorable battleground."

The defeat of Braddock's army at the forks of the Ohio was the signal for a wholesale defection of the valley Indians from the English cause. Braddock had been presented to them as "a great General" sent from "your Father, the King of Great Britain, to defeat the designs of the French in taking your lands without your consent." On his march to the Ohio, Braddock had met with a Delaware sachem named Shingas, and five other chiefs of the Shawnee, Mingo and Delaware nations, to secure their help in expelling the French. But when they asked what he intended to do with the land if he should drive out the French and their Indians, Braddock replied that the English would inhabit and inherit it; and when Shingas asked him if the Indians who were friends to the English might still have a hunting ground in the valley sufficient to support themselves and their families, Braddock reiterated, "no Savage Shoud Inherit the Land." The following morning Shingas and the other chiefs came and told Braddock that "if they might not have Liberty to Live on the Land they would not Fight for it."

Three months after Braddock's defeat, a party of Shingas' warriors appeared at a home on Penns Creek in the Susquehanna Valley and told the inhabitants, "We are Allegheny Indians, and your enemies. You must all die." The attackers then shot the owner of the farm, tomahawked his son and took his two daughters prisoner. During the next three days, seventeen settlers were killed, others taken captive, and farmhouses burned throughout the area. Later, Shingas sent a message to those Delawares who had remained in the Susquehanna Valley: "We, the Delawares of Ohio, do proclaim War against the English. We have been their Friends many years, but now have taken up the Hatchet against them, and we will never make it up with them whilst there is an English man alive."

The Penns Creek massacre began a reign of terror against the Pennsylvania frontier settlements by Delaware, Shawnee and Mingo warriors, and the bloodiest warfare in the history of the colonies. Farms were set afire, settlers and their families massacred and livestock slaughtered. "You cannot conceive what a vast Tract of Country has been depopulated by these merciless Savages," the Governor reported in mid-November; and the Indian trader George Croghan sent word that "almost all the women and children over Sasquehannah have left their habitations and the roads are full of starved, naked, indigent multitudes."

The Indian terror was not confined to the Pennsylvania highlands but followed the line of settlement to the Appalachian frontiers of Maryland and the valley of Virginia. When the waves of Scotch-Irish immigrants had entered the valley twenty years earlier, they had found it a grassland prairie, suitable for grazing and open for settlement. The prairie had been created by the Indians, although only two small villages of Tuscaroras and Shawnees inhabited it. Before the settlers came, the valley was their hunting ground. Every year they came over the mountain trails from their villages on the Ohio to hunt the buffalo that came to graze in its pastures. At the end of each season, the Indians set fire to the open ground to preserve it as a grassland. Now the Shawnees and other Indians of the Alleghenies returned to reclaim it.

Two weeks before Shingas' warriors appeared at Penns Creek, an outpost on the Shenandoah River reported attacks by a band of 150 natives:

They go about and commit their outrages at all hours of the day, and nothing is to be seen or heard of, but desolation and murder heightened with all barbarous circumstances, and unheard of instances of cruelty. They spare the lives of the young women, and carry them away to gratify the brutal passions of lawless savages. The smoke of the burning plantations darkens the day and hides the neighboring mountains from our sight.

While the Delawares, Shawnees and Mingos razed the back-country settlements, the defeats of Washington and Braddock in the Ohio Valley had thrown the Iroquois Confederacy into a state of confusion. For them, the conflict in the Ohio Valley was a source of bitter irony. "We don't know what you Christians French and English together intend," an Indian spokesman remarked. "We are so hemm'd in by both, that we have hardly a Hunting place left, in a little while, if we find a Bear in a Tree, there will immediately Appear an owner for the Land to Challenge the Property."

At the Albany Conference, the Mohawk sachem Hendrick summed up Iroquois concern: "Brethren.—The Governor of Virginia, and the Governor of Canada are both quarrelling about lands which belong to us, and such a quarrel as this may end in our destruction; they fight who shall have the land."

In terms of settlement, the Iroquois had more to fear from the English farmers than from the French traders. By the middle of the eighteenth century, the population of French Canada was only 55,000, compared to the 1,200,000 inhabitants of the thirteen British colonies. Yet the Iroquois had grown to greatness with the expansion of the English domain. Their sway over the tribes in the territory extending from New England to the valleys beyond the Allegheny was premised on English control of the fur trade and English supremacy in arms. Both were shaken by the defeats on the Ohio. Delawares, Shawnees and Mingos no longer heeded their "uncles" on the Onondaga Council. Even some Senecas and Cayugas now defected to the French, despite the League's formal declaration of neutrality.

In the east, however, the Mohawks joined the English defense of Albany. At Lake George, Hendrick, then approaching his eightieth year, led a band of two hundred warriors in the assault on Fort Edward. Before the battle, which was to be his last, the aged sachem warned the English that the troops available were not sufficient for the task. "If they are to fight, they are too few," he said; "if they are to die, they are too many."

Of all the campaigns launched by the British and colonial forces following Washington's defeat at Fort Necessity, only one was successful. The French Fort Beauséjour on the Bay of Fundy was captured and five thousand French inhabitants were deported from Nova Scotia. But at Niagara and Champlain, and at the forks of the Ohio, the French held their positions and made preparations to advance. Meanwhile, the English military failures solidified the Indian tribes north of the Ohio in their allegiance to the French cause.

Despite these setbacks, the colonies were still slow to muster their forces for the defense of the imperiled frontier. Governor William Shirley of Massachusetts, who had succeeded Braddock as Commander in Chief, urged the assemblies of Virginia, Maryland and Pennsylvania to mount a third effort to take Fort Duquesne. But the colonies felt the task was beyond them; only the mother country could undertake such an effort.

Appealing to England for military support a year earlier, Shirley had catalogued the colonies' weaknesses: New England was hemmed in by French fortresses from Cape Breton to Lake Champlain and unable to bring substantial aid to the threatened frontiers of New York and Pennsylvania; moreover, based on experience in past wars, Albany seemed likely to surrender to the French "if they could preserve their Trade by it"; Pennsylvania under its Quaker regimes had refused to organize a militia, build forts or engage the enemy, while its German immigrants, constituting half the population, were "indifferent about changing the English for a French Government, provided they could be eased of their Quit Rents, & have their Grants of Land enlarg'd to them"; nor could a substantial effort be expected from the colonies south of the Delaware, because of the vast number of "Negro Slaves capable of bearing Arms." The slaves would be "in great danger of being seduc'd from their Fidelity to their Masters by Promises of liberty, & Lands to settle upon." Moreover, "it is well known, how much those Colonies abound with Roman Catholicks, Jacobites, Indented Servants for long terms, & transported Convicts, who, far from being depended upon against the enemy, would doubtless, many of them instigate the Slaves to rebel, & perhaps join with them."

Shirley's fears were echoed by Dinwiddie. In a letter to the Earl of Halifax on the difficulties of using militia for frontier defense, the Governor of Virginia explained that he had "to leave a proper Number in each County to protect it from the Combinations of the Negro Slaves, who have been very audacious on the Defeat on the Ohio. These poor Creatures imagine the French will give them their Freedom."

Following Braddock's defeat, Dinwiddie made Washington Commander in Chief of all forces to be raised for the defense of the Virginia Colony. Despite reports of the depredations by Shawnee and Mingo warriors on the back settlements, however, recruitment proved difficult. Arriving in the Piedmont Region, Washington found that supplies were hard to secure and volunteers were unavailable. Draftees from among those unable to pay the ten-pound exemption fine had been pressed into service to fill the gap. Their protests had been so violent that they had been locked in the county jail, only to be released by their friends who broke in to free them. In frustration, Washington wrote to Dinwiddie requesting materiel and the enactment of stricter military regulations and harsher penalties. In the meantime, he instituted his own measures of flogging, imprisonment and threats of hanging to maintain order and sustain recruitment, even though (as he confessed) he had "no legal right to inflict punishment of the smallest kind."

Across the Blue Ridge, at the scene of the ravages, the situation did not improve. The effort to raise a militia had already failed before Washington arrived. "It was impossible to get above 20 or 25 men," he was told by the officer in charge. The frontiersmen "absolutely refused to stir, choosing as they say to die, with their Wives and Familys." This was all the more irritating to Washington, because he believed the Indians to be few in number and the settlers "more encompassed by Fear than by the Enemy."

Recruitment was only an aspect of the problem. "In all things," he wrote Governor Dinwiddie, "I meet with the greatest opposition. No Orders are obey'd, but what a Party of Soldiers, or my own drawn Sword, Enforces; without this, a single Horse, for the most urgent occasion cannot be had." The people had reached such a state of "insolence," he thought, because they had had every order in the past submitted for their approval. He himself had yielded on no essential point; "nor will I, unless they execute what they threaten, i.e., 'to blow out my Brains.' "

While panic prevailed on the frontier, it was impossible to get people "to act in any respect for their common Safety's." The individualism of the back-country inhabitants was a constant obstruction to efforts to organize the colony's defense. One militia captain was told to hasten with his company to the town of Winchester on the Shenandoah, Washington reported. But "with coolness and moderation this great Captain answered, that his Wife, Family and Corn was at stake; so were those of his Soldiers; therefore it was not possible for him to come . . . Such is the Example of the Officers! such the Behaviour of the Men; and such the unhappy Circumstances on which our Country depends!"

The following year the military situation worsened as the French took Fort Oswego on Lake Ontario, the most westerly British outpost and the key to the northern fur trade. But at the same time a series of diplomatic moves in Europe paved the way for a new level of British intervention in behalf of the colonial cause.

On May 18, 1756, the Crown formally declared war on France and the American conflict became part of a global struggle. Two months later, the Fourth Earl of Loudoun arrived in the colonies as the new Commander in Chief. Loudoun brought two military regiments, and authorization to recruit four battalions of "Royal Americans." Although he too experienced difficulty in mustering support, colonial leaders had begun to summon their constituencies to battle. In Virginia, the Reverend Samuel Davies called on the colonists to take up arms lest "Indian savages and French Papists infamous all the World over for Treachery and Tyranny, should rule Protestants and Britons with a Rod of iron. . . . Can you bear the Thought," he

asked without self-irony, "that Slavery should clank her Chain
in this Land of Liberty?"

To facilitate recruitment, Parliament voted a £115,000 sub-
sidy to the colonies as compensation for their losses in the first
year of the war. The sum eventually grew to exceed one million
pounds. The following year, Britain made America its main
theater of war.

Preparations were undertaken to send seventeen ships of the
line, five frigates and eight thousand regulars as a first stage in
the effort to expel France from the New World. An offensive
was planned against Fort Ticonderoga on Lake Champlain; Fort
Louisburg, which guarded the mouth of the Saint Lawrence
River; and Fort Duquesne on the Ohio.

In addition to providing men and money, London assumed
control of Indian policy, with an eye toward returning the
frontier tribes to the English fold. Sir William Johnson was
commissioned by the Crown as "Our Sole Agent and Superin-
tendant of the . . . Indians and their Affairs." He was empowered
to allay the fears and doubts of the natives "with respect to the
Lands which have been fraudulently taken from them" as well
as the other grievances that had accumulated in their dealings
with the colonies.

A series of conferences were held for this purpose, culminat-
ing in a gathering of more than five hundred Indians representing all the Six Nations and nine other tribes who met with the
governors of Pennsylvania and New Jersey at Easton, Pennsylvania, in October 1758. The military pressures on the French
along the northern frontier had already made it difficult for
them to supply their Indian allies, who as a result had begun
to show reluctance to continue the fight. The conference completed their disaffection from the French cause.

The Easton Treaty redressed the outstanding grievance of
the Delawares and Shawnees over lands belonging to them beyond the Alleghenies which had been sold by members of the
Six Nations. The Treaty pledged that "no white people should
make plantations or settlements on the lands to the westward
of those hills." This gesture, in the words of a colonial commander, "knocked the French in the head." The tribes renewed

Washington-Braddock Route
Braddock March
Forbes Road

0   10   20   30   40

OHIO
ALLEGHENY
Ft. Duquesne
(Forks of the Ohio)
YOUGHIOGHENY
FORBES ROAD
BRADDOCK
Raystown
Redstone
Old Fort
Gist's
REDSTONE CR.
Jumonville Camp
GREAT
MEADOWS
Ft.
Necessity
MONONGAHELA
WILLS CR.
WASHINGTON-BRADDOCK ROUTE
POTOMAC

Lake
Superior

OTTAWA

OTTAW

Michilmackinac

Green Bay

Lake Huron

Georgian
Bay

HURON

SAUK

WISCONSON RIVER

Lake Michigan

POTAWATOMI

Ft. St. Joseph

Ft. Detroit

Le

Ft.
Nia

SENE

FOX

MISSISSIPPI RIVER

ILLINOIS RIVER

Ft. St. Louis

MIAMI

Lake Erie

ERIE

Ft. Presque Is
Ft. Le Boeuf

FRENCH CR.

Venango

ALLEGHENY

ALLE

SU

ILLINOIS

WABASH RIVER

Pickawillany

MIAMI R.

SCIOTO R.

Logstown

Ft. Duquesn

Raystow

Ft.
Necessity

OHIO
RIVER

RIVER

(LA BELLE RIVIÈRE)

OHIO VALLEY

MONONGAHELA R.

YOUGHIOGHENY R.

SHAWNEE

KANAWHA

ALLEGHENY MTS.

SHENANDOAH

SHEN

GREAT

VALL

BLUE

RIDGE

PO

MISSISSIPPI RIVER

CUMBERLAND

RIVER

ROANOKE

TENNESSEE RIVER

CHEROKEE

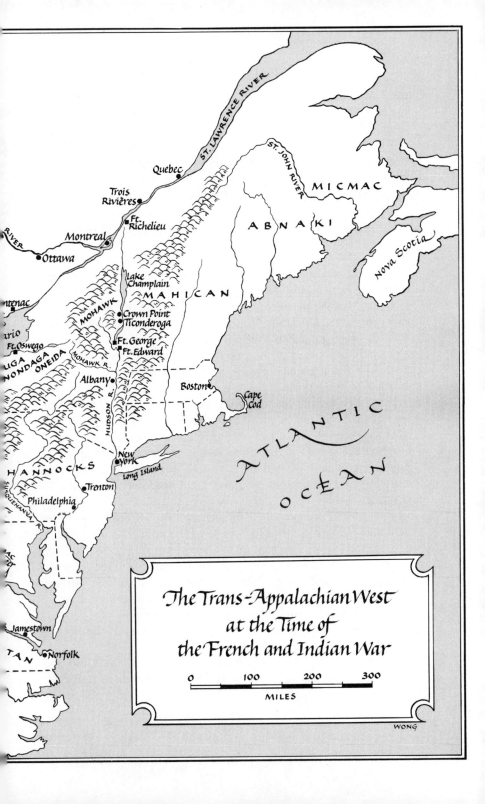

The Trans-Appalachian West
at the Time of
the French and Indian War

0   100   200   300

MILES

WONG

the Covenant Chain. Within a month of these events, the defenders of Fort Duquesne abandoned and burned it, and the English resumed control of the coveted forks of the Ohio.

The following year the military balance shifted decisively in favor of the British. The forts at Niagara, Ticonderoga, Crown Point and Frontenac were taken, and on September 17, 1759, the fortress city of Quebec. It was a year before Montreal capitulated and three before the European conflict came to an end. But for the colonies, the war was over; New France had fallen, and no military force barred their way west.

The western frontier had already begun to excite the imagination of Americans. In the region between the Appalachians and the Mississippi, noted Nathaniel Ames in his *Almanac* for the year 1758, lay lands larger than all France, Germany and Poland, "well provided with rivers, a very fine wholesome air, a rich soil, capable of producing food and physick, and all things necessary for the conveniency and delight of life. In fine, the Garden of the World!"

Even before the conquest of New France was complete, traders had set out toward the western El Dorado over the military roads that had been cut through the wilderness; settlers climbed the passes of the Blue Ridge to reoccupy their abandoned farms and pushed even farther beyond the mountains; and the land companies resumed their speculative activity in the Ohio Valley.

The Indian nations of trans-Allegheny watched these developments with a growing sense of betrayal. At the Easton conference and similar meetings where their allegiance had been sought against the French, they had been promised that no settlement would be permitted beyond the mountain barrier. After the taking of Fort Duquesne, the commanding English officer had told them, "We are not come here to take Possession of your hunting Country in a hostile Manner as the French did when they came amongst you."

But the English did not abandon the forks of the Ohio and withdraw from the territory as the Indians hoped. Instead they went on to occupy the other French forts along the rivers

of the Ohio Valley and the approaches to the Great Lakes,
taking possession of the key post at Detroit in November 1760.
The following year, another conference was held at Easton
with the Indians, who complained that the colonists were not
keeping their promises: "We ... are penned up like Hogs," a
Delaware spokesman said; "there are Forts all around us, and
therefore we are apprehensive that Death is coming upon us."

During the summer, two Senecas appeared at a meeting of
Ottawa, Wyandot, Chippewa and Potawatomi chiefs. The Sene-
cas called on the Great Lakes tribes to cut off the English at
Fort Detroit, saying they would do the same at Niagara and
Fort Pitt. Although nothing came of the Seneca plan, the drift
toward war was increasingly evident.

In 1762, the trader and Indian agent George Croghan reported the Indians' growing concern over the failure of the
British to supply them with presents and ammunition. "They
are a Rash Inconsistent people and inclined to Mischiff," he
warned, "& will never Consider Consequences tho itt May End
in thire Ruen." The tribes seemed divided at present, but if the
Senecas, Delawares and Shawnees should break with the English,
"it will End in a ginerall Warr with all the Western Nations."

While these events were taking place, a prophet appeared
among the Delawares of Cuyahoga, near Lake Erie. He traveled
about the country with a deerskin map, drawn, as he said, at the
direction of the "Great Spirit." The map showed a region of
bounty in which the Great Spirit had originally set the Indians,
and it showed the place of misery in which they now found
themselves. In its southwest corner, there was an open space
representing the avenue by which they could regain what they
had lost. "Look here!" the prophet exhorted his listeners. "See
what we have lost by neglect and disobedience ... by looking
upon a people of a different color from our own, who had come
across a great lake, as if they were a part of ourselves; by suffering them to sit down by our side, and looking at them with
indifference, while they were not only taking our country
from us, [but the path] leading into those beautiful regions
which were destined for us. Such is the sad condition to which
we are reduced."

To regain the path that had been taken from them, the Indians must act as the Great Spirit ordered:

"You are to make sacrifices . . . to put off entirely from yourselves the customs which you have adopted since the white people came among us. You are to return to that former happy state, in which we lived in peace and plenty, before these strangers came to disturb us; and above all, you must abstain from drinking their deadly *beson* which they have forced upon us for the sake of increasing their gains and diminishing our numbers. Then will the Great Spirit give success to our arms; then he will give us strength to conquer our enemies, to drive them from hence, and recover the passage to the heavenly regions which they have taken from us."

In April 1763, a war council was held on the Ecorse River, ten miles below Fort Detroit. Braves of the Ottawa, Wyandot, Potawatomi and Chippewa tribes were present. Before them stood Pontiac, the Ottawa chief. A man of "commanding and imperious" presence, Pontiac had fought with the French through many battles, and his Ottawas had taken part in Braddock's defeat. He was tall and his body was decked in ornaments: beads were set in his ears, there was a decorative stone in his nose and silver bracelets adorned his arms. His face was painted, and his black hair was cut in a warlock, narrowing at the back, in Ottawa fashion, to provide enemies less to grip.

As the assembled braves listened, Pontiac described the vision of the Delaware prophet. In his account, the Great Spirit spoke as a God of Wrath:

"I am the Maker of heaven and earth, the trees, lakes, rivers, and all things else. I am the Maker of mankind . . . The land on which you live I have made for you, and not for others. Why do you suffer the white men to dwell among you? My children, you have forgotten the customs and traditions of your forefathers. Why do you not clothe yourselves in skins, as they did, and use the bows and arrows, and the stone-pointed lances, which they used? You have bought guns, knives, kettles, and blankets, from the white men, until you can no longer do without them; and what is worse, you have drunk the poison firewater, which turns you into fools. Fling all these things away;

live as your wise forefathers lived before you. And as for these English—these dogs dressed in red, who have come to rob you of your hunting-grounds, and drive away the game—you must lift the hatchet against them. Wipe them from the face of the earth . . ."

Pontiac's speech sounded the war cry for the tribes of the Ohio Valley and the northern Great Lakes. Two weeks later, the Ottawas laid siege to the fortress at Detroit and began the final struggle for the trans-Appalachian frontier.

Following this attack, Ottawas and Wyandots surprised the garrison at Fort Sandusky on Lake Erie and captured the post. Two weeks later, Potawatomis took Fort St. Joseph in southwestern Michigan, killing or capturing all its defenders, while Miamis joined Ottawas in subduing Fort Miamis. In the east, Delawares and Mingos swept through the valley of the Monongahela, killing traders and back-country settlers, and launching a siege of Fort Pitt. On June 1, the conquerors of Fort Miamis joined with Wisconsin tribes to take Fort Ouiantenon on the Wabash River, while far to the north Chippewas and Sauks overwhelmed the garrison at Fort Michilimackinac. Two weeks later, Senecas took Fort Venango on French Creek and then Fort Le Boeuf. The following day, June 19, the Senecas joined with Ottawas, Wyandots and Chippewas to take Fort Presque Isle on Lake Erie, and shortly afterward, the British abandoned the isolated post of Fort Edward on Green Bay. Meanwhile, Shawnees, Delawares, Mingos and Senecas had returned to scourge the frontiers of Allegheny, putting its settlements to the torch, killing the inhabitants, often burning them alive, and leaving scenes of torment and desolation wherever they struck.

In less than two months, Pontiac and his forces had conquered every British post in the Ohio Valley and Great Lakes region except Detroit and Duquesne, which had recently been renamed Fort Pitt. Not since the days of Philip had there been so vast a rising on the Indian frontier.

Following the loss of the posts at Presque Isle, Le Boeuf and Venango, British General Jeffrey Amherst dispatched a letter to his field commander, Henry Bouquet, with the following postscript: "Could it not be contrived to send the *Small Pox*

among these disaffected tribes of Indians? We must on this occasion use every strategem in our power to reduce them.   J.A."

Bouquet, who was preparing to lead a force to relieve Fort
Pitt and the valley posts, agreed. He would try, he said, to
infect the Indians with some contaminated blankets, and he
expressed the wish that they could use English dogs to hunt
them, "as it is a pity to expose good men against them."

General Amherst approved the scheme: "You will do well to
try to inoculate the Indians by means of blankets, as well as to
try every other method that can serve to extirpate this execra-
ble race. I should be very glad your scheme for hunting them
down by dogs could take effect, but England is at too great a
distance to think of that at present.   J.A."

No record confirms the execution of this plan, but months
later the smallpox ravaged the Indians of the valley. Meanwhile, Bouquet and his force advanced through the settlements
of western Pennsylvania toward the forks of the Ohio. As the
troops made their way over the wilderness road, they witnessed
scenes of grim destruction. "The list of the people known to
be killed, increases very fast every hour," Bouquet reported.
"The desolation of so many families, reduced to the last extremity of want and misery; the despair of those who have
lost their parents, relations and friends, with cries of distracted
women and children, who fill the streets,—form a scene painful
to humanity, and impossible to describe."

All across the western wilderness of Pennsylvania, Maryland
and Virginia, bands of Indians roamed among the settlements
and carried out their campaign of extermination. "From what
appears," ran a letter from the town of Carlisle, "the Indians
are travelling from one Place to another, along the Valley,
burning the Farms, and destroying all the People they meet
with." The eastern settlements were filled with fleeing settlers,
and "every Stable and Hovel in the Town was Crowded with
miserable Refugees, who were reduced to a State of Beggary
and Despair; their Houses, Cattle and Harvest destroyed....
On both Sides of the Susquehannah, for some Miles, the Woods
were filled with poor Families, and their Cattle, who make
Fires, and live like the Savages."

Despite the ravages on its western frontiers, Pennsylvania was still unable to marshal its defenses. Believing the reports from the frontier exaggerated, and regarding the Indian violence as a reaction to settler injustice, the Quaker government in Philadelphia was reluctant to raise an army against them. The frontiersmen themselves gave little help to Bouquet and his relief force, either in providing supplies or volunteers. Distrustful of the British regulars and fearful of the Indians, they refused to leave their families to join his expeditionary force. Like Braddock before him, Bouquet was left to complain: "I find myself utterly abandoned by the very people I am ordered to protect."

In August, Bouquet passed the Allegheny ridge. After a bloody victory over the Delawares and Shawnees at "Bushy Run," he lifted the siege of Fort Pitt. His success marked a decisive turn in the war. Pontiac still had not taken Detroit, and a relief force was on the way. With their ammunition nearly exhausted, Pontiac's allies began to waver.

In September, Sir William Johnson met with five Iroquois nations (the Senecas were not present) at his estate in the Mohawk Valley. Johnson was able to secure the neutrality of the Iroquois and even a partial commitment to enter the conflict against the western tribes.

Meanwhile, in London the Crown issued a proclamation conceding to the Indians their principal complaint. A line was drawn demarcating the lands beyond the Appalachians, reserving them to the Indian nations. This was done as "just and reasonable, and essential to our interest and the security of our colonies, that several nations or tribes of Indians with whom we are connected, and who live under our protection, should not be molested or disturbed in the possession of such parts of our dominions and territories as, are reserved to them . . . as their hunting-grounds."

The Crown further ordered all persons who had "either wilfully or inadvertently" settled on the lands west of the mountains to "remove themselves from such settlements" at once.

The proclamation was issued on October 7; but before it reached America, the revolt had collapsed. On October 12, the chief of the Chippewas came to Fort Detroit with a pipe of peace. He said that he had been sent also by the Potawatomis and Wyandots, who repented of their conduct and asked forgiveness. Of the Indians at Detroit, the Ottawas alone stood fast. But on the 31st of the month, French messengers arrived in Pontiac's camp with a letter addressed to all the nations of "*La Belle Rivière et le Lac*." It had long been Pontiac's hope that a French force would sail up the Mississippi from New Orleans to join his struggle. The letter, which had been solicited from the French by General Amherst, dispelled his illusion. The French and English were now at peace; Pontiac could expect no assistance from that quarter.

A day after the French messengers arrived, the commander of Fort Detroit dispatched a letter to Amherst: "This moment I received a message from Pontiac, telling me that he should send to all the nations concerned in the war to bury the hatchet; and he hopes your Excellency will forget what has passed." He added that if Amherst intended to punish the Indians further, "it may easily be done without any expense to the Crown, by permitting a free sale of rum, which will destroy them more effectually than fire and sword."

This ended the war with Pontiac and the western Indians. Fighting continued for several years; the Shawnees and Delawares kept up their harassment of the frontier settlements, and Pontiac himself sought to organize a new alliance among the Mississippi tribes. But the British were able to keep the frontier firmly under control. About this time, the struggle between settlers and natives was overtaken by a new and more portentous conflict, between the American colonies and the English Crown.

3

Declaring Independence

FOR nearly two centuries, Britain had provided a shield for its American colonies against the expansive empires of France and Spain. With the end of the war that had begun in defense of the Ohio frontier, the English Crown acquired all of French Canada and North America east of the Mississippi, as well as Spanish Florida to the Apalachicola River. America's frontiers were now uncharted wilderness and limitless ocean. For the first time since their settlement, the colonies were free from external menace.

Enclaves had been left to the French and Spanish at New Orleans and in the Caribbean. But these were viewed as political hostages rather than territorial threats. "While we retain our Superiority at Sea," wrote Benjamin Franklin in 1763, "I cannot but look on the Places left or restor'd to our Enemies on this Side of the Ocean, as so many Pledges for their Good Behaviour. Those Places will hereafter be so much in our Power, that the more valuable they are to the Possessors, the more cautious will they naturally be of giving us Offence."

New territory created new expectations and opportunities. The colonial economies prospered; colonial prospects expanded. Imperceptibly, the balance of empire had changed. Obligations long borne by the colonists began to seem arbitrary and unreasonable; new grievances became potential premises of revolt. Within a year of the fall of New France, while England was still at war in Europe, the bond between imperial parent and colonial offspring developed its first significant crack.

Under the mercantile theory of empire, the dependencies in America were regarded as instruments of British welfare. Colonial commerce was regulated for the profit of British markets; colonial manufactures competitive with British products were discouraged. Yet, even under this system, the colonies had managed, in little more than a century and a half, to establish a formidable position in international trade.

In part this was because the prosperity of the mother country was seen to depend on the self-sufficiency of the empire as a whole. Colonial products were also protected and encouraged by imperial policy. Land was granted to the settlers on generous (though unequal) terms. Labor was made abundant by policies which admitted immigrants of other countries, thereby increasing colonial production and trade.

Although taxed and restricted by imperial regulations, the colonial economies were also stimulated. As a result of the Navigation Act of 1660, and the expulsion of the Dutch from the American trade, the New England maritime industry became a thriving enterprise. Ships trading in the empire were required to be built in England or her colonies. By 1775, it was estimated that one in every three vessels plying the trade of Britain's global empire had been made in American shipyards.

Most often the imperial system failed to impede the colonies' growth for simpler reasons: the vast distances and liberal framework of the empire made its negative regulations difficult to enforce. When, for example, competition from the colonies' infant iron industry began to threaten English manufactures, Parliament passed an act prohibiting the erection of new steel mills. But twenty-five years later, there were more furnaces in operation in the colonies than in England and Wales, while the amount of bar and pig iron produced was larger than the total output of Great Britain.

In trade, too, evasion of regulations was common. Illegal smuggling to Dutch and French ports had long been a prevalent activity of New England's business. During the French and Indian War, however, the practice suddenly acquired new overtones.

At the beginning of the Ohio campaign, General Braddock had complained to Pennsylvania's governor about the lack of colonial support. The reply was sympathetic. Pennsylvania was rich, its treasuries full, its people "burthened with no Taxes," wrote the Governor. Yet, like almost all the other colonies, Pennsylvania had refused to contribute to the defense of the frontier, and by its inaction had "suffered the French to take quiet Possession of the most advantageous Places." Worse, the very supplies being denied to Braddock and the British regulars were being sold illegally by the colonists to the enemy: "The Trade that has been carried on from these Colonies with the French at Cape Breton," observed the Governor, "has certainly enabled them to support an Army on the back of Us which they could not otherwise have done."

The following year, the King's Council issued orders to stop the treasonous flow of goods. Yet the merchants who were supplying the enemy represented a powerful interest in colonial society, and the practice continued. In August 1760, the Prime Minister sent an even stronger letter to the colonial governors demanding their aid in suppressing the trade "by which the Enemy is, to the greatest Reproach & Detriment of Government, supplyed with Provisions and other Necessities whereby they are, principally, if not alone, enabled to sustain, and protect this long and expensive War."

Within six months, the attempt to enforce this order had led to the first clash of principle between the American colonies and their king.

In conducting searches to halt the flow of smuggled goods, customs officials were required to have warrants or "writs of assistance" from the courts. These writs were general in nature and limited in time only by the life span of the King. They had been issued by the Massachusetts Superior Court in each of the three years previous, with no protest.

On October 25, 1760, King George II died, which caused the terms of the general writs to lapse. The following month, New France surrendered, and a month later, the head of customs attempted to renew the writs in Massachusetts. But a group of sixty-three Boston merchants filed suit against the petition. In the ensuing court test in Boston, a new spirit of self-assertion and even truculence was revealed, a readiness of some colonial leaders to challenge the authority of the Crown.

Much of the trial's impact was due to the oratory of James Otis, a moon-faced politician whom the merchants had retained as one of their attorneys. Unlike his co-counsel, whose arguments were confined to legal precedents and technical points of the law, Otis' case was set in the explosive frame of fundamental principles and natural rights. John Adams, who was present in the courtroom, recalled Otis' argument: "Every man, merely, natural, was an independent sovereign, subject to no law, but the law written on his heart, and revealed to him by his Maker ... His right to his life, his liberty, no created being could rightfully contest. Nor was his right to his property less incontestable." To his dying day, Otis said, he would "oppose all such instruments of slavery on the one hand or villany on the other as this writ of assistance." The writs represented the kind of power "which in former periods of English history, cost one King of England his head and another his throne."

"Otis was a flame of fire," Adams recalled; "he hurried away all before him. ... Every man of an immense crowded audience appeared to me to go away, as I did, ready to take arms against Writs of Assistance. Then and there, was the first scene of the first act of opposition, to the arbitrary claims of Great Britain. Then and there, the child Independence, was born."

The court reserved judgment on the writs, referring the case to higher authority. A year later, their legality was upheld, but sentiment was already so strong that they were never effectively enforced. Meanwhile, Otis was elected to the Massachusetts Assembly and became a leader of the opposition to what radicals now began to portray as a conspiracy of Parliament to deprive the colonists of their rights as Englishmen, and to subject them to increasingly despotic rule.

About the time of the writs case in Massachusetts, a similar portent of rebellion appeared in a court case in the King's oldest, most populous and most productive colony, Virginia. There, too, a popular leader appeared to give it expression.

For as long as tobacco had been the staple of Virginia's economy, it had functioned as a money payment for goods and services. Some groups, such as the clergy, received their salaries in tobacco. Planters paid their often heavy obligations to British merchants in quantities of the leaf. In 1755, a drought cut the tobacco crop drastically, driving prices up to six cents a pound, or three times their normal level. To meet the situation, the Assembly passed a "Twopenny Act" allowing Virginians to discharge their tobacco debts in money at the rate of two cents a pound, thereby depriving their creditors of a windfall gain. Three years later, another drought again brought high prices to tobacco markets. A new Twopenny Act was passed. Although there had been no objections to the previous measure, the Anglican clergy now appealed to the Crown, which responded by suspending the Virginia law. The clergy then sued its debtors for the difference in value, in a movement that became known as the "Parsons' Cause."

One of the trials of the parsons' suits was argued by a young lawyer named Patrick Henry. Like Otis, he employed a logic that magnified the significance of the issues at hand. By disallowing the Twopenny Act, he declared, the King denied his subjects their proper protection and thus "from being the Father of his people degenerated into a Tyrant, and forfeits all rights to his subjects' Obedience."

At these words, the opposing counsel, Peter Lyons, called out to the bench that "the gentleman had spoken treason" and wondered that "their worship could hear it without emotion or any mark of dissatisfaction." Cries of "Treason, treason" from some of the spectators supported Lyons' objection, but did not halt the flow of inflammatory rhetoric or elicit any disapprobation from the court. When the case was concluded, the jury reached an immediate verdict: the plaintiff was awarded one penny in damages. Henry was lifted onto the shoulders of cheering supporters and carried in triumph from the courtroom. Reporting this result to a friend, the clergyman plaintiff wrote that "the ready road to popularity here, is to trample under foot the interests of religion, the rights of the church, and the prerogative of the crown."

The opposition to the Parsons' Cause had partly reflected sentiment in the Virginia back communities among Presbyterians, New Lighters and other dissenters against the established Anglican Church. Partly it reflected the self-assurance that flourished in the aftermath of the victory over the French. The same confidence was also manifest in the imperial designs of the Tidewater planters, whose sights were set on the wilderness lands beyond the mountains. This territory was reserved to the Indians by the Proclamation of 1763. It now became a third area of conflict with the British Crown.

The leaders of the westward movement were prominent figures in the colonial societies, particularly those of Virginia and Pennsylvania, whose boundaries extended into the Ohio and Mississippi valleys. In Virginia, they included such men as William Byrd, Patrick Henry, Richard Henry Lee and George Washington. Since resigning his commission after the fall of Fort Duquesne, Washington had acquired through marriage a substantial estate in slaves, securities and land, and thereby transformed himself into a major planter with holdings suitable to his position as the colonies' foremost military figure.

Even before his marriage, Washington had turned his attention toward the west. In the summer of 1758, he laid plans to patent his share of the 200,000 acres on the Ohio that had been promised to the original volunteers who went to defend the Ohio Company outpost. Five years later, under Washington's leadership, the veterans of the Ohio filed a formal petition to the King for the claim.

Washington's view of the western prospect was expansive. "There is a large field before you," he wrote to a captain who had served under him in one of the Ohio campaigns, "... where an enterprising man with very little money may lay the foundation of a noble estate in the new settlements upon Monongahela for himself and posterity." For proof, one had only to look at Frederick County in the Piedmont, Virginia's previous frontier, "and see what fortunes were made by the ... first taking up of those lands ... Nay, how the greatest estates we have in this colony were made. Was it not by taking up and purchasing at very low rates the rich back lands which were thought nothing of in those days, but are now the most valuable lands we possess?"

Shortly after Washington filed the claim in behalf of the Ohio veterans, the Ohio Company itself sent one of its members to represent its claim to the King in London. Ohio Company shareholders were concerned not merely because of the Crown's restrictions on settlement but because their original grant of a million acres had lapsed. The families they had undertaken to settle within seven years, as a condition of the grant, were not settled, and the forts they had undertaken to build had not been built.

At the same time, members of the Ohio Company, including Washington and Richard Henry Lee, joined with several prominent Marylanders to found a new company to speculate in western lands. The Mississippi Company, which they organized, hoped to obtain two and a half million acres of land from the Crown, extending from the juncture of the Ohio and Mississippi east to the Wabash and south to the Tennessee. Interest in these lands was also shown by a Virginia land company whose prime mover was Patrick Henry and by another whose shareholders included Peter Jefferson and Thomas Walker, who after Jefferson's death became the guardian of his young son Thomas.

Southern planters were in the forefront of the speculative movement in western lands; the exhaustion of the soil, caused by the cultivation of tobacco, and the availability of an expanding supply of slave labor made such acquisitions attractive to them. But they were not alone; the mercantile interests of Philadelphia and New York were also active in laying claim to the rich territories in the west.

The most prominent Pennsylvanian, Benjamin Franklin, had long dreamed of settling the lands on the far side of the mountains. "The great country back of the Appalachian mountains, on both sides the Ohio, and between that river and the lakes," he had written at the beginning of the war with the French, is "one of the finest in North America.... If two strong colonies of English were settled between the Ohio and lake Erie... they would be a great security to the frontiers of our other colonies."

When the Treaty of Paris was signed in 1763, ending the Seven Years War, Franklin saw it as a propitious moment to implement his plan. "Since all the Country is now ceded to us on this Side the Mississippi," he wrote to his legal adviser, "is not this a good time to think of new Colonies on that River, to secure our Territory and extend our Commerce...? What think you now of asking for a Slice of Territory, to be settled in some manner like that I once propos'd?"

Franklin actively promoted the creation of these colonies, called Vandalia and Charlotta, and—with his illegitimate son William, who was Governor of New Jersey; the Indian agent George Croghan; the Quaker banking house of Baynton, Wharton and Morgan; and the Jewish firm of David Franks—he became involved in a series of companies and schemes for acquiring western lands and settling them for a profit.

Ironically, the Proclamation of 1763, which barred Franklin and the other colonial speculators from access to the lands, was at the same time a stimulus to the land fever. For speculators regarded the proclamation as merely a temporary injunction, providing a propitious opportunity before the lands were legally opened. Thus, writing to a former captain in his Ohio regiment, Washington proposed a joint effort "to secure some of the most valuable lands in the King's part," which they could accomplish "notwithstanding the proclamation, that restrains it at present, and prohibits the settling of them at all; for I can never look upon that proclamation in any other light (but this I say between ourselves), than as a temporary expedient to quiet the minds of the Indians. Any person, therefore, who neglects the present opportunity of hunting out good lands, and in some measure marking and distinguishing them for his own, (in order to keep others from settling them) will never regain it."

The territory which held such promise for Washington and other colonial speculators was viewed more complexly from the island center of the empire. A costly effort to suppress the western tribes had just been concluded. Hasty expansion into the region might arouse the tribes again and endanger London's fur trade. The ministry's priority lay not in settling the new territory but in paying the costs of defending it. The war for the frontier had left a public debt greater and more burdensome than any in England's history. The expense of maintaining troops to patrol it was considerable. Consequently, the ministry resisted pressures from the colonial expansionists for new land, while moving swiftly (and imprudently as it proved) to impose new and unprecedented taxes on the Crown's subjects across the sea.

When the King's chief minister, George Grenville, opened the discussion of the budget in the House of Commons on March 9, 1764, he presented the members with a picture of growing national crisis. The national debt had risen to £147 million, virtually double its prewar level. During the preceding year, attempts to increase taxes on the already overburdened populace had resulted in a wave of protests. "This hour is a very serious one," the Prime Minister warned. Since the tax load on the King's subjects in England was already twenty-six shillings a head, while in America it was only one shilling or even less, it was not strange that Grenville's thoughts turned in that direction. "We have expended much in America," Grenville told the Commons, "let us now avail ourselves of the fruits of that expense."

A voluntary contribution from the American colonies, however, seemed unpromising. During the war, it had been necessary for Parliament to make a series of appropriations in excess of a million pounds to induce the colonies to raise supplies and manpower for their own defense. Even then, the three colonies most directly threatened by French armies had accounted for 70 percent of the entire contribution. If the colonists had been so reluctant to contribute funds to their own defense in the midst of war, it was unlikely that they would be willing to do so when the battles had been won. Taxes had never been levied on the colonies by Parliament. Yet a tax now seemed inevitable.

Grenville's first proposal was a charge of threepence per gallon on all foreign molasses imported into North America. This was merely the renewal of an old but weakly enforced tariff, and the rate it proposed was only half the original, an effort to balance the fact that it would now be enforced. Even the colonies' agents in London accepted the measure in principle. Its purpose—to raise revenue to pay for the defense of British North America (and in particular the newly acquired territories)—seemed unobjectionable. "There did not seem to be a single man in Parliament," reported the agent of Massachusetts, "who thought that the conquered provinces ought to be left without Troops, or that England after having run so deeply in Debt for the conquering of these provinces, by which Stability & Security is given to all the American Governments, should now tax itself for the maintenance of them."

But the colonists thought otherwise. A sharp rebuke was issued by the Massachusetts legislature to its London agent for failing to oppose so "burthensome" and "unconstitutional" a scheme as that of obliging the colonies to maintain an army, and taxing them without their consent. "If all the colonies are to be taxed at Pleasure, without any Representation in Parliament, what will there be to distinguish them in point of Liberty from the Subjects of the most absolute Prince? . . . If we are not represented, we are slaves."

In part, the strength of the colonial reaction stemmed from the fact that the Molasses Act was seen as only the first in a series of taxes that Parliament intended to lay on the colonies' wealth. At the time that Grenville introduced the act, he indicated that it would be followed by a stamp duty. Since this would represent the first direct tax ever levied on the colonies, however, he agreed to defer the measure for a year. Massachusetts' agent explained the delay, saying that the Prime Minister was "willing to give the Provinces their option to raise that or some equivalent tax. Desirous as he expressed himself to consult the ease, the quiet and the Good will of the Colonies."

Grenville sought to appease the colonies further by providing that all the Stamp Act agents would be Americans and all the revenues would be spent in America. When he met with the colonial representatives, including Benjamin Franklin (who had suggested a similar tax during the war), he told them that the tax seemed the best way to meet the financial problem, but if they could suggest a better way, he would adopt it.

Grenville also broached the question of parliamentary representation. In the first place, he noted, the colonies had not indicated that they actually desired to send members to Parliament. In the second, there were many reasons for them not to: the expense would be great; they could not expect a majority in the Commons, and the distance would create the same problems between them and their representatives as it now did between them and Parliament.

Following these observations, he asked whether they meant that a breach between them was inevitable. "What then? Shall no Steps be taken and must we and America be two distinct Kingdoms?" Grenville thought that the nature of their situations made it possible and likely that one day they would in fact be two kingdoms, "but we trust even you wont say you think yourselves ripe for that event as yet. You are continually increasing in numbers and in strength; we are perhaps come, at least to our full growth. Let us then leave these possible events to the disposal of providence." Grenville concluded with the hope that mutual interest and duty would keep the parties on both sides "within the bounds of justice."

Despite the fact that the Stamp Act represented a major departure in policy, the assembled colonial agents, including Franklin, accepted it in principle and took steps to participate personally in the collection of the new duties. Neither the representatives of the colonies nor of the Crown suspected the reaction that was to follow.

The first of the colonial assemblies to challenge the new Stamp Act was Virginia's. Led by Patrick Henry, the House of Burgesses passed a series of resolves proclaiming that Virginians enjoyed "all the liberties, Privileges, Franchises and Immunities... possessed by the people of Great Britain," and therefore had the exclusive right to tax themselves. Any attempt by any power other than their own assembly to lay a tax on them would have "a Manifest Tendency to Destroy American Freedom." Another resolve, rejected by the burgesses but widely published in the colonial press, declared that anyone supporting such a tax in word or deed would be regarded as "an *Enemy* to his *Majesty's Colony*."

In presenting these resolutions, Henry once more resorted to the rhetoric that had become his political trademark. "Tarquin and Caesar had each his Brutus, Charles the First his Cromwell, and George the Third—" he declared, and was interrupted with a cry of "Treason!" whereupon he continued: "—may profit by their example. If *this* be treason, make the most of it."

In Massachusetts, Governor Francis Bernard was convinced that there would be compliance with the new measure despite "murmurs" against it. Thomas Hutchinson, the Chief Justice, opposed the tax, reporting to London that "the stamp act is received among us as decently as could be expected. . . . The act will execute itself." But news of the Virginia resolves, in the words of Bernard, was "an Alarm Bell to the disaffected." One colonial assembly after another announced its opposition to the act, while popular resistance took a suddenly violent turn.

On the morning of August 18, 1765, on High Street in the heart of Boston, an effigy of Andrew Oliver, the stamp distributor for Massachusetts, was found hanging from a large elm. Several thousand people gathered at the site, which was afterward known as the Liberty Tree, and at dusk "an amazing mob" brought the effigy through the courthouse in an effort to intimidate the Council, which was in session. The crowd then marched to the docks, setting fires, breaking fences and stealing liquor as they went, and finally came to a small building which Oliver had just erected as the new stamp office. Within a few minutes, it was leveled to the ground.

The effigy was then taken to Oliver's house, where in the helpless presence of the Sheriff and Chief Justice, the crowd burned it and attacked the house itself. Then, after breaking the windows and doors, and finding the Olivers gone, they finally dispersed.

The following morning, the Governor called his Council together. But all the councilors could do was admit their powerlessness to affect or control the events. That afternoon, Oliver was approached by a group of men who warned him that if he did not resign his office at once, "his house would be immediately Destroyed and his Life in Continual Danger." Oliver quickly complied.

Two weeks later, a mob again gathered in Boston and lit a bonfire in front of the Town House, while the crowd around it chanted, "Liberty and Property." When the people were properly aroused, they attacked and destroyed the residences of two officials whose offices were connected with the Stamp Act, and then proceeded to the mansion of Chief Justice Thomas Hutchinson, descendant of Anne Hutchinson and scion of one of New England's most prominent families. The Hutchinsons had scarcely time to flee the supper table before the rioters smashed the doors with axes and swarmed into the house, ripping curtains and wainscotting, splintering furniture and scattering the archive of Massachusetts history that Hutchinson had painstakingly compiled into the mud of the New England night.

For three hours the mob worked with frenzied diligence at the cupola that crested the Hutchinson house before they could get it down. Only the brickwork construction of the walls prevented them from leveling the building entirely. The next day the streets "were scattered with money, plate, gold rings, etc. which had been dropped in the carrying off."

In the morning, Chief Justice Hutchinson appeared in court without his robes and "with tears starting from his eyes and a countenance which strongly told the inward anguish of his soul." The clothes he was wearing were all that he had, he apologized, and even some of them were borrowed. "I call to my Maker," he said, "to witness that I never, in New England or Old, in Great Britain or America, neither directly nor indirectly, was aiding, assisting, or supporting or in the least promoting or encouraging what is commonly called the Stamp Act, but on the contrary, did all in my power, and strove as much as in me lay, to prevent it." It was not from timidity, he added, that he made this declaration, "for I have nothing to fear. They can only take away my life, which is of but little value when deprived of all its comforts, all that is dear to me, and nothing surrounding me but the most piercing distress."

Although similar incidents in other colonial cities did not attain the ferocity of the Boston events, the intimidation of local officials became the central feature of colonial opposition to the Stamp Act. A secret military organization, the Sons of Liberty, was formed to spearhead the vigilante actions. The rank and file of the new organization was composed of sailors, artisans and mechanics, who carried out its violence; but its promoters and leaders were lawyers and merchants from the wealthiest families, often with old scores to settle with the customs officials. "The Lawyers," complained General Thomas Gage, commander of the British forces in America, "were the Source from whence the Clamors have flowed in every Province. In this Province Nothing Publick is transacted without them. . . . The whole Body of Merchants in general, Assembly Men, Magistrates, &c. have been united in this Plan of Riots, and without the Influence and Instigation of these the inferior People would have been quiet. Very great Pains was taken to rouse them before they Stirred. The Sailors who are the only People who may be properly Stiled Mob, are entirely at the Command of the Merchants who employ them."

In October a congress of the colonies convened in New York to hammer out a united policy. It was the first such gathering that had not been prompted by London. The Congress accepted Parliament's right to make laws for the colonies, but rejected its right to tax them. Not even representation would change their attitude on this question. "The people of these colonies," they resolved, "are not, and from their local circumstances cannot be, represented in the House of Commons in Great Britain."

On November 1, the day the stamps were scheduled to go on sale, there were none available. Nearly every distributor had resigned his post as a result of the threats and pressures of the Sons of Liberty. In addition, the merchants of New York, Philadelphia and Boston had agreed to boycott British goods until the Stamp Act was repealed.

The day began overcast as the colonists in mock funeral corteges paraded Liberty in her coffin through the streets of the main towns. Persons of all ranks filled the columns in Newport "from the highest even down to the blacks, who seem'd from a sense of their masters suffering to join the mourning course." In Portsmouth, the coffin the demonstrators carried to the burial ground was inscribed "Liberty—aged 145," an allusion to the Pilgrims' first landing at Plymouth. After the funeral oration, the mood of the demonstrators shifted and the inscription was altered, so that it read "Liberty Revived," and the "Stamp Act" was buried instead in the grave. In Newport, the day ended with bells ringing and the crowd lifting their voices in song:

> The birthright of Britons is *Freedom*,
> The contrary is worse than Death's pangs.
> Huzza for George the Third.
> Britannia's Sons despise Slavery,
> And dare nobly to be free!

The mock burials of the Stamp Act proved to be more than symbolic. Unable to enforce its writ in the colonies, Parliament repealed the legislation six months after its enactment.

But the events themselves could not be repealed. They had "laid the basis of an alienation which will never be healed," wrote Ezra Stiles, who was later president of Yale. "Henceforth the *European* and *American* interests are separated never more to be joined."

Half a century later, in a letter to Thomas Jefferson, John Adams reflected on the meaning of "the Revolution" that had broken the imperial ties: "What do we mean by the Revolution? The War? That was no part of the Revolution. It was only an Effect and Consequence of it. The Revolution was in the Minds of the People, and this was effected, from 1760 to 1775, in the course of fifteen Years before a drop of blood was drawn at Lexington."

Adams' choice of the year 1760 as the beginning of the Revolution was illuminating. Five years before, a student at Harvard, he had revealed his own sense of America's destiny to a friend: "Soon after the Reformation, a few people came over to this new world for conscience sake," he wrote. "Perhaps this apparently trivial incident may transfer the great seat of empire into America."

> It looks likely to me: for if we can remove the turbulent Gallicks, our people, according to the exactest computations, will in another century become more numerous than

England itself. Should this be the case, since we have, I may
say, all the naval stores of the nation in our hands, it will
be easy to obtain the mastery of the sea; and then the
united force of all Europe will not subdue us. The only
way to keep us from setting up for ourselves is to dis-
unite us. *Divide et impera.*

With the surrender of Quebec in 1759, the Gallic threat had
been removed. On the other hand, the disunity that Adams
feared was already a basic fact of colonial existence. Intercolonial rivalry had confronted London with its most formidable problem in the recent war. The new conquests had
intensified these rivalries by providing a new arena of competition. But by an irony of fate, they had also diminished them.
The taxes demanded by the Crown to pay the costs of conquering and defending the territory now worked to overcome
the divisions. Land speculation was the prerogative of the few;
taxes burdened the many. Reaching down across class and
sectional lines, taxation posed the issue of authority at the most
basic constitutional level. The attempt to tax the colonies united
them, and made them conscious of their strength.

More than any other American, Benjamin Franklin personified
the profound shift in colonial attitude that followed the French
defeat. During the Parliamentary debates over the repeal of the
Stamp Act, he was called before the House of Commons to
present the Americans' views. In answering the claim that the
colonies owed a debt to Britain for their defense in the last
war, Franklin ignored and then rewrote the historical record.

In 1754, he himself had warned the Albany Congress of the
impending disaster to the colonies if they failed to stop the
French advance. The French intended to surround the British
colonies, he declared, "to fortifie themselves on the Back thereof
to take and keep Possession, of the heads of all the Important
Rivers, to draw over the Indians to their Interest, [for] a
General Attack on the Several Governments," and the subjection of "the whole Continent" to the French Crown. It was
"absolutely necessary," he told the delegates, "that Speedy and
Effectual measures be taken to Secure the Colonies from the
Slavery they are threatened with."

Facing the British Parliament a decade later, however, he dismissed the war as a remote adventure of empire, in which Americans had become unwillingly involved: "I know the last war is commonly spoken of here as entered into for the defence, or for the sake of the people of America. I think it is quite misunderstood. It began about the limits between Canada and Nova Scotia, about territories [to] which the crown indeed laid claim, but were not claimed by any British colony.... We had therefore no particular concern or interest in the dispute."

Even the circumstances of the war's origins in Washington's efforts to protect the Ohio Company's claims in the Ohio Valley proved no obstacle to Franklin's revision. Although its principal shareholders were leading citizens of Virginia, including the colony's governor, and although they expected vast personal tracts of territory for their efforts, the Ohio Company was presented in Franklin's account as simply a British trading corporation with local "factors" and "correspondents."

> As to the Ohio, the contest there began about your right of trading in the Indian country, a right you had by the Treaty of Utrecht, which the French infringed ... they took a fort which a company of your merchants, and their factors and correspondents, had erected there to secure that trade, Braddock was sent with an army to re-take that fort ... and to protect your trade. It was not until after his defeat that the colonies were attacked. They were before in perfect peace with both French and Indians.

Franklin's version freed the American colonies from their sense of obligation to the parent country. A similar result was achieved in other briefs for the colonial cause, which began to appear at this time. In his *Inquiry into the Rights of the British Colonies*, published in 1766, the Virginian Richard Bland maintained that "*America* was no Part of the Kingdom of *England;* it was possessed by a savage People, scattered through the Country, who were not subject to the *English* Dominion, nor owed Obedience to its Laws." America was an "independent Country" which had been "settled by *Englishmen* at their own Expense."

Before the Stamp Act crisis, Thomas Hutchinson "could not think it possible" that the idea of independence "should enter into the heart of any man in his senses, for ages to come." Now he was convinced that he had been mistaken, and that only "the united endeavours of the friends to Britain and her colonies, in Europe and America" could "restore the colonists to a true sense of their duty and interest."

While identifying himself as one such friend, in a letter to Lord Kames, however, Franklin indicated that even a union based on equality between Britain and the colonies was now a matter of indifference to Americans, its advantage being "not so apparent." America might suffer at present under the "arbitrary power" of Britain, and she might suffer in separation from it, but these were "temporary evils that she will outgrow." The colonies' situation was different from that of other dependencies like Scotland and Ireland. "Confined by the sea, they can scarcely increase in numbers, wealth and strength so as to overbalance England. But America, an immense territory, favoured by Nature with all advantages of climate, soil, great navigable rivers, and lakes &c. must become a great country, populous and mighty; and will, in a less time than is generally conceived, be able to shake off any shackles that may be imposed on her, and perhaps place them on the imposers."

Nor was Franklin alone in his optimism that the power of the American child would soon outgrow its English parent's, and that this fact would determine the fate of the empire. The fifth number of the *American Whig*, which appeared in 1767, and which was written by Robert R. Livingston and other prominent patriots, exclaimed, "Courage, then Americans! The finger of God points out a mighty empire to your sons. . . . The day dawns, in which this mighty empire is to be laid by the establishment of a regular American Constitution. . . . The transfer of the European part of the family is so vast, and our growth so swift, that, before seven years roll over our heads, the first stone must be laid." Nothing could prevent this development: "Peace or war, famine or plenty, poverty or affluence,—in a word, no circumstance, whether prosperous or adverse can happen to our Parent; nay, no conduct of hers, whether wise or imprudent—no possible temper of hers, whether kind or cross-grained—will put a stop to this building. There is no contending with Omnipotence: and the pre-dispositions are so numerous and well adapted to the rise of America, that our success is indubitable."

By the time British officials were forced to repeal the Stamp Act, they had come around to the view that the colonists' real desire—despite continued protests of loyalty—was independence. This suspicion now became a guiding theme of British policy. Concessions continued to be made in the face of American resistance, as was inevitable. An empire like Britain's, based on consent and lacking a standing army, could not enforce its will against a popular consensus. But in the last analysis, London was not willing to relinquish the supremacy it could no longer sustain. While conceding particulars, imperial policy hardened on principles, especially the principle of authority. The resulting combination, at once arbitrary and impotent, served to provoke the consequence most feared.

The repeal of the stamp duty, a major concession, was accompanied by a Declaratory Act asserting the prerogative that had just been surrendered. The act proclaimed Parliament's authority to make laws "of sufficient force and validity to bind the colonies and people of America, subjects of the crown of Great Britain, in all cases whatsoever."

It was an idle declaration. As Governor Hutchinson observed, already in America "the authority is in the populace, no law can be carried into execution against their mind." Undaunted, Parliament passed a series of new measures in 1767 known as the Townshend Acts. These were designed to take advantage of an apparent loophole in the colonies' stand against taxation. In his testimony, Franklin had told the Commons that while the colonies objected to "internal taxes," they would have no such objection to "external taxes," levied as charges on trade. The colonists recognized the service that Britain's great empire rendered to their commerce: "The sea is yours; you maintain, by your fleets, the safety of navigation in it, and keep it clear of pirates."

But Franklin had no authority to make such a claim, and the

Stamp Act Congress had already rejected any distinction between taxes. Accordingly, the Townshend Acts were greeted by new protests and economic boycotts of British goods.

"Our enemies very well know that dominion and property are closely connected; and that to impoverish us, is the surest way to enslave us," warned an article in the *Boston Evening Post*. "Therefore, if we mean still to be free, let us unanimously lay aside foreign superfluities, and encourage our own manufacture. SAVE YOUR MONEY AND YOU WILL SAVE YOUR COUNTRY!"

In 1770, this resistance once again forced Parliament to retreat and repeal its measures. Once again, however, the British sought to maintain in principle what they had been unable to sustain in practice. The Townshend duty on tea was not lifted, its preservation being regarded "as a mark of supremacy of Parliament, and an efficient declaration of their right to govern the colonies."

The colonists did not yet challenge this right; expressions of loyalty to the King accompanied every protest against the oppressions of Parliament. Beneath the surface of the colonial mind, however, the justification for a more drastic step was already forming. With each new act of taxation, the colonists began to discern an increasingly sinister design in British policy, until its measures were no longer seen as efforts to raise revenues in strained circumstances, but as manifestations of a plot to destroy liberty itself.

In the very year the Townshend Acts were repealed, the Boston Town Meeting concluded that "a deep-laid and desperate plan of imperial despotism has been laid, and partly executed, for the extinction of all civil liberty," and that "the august and once revered fortress of English freedom—the admirable work of ages—the British Constitution seems fast tottering into fatal and inevitable ruin." The threat of such a catastrophe and the "universal havoc" it would bring confronted the colonists with "*an awful warning to hazard all*" to prevent it.

This warning was followed by a further abatement in the colonies' grievances and a general prospering of the colonial economies. But two years later, in protesting a measure to pay judges' salaries out of import duties, the Boston Town Meeting once again sounded the alarm: "The Plan of *Despotism*... is rapidly hastening to a completion... under a constant unremitted uniform Aim to inslave us." The following year, Parliament passed a new Tea Act and set in motion the sequence of events that would lead to a final break.

In an effort to rescue the faltering East India Company by permitting it to sell directly to America, the Tea Act eliminated English duties and middlemen, promising cheaper tea to Americans. Since the Townshend duty on tea would still be collected, however, the act would also serve to establish Britain's authority to tax her colonies. Thus the constitutional issue was joined. In addition, the new measure would permit the East India Company to undersell colonial merchants (who had been importing illegal Dutch tea), a fact which encouraged them to regard the measure as the first step in a monopolistic plan to destroy them. "Despotism with all its horrors stares us full in the face," declared the *Massachusetts Spy*. "Taxation without consent and monopoly of trade" portended "the most dreadful train of intolerable evils that ever overwhelm a people!"

In December 1773, the East India tea began to arrive in the ports of Charleston, Boston, New York and Philadelphia. On the night of the 16th, thirty to sixty men disguised as Mohawk Indians climbed aboard the vessels in Boston harbor and, before a crowd of hundreds, pitched forty-five tons of tea into the dark waters below.

When news of the "Tea Party" reached London a month later, the King's minister was appalled. He had given the colonists "a relief instead of an oppression." If they rebelled against even conciliatory duties, the issue was not taxes but authority. Crown and Parliament agreed. "We must master them," the King observed, "or totally leave them to themselves and treat them as aliens."

In March, Parliament passed a series of acts, which the colonists called "coercive" and "intolerable." The port of Boston was ordered closed until the town compensated the East India Company for its lost tea. The charter of Massachusetts was in effect annulled and its Provisional Council made appointive to conform to the practice in other royal colonies. General Thomas

Gage was appointed Governor and provided with two regiments to enforce the Parliamentary measures.

These steps, more drastic than any previously taken, provoked a wave of reaction as support for Boston spread through the colonies. The Virginia Assembly denounced the sending of troops as a "hostile invasion" and declared June 1, the date the act was to become effective, "a day of fasting, humiliation and prayer." Richard Henry Lee and other Virginia leaders proposed the convening of a Continental Congress. Franklin's old motto "Join or Die" was revived, and the figure of a snake— severed and united—became the symbol of the colonies' revolt. When the snake and its motto appeared opposing a Britannic dragon, however, one loyalist asked,

> Ye sons of Sedition, how comes it to pass
> That America's typed by a snake—in the grass?

On September 5, the First Continental Congress assembled in Philadelphia. During the debates, Patrick Henry declared, "Government is dissolved.... We are in a state of nature ... The distinctions between Virginians, Pennsylvanians, New Yorkers, and New Englanders, are no more. I am not a Virginian, but an American."

A Declaration of Rights was passed stating that the laws of nature, the principles of the English Constitution and the various colonial charters entitled Americans "to life, liberty and property," which they had never ceded to any sovereign power to dispose of without their consent.

The Congress expressed its "ardent desire, that harmony and mutual intercourse of affection and interest may be restored" with the mother country. But it also stated that "since the last war," measures taken by Parliament revealed "a system formed to enslave America."

Just before the Congress assembled, a new Parliamentary measure declared all of the coveted valley north of the Ohio and east of the Mississippi a part of Quebec.

The Quebec Act was a gesture of redress by Parliament to the *habitants* of the conquered Illinois country. It permitted them to retain the French legal code and allowed the Catholic

Church to collect tithes as it had under French rule. But it was also a powerful blow to the western ambitions of the colonists and aroused the anti-Papist fears of the New England Puritans: "Nor can we suppress our astonishment," the Continental Congress exclaimed in its rehearsal of grievances, "that a British Parliament should ever consent to establish in that country a religion that has deluged your island in blood, and dispersed impiety, bigotry, persecution, murder and rebellion in every part of the world."

Like previous measures, it was portrayed by the radicals as part of a more encompassing design: "Popery and French laws in Canada," wrote Tom Paine, "are but a part of a system of despotism which has been prepared for the colonies."

At its conclusion, the Congress resolved to boycott British goods and to hold a second congress in May, if their grievances were not redressed.

In mid-September, while the Congress was in session, the King reaffirmed the Parliamentary course: "The dye is now cast," he wrote, "the colonies must either submit or triumph." For the moment, no additional steps should be taken, but there should also be no retreat. Pursuit of the measures already adopted would lead the colonists to submit. Afterward, it would be all right to let them see that there was no inclination at present to lay fresh taxes on them: "But I am clear there must always be one tax to keep up the right, and as such I approve of the tea duty."

The ability to enforce the right, however, was still to be tested. On both sides there were parties still strong for conciliation. "Which is better," the Reverend Mather Byles asked his fellow Bostonians, "—to be ruled by one tyrant three thousand miles away or three thousand tyrants not a mile away?" And Edmund Burke explained to Parliament that the "disobedient spirit in the colonies" was "laid deep in the national constitution of things." No device could prevent the distance between them from weakening the authority of empire: "Seas roll, and months pass, between the order and the execution: and the want of a speedy explanation of a single point is enough to defeat a whole system." Therefore, the only reasonable course was "to comply with the American spirit as necessary; or, if you please to submit to it, as a necessary evil."

But stronger forces were moving the sides toward conflict. In October, Massachusetts Bay had become virtually independent when its Assembly was dissolved by Governor Gage, and reconvened as a "Provincial Congress" in Concord, with John Hancock as president. In February a second Provincial Congress met, and came to the conclusion from the "disposition" of the British government that the "sudden Distruction of this Colony in particular is intended," and therefore took steps to ready a militia and a force of "Minute Men" to respond in kind.

In Virginia, the Assembly had been dissolved by the Governor, the Fourth Earl of Dunmore, for its denunciation of the Boston Port Act. It was now convened at St. John's Church in Richmond in order to prepare for the Second Continental Congress. On March 17, the *Virginia Gazette* reported several developments that seemed to encourage hopes of a conciliation. The King's minister, Lord North, was said to be desirous of obtaining more information concerning sentiments in America; the greater part of the military force was to be removed from Boston, the fleet being left to enforce the blockade; and British merchants were preparing an appeal to the House of Commons in behalf of the colonies, while public opinion in England and Scotland had swung to the colonial side.

Six days later, in Richmond, Patrick Henry presented the Assembly with resolutions stating that a militia was the "only security of a free government" and proposing that the colony be "immediately put into a posture of defense." Henry then rose to take the floor and in dramatic accents declared, "The war is actually begun! The next gale that sweeps from the North will bring to our ears the clash of resounding arms! . . . Is life so dear, or peace so sweet as to be purchased at the price of chains and slavery? Forbid it, Almighty God! I know not what course others may take, but as for me, give me liberty, or give me Death!"

Richard Henry Lee and Thomas Jefferson led the triumphant support for Henry's resolutions. A committee was named to oversee the organization of the colony's defense. Its members included several officers of the French and Indian War, among them their commander, George Washington.

Since returning from the Ohio campaigns, Washington had devoted his energies to building and enlarging his worldly estate. In his efforts to become a great landed proprietor, he had made seven trips to the west and had organized a group of investors to acquire and drain the Great Dismal Swamp between the lower James and Albemarle Sound. When news of the Boston Tea Party reached Virginia, he was preoccupied with problems over tenants and leases, claims and property disputes arising from his speculative ventures. As a burgess, he had voted for the resolutions in support of Boston, but he had not approved the lawless actions of the Sons of Liberty. It was the punitive British response that changed his attitude. After the Coercive Acts, he was convinced that a crisis had arrived. "We must assert our rights," he wrote, "or submit to every imposition, that be heaped upon us, till custom and use shall make us as tame and abject slaves, as the blacks we rule over with such arbitrary sway."

Days after Washington left the Richmond convention, he was told that Lord Dunmore had voided the twenty-year-old land claims of the Ohio veterans, which he had spent so much effort to secure. He personally stood to lose 23,000 acres in addition to the considerable costs he had borne in the process of surveying, filing and seating the claims. Stunned by the action, he dispatched a letter to the Governor in a vain appeal for a reversal of his decision: "I hardly know yet how to persuade myself into a belief of the reality of it."

Meanwhile, he turned his attention to the task of mustering a Virginia militia. In the last week of April, he received word that the captain of a British vessel had landed on the banks of the James with fifteen marines and taken the powder stored in the Williamsburg magazine. The local population was indignant at the seizure. Although they could not admit the true source of their outrage, the colony's leaders made a protest to the Governor, complaining that the magazine was needed in case of a rebellion by the slaves. Dunmore replied with equal disingenuousness that it was only reports of a slave insurrection in a neighboring county that had led him to requisition the powder in the first place. He assured them that it could be returned in half an hour if required to put down an uprising.

The Virginians were neither convinced nor reassured by Dunmore's explanation. Members of the militia assembled on horseback in Fredericksburg and prepared to retrieve the missing powder, or at least compel the Governor to compensate the loss. Only the cautious remonstrances of Washington and others restrained them from marching on Williamsburg. When Dunmore heard of the Fredericksburg gathering, he immediately issued a warning to the rebels. If any harm should come to him or his affairs, he told them, he would "proclaim liberty to the slaves and reduce Williamsburg to ashes."

No threats or cautions deterred Patrick Henry, however. Setting out from Hanover with a company of militia, he marched on the capital. At his approach, Dunmore quickly produced compensation for the powder. But when Henry's troops dispersed, the Governor issued a proclamation declaring him an outlaw and warning anyone against aiding and abetting him. It was an act recalling Governor Berkeley's edict against Nathaniel Bacon, a hundred years before.

On April 19, the day prior to Dunmore's seizure of the powder stores, a British infantry force appeared in the village of Lexington, ten miles northwest of Boston, on a similar mission. When the troops arrived, they were met by seventy armed villagers, who had been warned by riders of their approach. A musket was fired, and in the battle that ensued eight Americans were killed. The British then marched to Concord, where another battle took place. Two Americans and three British regulars were killed. The British then retreated toward Boston, but all along the way their column was sniped at from stone walls, barns and buildings. By the time they reached Boston, seventy of them had been killed.

"A brother's sword has been sheathed in a brother's breast," wrote Washington, when he was informed of the events, "and ... the once happy and peaceful plains of America are either to be drenched with blood or inhabited by slaves."

On May 10, the Second Continental Congress met in Philadelphia, and the following month Washington was selected as General and Commander in Chief of the Army of the United Colonies, organized "for the defence of American Liberty."

The defense of American liberty was not yet identified with independence or rebellion, however. Unwilling to contemplate the betrayal of allegiance and the breach of authority that such a step entailed, the colonists regarded their oppression as authored by Parliament and not the King. On July 8, Congress sent an "Olive Branch Petition" to the Crown. The colonists, it avowed, were "attached to your Majesty's person, family and government with all the devotion that principle and affection can inspire." They were "connected with Great Britain by the strongest ties that can unite societies," and intended to remain so. "We solemnly assure your Majesty, that we not only most ardently desire the former harmony between her and these colonies may be restored, but that a concord may be established between them upon so firm a basis, as to perpetuate its blessings uninterrupted by any future dissentions to succeeding generations in both countries."

The petition pleaded with the King to use his authority to stop the war, repeal the Coercive Acts of Parliament and bring about "a happy and permanent reconciliation." But military events were rapidly moving the parties beyond the possibility of reconciliation.

In Virginia, civil war had already begun. On June 8, the Governor fled the capital by night and took refuge aboard a British man-of-war, anchoring his flotilla off Norfolk at the mouth of the James. With the Governor in flight, the House of Burgesses agreed to put the colony on a war footing. Two regiments were organized, one of which was led by Patrick Henry. Many of the militia soldiers wore hunting shirts with the motto "Liberty or Death" inscribed on them, and carried tomahawks and scalping knives. The burgesses assured Dunmore that he was in no personal danger but expressed their displeasure that "a Scheme, the most diabolical, had been meditated, and generally recommended, by a Person of great Influence, to offer Freedom to our Slaves, and turn them against their Masters."

The scheme, however, had already been put into action, and

the British war sloop *Otter* was busy raiding plantations along the Chesapeake and liberating Virginians' slaves. "Lord Dunmore sails up and down the river," reported a Norfolk resident, "and where he finds a defenceless place, he lands, plunders the plantation and carries off the negroes."

With the freed slaves, Dunmore organized an "Ethiopian Regiment" nearly three hundred strong and fitted them with uniforms before sending them out to meet the American rebels. Across their breasts, as a challenge to Henry's militiamen, he had emblazoned the inscription "Liberty to Slaves."

On November 7, Dunmore issued a formal proclamation of emancipation: All indentured servants and Negroes joining His Majesty's troops were declared from that time *free*.

"Hell itself could not have vomitted anything more black than this design of emancipating our slaves," complained a Philadelphia correspondent, reflecting widespread feeling in the south. Edward Rutledge, one of four South Carolina delegates to the Continental Congress, thought that Dunmore's proclamation acted "more effectually to work an eternal separation between Great Britain and the Colonies, than any other expedient, which could possibly have been thought of." And from his military headquarters, General Washington advised, "If Virginians are wise, that arch-traitor to the rights of humanity, Lord Dunmore, should be instantly crushed ... otherwise like a snow-ball, in rolling, his army will get size, some through promises and some through inclination, joining his standard; but that which renders the measure indispensably necessary, is the Negroes."

Meanwhile, the conflict had assumed major dimensions in the north. The Continental Congress had hardly met when it was told that Ethan Allen had crossed Lake Champlain and seized Forts Ticonderoga and Crown Point, opening the invasion route to Canada. Just after leaving the Congress on June 23 to take command of the Continental Army, Washington was informed that a major battle had taken place at Bunker Hill in Boston. Over a thousand British regulars had been killed, a devastating loss for the King's forces. "Those people shew a spirit and conduct against us," wrote General Gage, "they never shewed against the French."

In August, Washington announced his intention to conquer Canada. "The acquisition of Canada is of immeasureable importance to the cause we are engaged in," he explained. It was "the only link wanting in the great continental chain of union." In England, the Crown declared its colonies to be in a state of "open and avowed rebellion" and refused to receive their "Olive Branch" of peace.

Washington's campaign against Quebec was launched in September. The following month, the King appeared before Parliament. The "rebellious War" in the American territories had become more general, he announced, and was "manifestly carried on for the Purpose of establishing an independent Empire." There could be no thought of yielding to such a purpose or giving up the colonies which England had "planted . . . nursed . . . and defended at much expence of blood and treasure." Twenty thousand troops were dispatched to suppress the revolt. A Prohibitory Act embargoed all colonial trade, ordered the seizure of all American ships and proclaimed any resistance treason.

While these forces and directives were crossing the Atlantic, a pamphlet called *Common Sense* appeared in the colonies. Written by an Englishman only recently arrived in America, it took the argument between imperial parent and colonial offspring to its penultimate stage. With the publication of Tom Paine's tract, the goal of independence—hitherto disavowed, disclaimed and denied—surged irrepressibly to the surface of the colonial mind.

A writer in the *Connecticut Gazette* summarized the impact of Paine's words: "You have declared the sentiments of Millions. Your production may justly be compared to a land-flood that sweeps all before it. We were blind, but on reading these enlightening works the scales have fallen from our eyes . . . The doctrine of Independence hath been in times past, greatly disgustful; we abhorred the principle—it is now become our delightful theme, and commands our purest affections."

Paine's argument was as sweeping as its influence. To those who asserted that America had flourished under the connection with Britain, Paine asserted that the colonies would have done as well or better without it. To those who pointed to the protection Britain provided from other empires, Paine replied that she had only preserved the colonies from her own enemies on her own account. Extending Franklin's historical revision even further, he argued that "France and Spain never were, nor perhaps ever will be our enemies as *Americans*, but as our being *subjects of Great Britain*."

If Paine had difficulty in discerning the colonies' debt to Britain, he had none in discovering reasons to end their relation. "Small islands not capable of protecting themselves are the proper objects for kingdoms to take under their care," he observed, "but there is something very absurd, in supposing a continent to be perpetually governed by an island." It was as though after all the constitutional arguments and philosophical appeals, Paine had blurted out the calculations of a practical colonial mind: "It is not in the power of Britain or of Europe to conquer America," he reasoned, ". . . if they cannot conquer us, they cannot govern us."

He had never met with anyone either in England or America, he emphasized, who had not "confessed his opinion, that a separation between the countries would take place one time or other." It was only a matter of finding the right time. But this had already been settled: "*The time hath found us.*"

The only obstacle that remained to independence was the colonists' lingering sense of obligation to the mother country and the monarch, to whom loyalty had been sworn on every public occasion. Until the appearance of *Common Sense*, the colonial rebels had attempted to draw a sharp distinction between Parliament, which represented the inhabitants of Britain, and the King, who presided over the empire and its provinces. The despotic design which they perceived in the measures against them was in their eyes "ministerial," not royal; acts of the Commons, not edicts of the Crown, oppressed them. In their appeals they petitioned the King as "the loving father" of all his peoples, and sought redress of their grievances against the Parliament of Britain.

As the conflict progressed, this distinction became more and more difficult to maintain. But it remained crucial to the colonial cause. The sacrosanct position of the Crown preserved the authority of colonial law and the colonists' sense of loyalty and honor. In 1775, John Adams maintained that Parliament had no authority in America and never had, but still insisted, "We owe allegiance to the person of His Majesty, King George III, whom God preserve." The colonies themselves were united under the King, who was "King of Massachusetts, King of Rhode Island, King of Connecticut &c." This same view was taken by Congress in answering the King's declaration that they were in a state of rebellion: "What allegiance is it that we forget? Allegiance to Parliament? We never owed—never owned it. Allegiance to our King? Our words have ever avowed it—our conduct has ever been consistent with it."

But as the crisis deepened and the King formally declared their acts treason, the colonists' devotion became untenable. Paine's pamphlet characteristically cut the knot by ignoring the pledges and oaths Americans had made for a hundred years: "But where, says some, is the King of America? I'll tell you. Friend, he reigns above, and doth not make havoc of mankind like the Royal Brute of Britain."

Common Sense rejected not only the monarch, but monarchy itself: "Government by Kings was first introduced into the world by the Heathens, from whom the children of Israel copied the custom. It was the most prosperous invention the Devil ever set on foot for the promotion of idolatry."

Reference to the history of religion was supported by arguments from economy. In absolute monarchies, the king had weighty affairs to conduct, but this was hardly the case in limited monarchies like Britain: "In countries where he is neither a judge nor a general, as in England, a man would be puzzled to know what *is* his business." The nearer any government approached a republic, "the less business there is for a king." While this reasoning seemed to give away an important part of the colonists' case against the tyranny of the English monarch, it made the point that America could manage without one.

Just as the colonies, in Paine's view, had no use for monarchs, so they had no need for parents: "The infant state of the Colonies, as it is called, so far from being against, is an argument in favor of independence. . . . History sufficiently informs us, that the bravest achievements were always accomplished in the non-age of a nation."

Paine projected the particulars of the family quarrel into a universal frame and rekindled the fires of the original colonial mission. "The cause of America," he exclaimed, "is in great measure the cause of all mankind."

In the spring of 1776, when *Common Sense* first appeared and persuaded many, the middle colonies—Pennsylvania, New York, New Jersey and Maryland—still opposed the dread step of independence. One delegate from New Jersey expressed his opposition, saying, "We ourselves have happily lived and enjoyed all the liberty that men could or can wish," and gave it as his opinion that the cry for independence went up from men who wanted "a new empire." The main reluctance among the delegates, however, was that "the people of the middle colonies ... were not yet ripe for bidding adieu to [the British connection]."

While the Continental Congress deliberated, the military situation grew more serious. An emissary was sent to France to sound out the hated Papists about military aid. But alliance presumed sovereignty and thus raised the issue of independence in a new and critical way.

"It is not choice but necessity calls for Independence, as the only means by which foreign alliance can be obtained," wrote Richard Lee, head of the Virginia delegation. On June 7, Lee introduced a resolution: "That these United Colonies are, and of right ought to be, free and independent States."

One month later, on July 4, 1776, Congress adopted a *Declaration of Independence*, drafted by another Virginian, Thomas Jefferson. Like Paine's pamphlet, the *Declaration* indicted the King for attempting to establish "an absolute Tyranny over these States." It did not mention Parliament, the author of the specific acts against the colonies, and the authority by which the King himself ruled. Like Paine's pamphlet, the *Declaration* also elevated America's grievances to a universal cause: "We hold these truths to be self-evident, that all men are created equal, that they are endowed by their Creator with certain unalienable Rights, that among these are Life, Liberty, and the Pursuit of Happiness."

The following day, Americans held mock funerals of King George, the father of the colonial peoples, to symbolize the birth of a new nation.

Afterward, Americans who had opposed independence were perplexed by the revolutionary turn of events. "The downfal of the ancient monarchies," wrote Jonathan Boucher from his exile in England, "was preceded by causes, and effected by means, which were not wholly inadequate to the event. To their tyranny the Tarquins owed their expulsion; and to a system of government . . . oppressive and feeble, Spain may ascribe her loss of Holland and the kingdom of Portugal. But there was no such concurrence of adequate causes to produce the defection of America." Never in history, agreed the Tory Daniel Leonard, had there been so much rebellion with so "little real cause."

The revolt of the colonies, observed Peter Oliver, former Chief Justice of Massachusetts, was "as striking a Phaenomenon, in the political World, as hath appeared for many Ages past; & perhaps it is a *singular* one." Far from being oppressed, the colonies had been tenderly nursed in infancy with care and affection, and "indulged with every Gratification that the most froward Child could wish for . . . had been repeatedly saved from impending Destruction, sometimes by an Aid unsought-at othertimes by Assistance granted to them from their own repeated humble Supplications." Revolt in such circumstances was astonishing—enough to cause an attentive mind to "wish for a Veil to throw over the Nakedness of human Nature." The colonists had shown a temper of mind conforming exactly to the wayward children of Israel described by the poet Dryden:

> The *Jews*, a head strong, moody murmuring Race,
> As ever tried th'extent and stretch of Grace:
> *God's* pamper'd People, whom, debauch'd with Ease,
> No King could govern, nor no God could please.

The colonists had found a veil for the ambition that set them against a parent who protected them from their enemies: "This, in private Life would be termed, base Ingratitude: but Rebellion hath sanctified it by the Name of, Self Defence."

Indeed, the *Declaration* that Jefferson drafted as "an appeall to the tribunal of the world ... for our justification" was regarded by the American loyalists with a mixture of contempt and disbelief. From his exile, Thomas Hutchinson asked its author and other delegates of the slaveholding colonies "how their constituents justify the depriving more than an hundred thousand Africans of their rights to liberty and *the pursuit of happiness*, and in some degree to their lives, if these rights are so absolutely unalienable?"

The contrast between the liberty the colonists championed for themselves and mankind, and the slavery they imposed on black Africans was not newly discovered. It had been invoked during the struggle with Britain as an indictment of the colonial cause: "Blush ye pretended votaries for freedom!" a Baptist minister had written in 1774; "ye trifling patriots! who are making a vain parade of being advocates for the liberties of mankind, who are thus making a mockery of your profession by trampling on the sacred natural rights and privileges of Africans." If taxes were an oppression to justify America's revolt against British rule, how much greater the cause for America's slaves to revolt against their masters: "What is a trifling three-penny duty on tea," the minister asked, "compared to the inestimable blessings of liberty to one captive?"

American slavery refuted the revolutionary argument, and confounded the patriotic vision of America's birth as a divine plan "for the illumination of the ignorant, and the emancipation of the slavish part of mankind all over the earth." For none could fail to be conscious that America was then the chief country of human bondage, that slavery was expanding in the New World at the very moment it was being abolished in the Old.

The exalted ideals and harsh realities of the American experience were connected in the American mind by sinews of unexpiated guilt. The very fear the patriots expressed as a rationale for their rebellion—that the King of England intended their enslavement—seemed to draw its sustenance from a bad conscience. "Enslaving the *Africans* is one of the crying sins of our land, for which Heaven is now chastizing us," a Connecticut Town Meeting concluded in 1774. "The Common father of all men," a Philadelphia minister agreed, "will severely plead a Controversy against these Colonies for Enslaving Negroes, and keeping their children born British subjects in perpetual slavery—and possibly for this wickedness God threatens us with slavery." Paine himself drew this conclusion in 1775: "How suitable to our crime is the punishment with which providence threatens us? We have enslaved multitudes ... and now are threatened with the same."

The uneasy connection between the colonists' guilt and their revolutionary indignation was manifest in Jefferson's draft of the *Declaration*. Its catalogue of royal crimes was climaxed by a searing indictment of the King's participation in the Atlantic slave trade: "He has waged cruel war against human nature itself, violating it's most sacred rights of life & liberty in the persons of distant people who never offended him, captivating & carrying them into slavery in another hemisphere, or to incur miserable death in their transportation thither. this piratical warfare, the opprobrium of *infidel* powers, is the warfare of the CHRISTIAN king of Great Britain."

Yet, the very passion of Jefferson's argument seemed to betray the embarrassment of its premises. Slavery in England had been effectively abolished four years before. The distinction Jefferson sought to make between the traffic in slaves and slavery itself was suspiciously fine. As if to counter such objections, Jefferson extended his argument and accusations to implausible lengths. In the following clause, he indicted the King for imposing slavery on Americans and then for instigating the slaves, whose liberty *he* had destroyed, to revolt (an injury Jefferson felt personally when his own slaves subsequently defected to the British): "... and that this assemblage of horrors might want no fact of distinguished die, he is now exciting these very people to rise in arms among us, and to purchase that liberty of which *he* has deprived them, by murdering the people upon whom *he* also obtruded them; thus paying off former crimes committed against the *liberties* of one people, with crimes which he urges them to commit against the *lives* of another."

Jefferson's clause was eventually struck from the *Declaration* in deference to the interests of American slave traders north and south. But this did not resolve the paradox of the American purpose and its revolutionary ideals.

In part the paradox sprang from the very conservatism of the American cause. America's patriots—slaveowners, merchants and men of the frontier—intended no revolution of society, but the preservation of its liberty and property. Liberty to them was "liberty according to English ideas, and on English principles," as Burke had noted. It was not the British Empire that the patriots rejected, or even the imperial system, but only America's subordinate place within it. There was a shrewd truth in the King's charge that what Americans wanted was an empire for themselves.

Yet to admit as much would have been to accept the guilt of a primal disobedience. It would have been to acknowledge self as the paramount interest of the revolutionary cause. This was the argument of the loyalist opposition. The sin of pride and the sacred obligation of Christians to obey authority were the burdens of the sermons they preached. "Submit yourselves to every ordinance of man, for the Lord's sake," the Apostle Peter had enjoined in a favorite text, "whether it be to the King as supreme, or unto GOVERNORS."

Exculpation was the countertheme of the revolutionary litanies. Franklin even proposed a formula of absolution to serve as the official motto of the new republic: "Rebellion to tyrants is obedience to God." The sentiment so impressed Jefferson that he had it engraved on the official seal of Virginia and made it his personal stamp.

A guilt in the heart of the national deed inspired the exaltation of the national ideals. The purity of their motives was proved when patriots aspired to rights for mankind, rather than power for themselves; their loyalty and honor were preserved in discovering the King to be the true author of subversive acts. "I ... should much distrust my own judgement," Washington wrote in explaining his support for rebellion, "if my nature did not recoil at the thought of submitting to measures, which I think subversive of every thing that I ought to hold dear and valuable, and did I not find, at the same time, that the voice of mankind is with me."

Slavery was not the only legacy that illuminated the inner conflict of the American mission. The conquest of the land provided another. "Whoever shall attempt to trace the claims of the European Nations to the Countrys in America from the principles of Justice," Jefferson wrote, "or reconcile the invasions made on the native Indians to the natural rights of mankind, will find that he is pursuing a Chimera, which exists only in his imagination, against the evidence of indisputable facts."

The *Declaration* made only one reference to America's natives. Like the stricken passage on the slave trade, it disclosed the colonists' own ambivalence about rebellion, accusing the King of subverting the colonial peace: "He has excited domestic Insurrections amongst us, and has endeavoured to bring on the Inhabitants of our Frontiers, the merciless Indian Savages, whose known Rule of Warfare, is an undistinguished Destruction, of all Ages, Sexes and Conditions."

In the months prior to the *Declaration*, both parties to the conflict had sought the allegiance of the wilderness tribes. At first, the natives attempted to maintain a neutral ground. When colonial representatives met with the Iroquois at Albany, they were told, "This is a Quarrell between Father and Children; we shall not meddle with it." But as the war progressed, the hostility of the colonial settlers and the continuing press of their claims to Indian lands caused a majority of the tribes to join the British side. Delaware and Shawnee, Mohawk and Seneca, Cherokee and Chippewa, one after another "took up the hatchet" against the Americans. The fighting was waged with the same implacable violence that had characterized the previous struggles for the wilderness frontier. During a scourge of Iroquois towns in New York, officers of the patriot army proposed a July 4th toast of "Civilization or death to all American savages." As in earlier contests, the natives were vanquished by the superior arms of their colonial opponents.

Following their victory, the Americans continued the course of expansion and settlement that had carried their banners from the ocean coasts of Virginia and New England across the

Appalachian chain to the Mississippi Valley. As Commander in Chief of the American armies, Washington favored the purchase of native lands whenever possible, preferring "the expediency of being on good terms with the Indians" to attempting to drive them "by force of arms out of their Country." In the past, he recalled, such efforts had been "like driving the wild Beasts of the forest, which will return as soon as the pursuit is at an end, and fall perhaps upon those that are left there." Better to proceed prudently, for "the gradual extension of our settlements will as certainly cause the savage, as the wolf, to retire."

To clear the wilderness for the advancing civilization was the mission of the American pioneer, not only for Washington and the patriot rebels, but also for the Puritan Saints who had set out more than a hundred years earlier in the New World to conquer Satan's armies and bring light to the primeval dark.

When Washington assumed the Presidency of the Republic, he invoked the Pilgrim vision of a divine covenant: "No People can be bound to acknowledge and adore the invisible hand, which conducts the affairs of men more than the People of the United States," he declared. "Every step, by which they have advanced to the character of an independent nation seems to have been distinguished by some token of providential agency." In the economy of nature there was "an indissoluble union between virtue and happiness." Americans enjoyed the protection of providence, because they honored the covenant in their deed. For "the preservation of the sacred fire of liberty, and the destiny of the Republican model of Government, are justly considered as *deeply*, perhaps as *finally* staked, on the experiment entrusted to the hands of the American people." America, Jefferson agreed in his own presidential address, was "a chosen country."

Like the Jews of Exodus, the diverse peoples of America's settlements were a "community of fate." They had endured a wilderness to build Jerusalem in a promised land. At the Sinai of their deliverance, they proclaimed an ethical doctrine for mankind. They saw the God of their right prevail in all their victories, and were rewarded afterward with the lands of the tribes they had conquered.

The root of the new American nation sprang not from a common soil, or language or inheritance of blood, but from the communal deed of its wilderness creation, and the messianic promise that justified its course. One nation conceived in liberty: an ark of refuge and redemption for the race. "A situation similar to the present," declared the prophet of *Common Sense,* "hath not happened since the days of Noah until now ... We have it in our power to begin the world over again."

In 1776, Americans stood once more on the shores of a new Jordan, and beheld a new world. To the west, a country vaster than they had conquered waited for them to take possession. Beyond stretched oceans that their children would cross. Generations would hear a Manifest Destiny summon them to expand the realm of freedom. On an ever-renewed frontier of possibility, they would re-enact the drama of a pilgrim birth.

Selected Bibliography

In writing history, every author is indebted to his predecessors. But the creation of the work grows primarily out of a silent dialogue between the sources and the author himself. What he believes of the accounts available, the perspective he draws on motives and events, the choices he makes of what to emphasize or to ignore, are the crucial decisions that create a historical vision.

I have incurred, in writing this book, special debts to E. S. Morgan's *American Slavery, American Freedom* and to Lawrence Henry Gipson's 13 volumes on *The British Empire Before the American Revolution*. Morgan's social portrait of colonial Virginia, the crucible of American democracy, was invaluable in shaping my own conception, which differs from his mainly in its emphasis on the psychological dimension of what he calls "the American paradox": the interdependence of American slavery and American freedom. In seeking an understanding of the conflict which led to America's independence from Britain, I have drawn on Gipson's massive analysis of imperial-colonial relations in the period 1760 to 1775. Gipson and the imperial historians have been criticized by Morgan in an essay included in *The Challenge of the American Revolution*. If the views of Gipson and the imperial school are accepted, he asks, how can the Revolution be understood at all? For if the empire is seen as on balance beneficial to the colonies, then it is necessary to regard men of broad vision like Washington, Adams, Jefferson and Franklin as parochial and narrow-minded, or "dupes of agitators." By taking a more psychological view of the actors and events, I have attempted to resolve this difficulty while giving proper weight to the historical evidence, which I believe supports the imperial school. This resolution also avoids the pitfalls of other standard views, which are compelled to regard the patriots as motivated solely by economic interests, or as political idealists of a rarity not usually encountered outside the pages of academic histories.

In researching this book, I have found useful the various editions

228

and writings of Samuel G. Drake, Alden Vaughan's *New England Frontier* (unfortunately marred by its apologetics in behalf of the Puritans), Winthrop Jordan's *White over Black*, Richard Morton's *Colonial Virginia*, Wilcomb Washburn's *The Governor and the Rebel*, Thomas Abernethy's *Western Lands and the Revolution*, Charles Howard McIlwain's essay on the fur trade in Wraxall's *An Abridgement of the Indian Affairs*, and Douglas Southall Freeman's *George Washington*. Also Francis Jennings' *The Invasion of America*, which contains an interesting, if not always persuasive, critique of Puritan and colonial sources.

Direct quotations in the text are from contemporary sources. With few exceptions, these are listed in the "A" sections of the Bibliography. The exceptions occur where quotations have been cited from secondary sources. These are listed in the "B" sections, with the other principal references used in this work.

An effort has been made to preserve the spelling and punctuation of the original sources in the text citations. On occasion, minor alterations have been made in the interest of intelligibility. In one instance (see pp. 63–64) the changes required in the excerpt from John Easton's "Relacion" amount to an interpolation of the original.

PART I. THANKSGIVING IN NEW ENGLAND

A. Contemporary Sources

1. Patuxet

Arber, Edward. *The Story of the Pilgrim Fathers, 1606–1623 A.D. as told by Themselves, their Friends, and their Enemies.* London, 1897.

Bradford, William. *History of Plymouth Plantation 1620–1647.* Ed. Worthington C. Ford. 2 vols. New York, 1968.

Cotton, John. *Gods Promise to His Plantations.* Old South Leaflets, III, no. 53. Boston, n.d.

Cushman, Robert. "Cushman's Discourse." In Alexander Young, ed., *Chronicles of the Pilgrim Fathers of the Colony of New Plymouth, from 1602–1625.* Boston, 1844.

Higginson, Francis. *New-England's Plantation.* Salem, 1908.

Johnson, Edward. *Johnson's Wonder-Working Providence of Sion's Saviour in New England.* Ed. J. Franklin Jamieson (*Original Narratives of Early American History*). New York, 1910.

Morton, Nathaniel. *New-England's Memoriall.* In Young, *Chronicles of the Pilgrim Fathers.* Boston, 1844.

Morton, Thomas. *The New English Canaan* (1632). In Peter Force, *Tracts and Other Papers, Relating Principally to the Origin,*

Settlement, and Progress of the Colonies in North America, from the Discovery of the Country to the Year 1776. Vol. 2. 4 vols. Washington, D.C., 1836–1846.

Mourt, G. *Mourt's Relation; A Journal of the Pilgrims at Plymouth* (1622). Ed. Dwight Heath. New York, 1963.

White, John. *The Planters Plea. Or The Grounds of Plantations Examined, And Usuall Objections Answered* (1630). In Force, op. cit.

Winslow, Edward. "Good Newes from New England." In Arber, op. cit.

———. "Winslow's Brief Narration." In Young, op. cit.

Winthrop, John. *Winthrop Papers.* Massachusetts Historical Society. Boston, 1929.

Young, Alexander, ed. *Chronicles of the Pilgrim Fathers of the Colony of New Plymouth, from 1602 to 1625.* Boston, 1844.

2. Magnalia Christi Americana

Bradford, William. *History of Plymouth Plantation 1620–1647.* 2 vols. Op. cit.

Chapin, Howard M. *Documentary History of Rhode Island.* 2 vols. Providence, 1916.

Gardiner, Lion. *A History of the Pequot War.* Cincinnati, 1860.

Gorton, Samuel. *Simplicities Defence against Seven-Headed Policy* ... (1646). In Force, op. cit., vol. 4.

Hubbard, William. *A Narrative of the Troubles with the Indians in New-England From the first Planting thereof to the present Time* (1677). Ed. Samuel G. Drake. 2 vols. Roxbury, Mass., 1865.

Mason, John. "A Brief History of the Pequot War." In *Massachusetts Historical Society Collections,* 2 ser., VIII, 1826.

Mather, Cotton. *Magnalia Christi Americana: or, the Ecclesiastical History of New-England from its First Planting in the Year 1620, unto the Year of our Lord 1698.* 2 vols. Hartford, 1820.

Mather, Increase. *A Relation of the Troubles which have hapned in New-England By reason of the Indians there. From the Year 1614 to the Year 1675.* Ed. S. G. Drake. Boston, 1864.

Underhill, John. "News from America." In *Mass. Hist. Soc. Coll.* 3 ser., VI, 1837.

Vincent, Philip. "A True Relation of the Late Battel Fought in New England, between the English and the Pequot Salvages." In *Mass. Hist. Soc. Coll.,* op. cit.

Williams, Roger. *The Bloody Tenent of Persecution for Cause of Conscience.* London, 1848.

———. *A Key into the Language of America: Or, An help to the Language of the Natives in that part of America, called New-*

England ... (1643). Ed. James Trumbull. In Narragansett Club, *Publications* I. Providence, 1866.

————. *Letters of Roger Williams, 1632–1682.* Ed. John Russell Bartlett. Narragansett Club, *Publications* VI. Providence, 1874.

Winthrop, John. "A Modell of Christian Charity." In D. Boorstin, ed., *An American Primer.* New York, 1968.

————. *Winthrop's Journal, "History of New England," 1630–1649.* Ed. James K. Hosmer. 2 vols. New York, 1908.

3. METACOMET

Borden, John. Remarks on Philip in Theodore Foster, "Materials for a History of Rhode Island." *Collections of the Rhode Island Historical Society,* vol. VII, 1885.

Church, Thomas. *The History of Philip's War, Commonly Called the Great Indian War, of 1675 and 1676.* Ed. S. G. Drake. Exeter, Mass., 1829.

Drake, S. G. *Old Indian Chronicle ... and Chronicles of the Indians.* Boston, 1836.

Easton, John. "A Relacion of the Indyan Warre." In Charles H. Lincoln, ed., *Narratives of the Indian Wars, 1675–1699.* New York, 1913.

Eliot, John. *A Brief Narrative of the Progress of the Gospel Among the Indians of New England, 1670.* Ed. W. T. R. Marvin. Boston, 1868.

————. "The Christian Commonwealth: or, The Civil Policy of the Rising Kingdom of Jesus Christ" (1660). In *Massachusetts Historical Society Collections,* 3 ser., IX, 1846.

Gookin, Daniel. "An Historical Account of the Doings and Sufferings of the Christian Indians in New England, in the Years 1675, 1676, 1677." In *Transactions and Collections of the American Antiquarian Society,* II, 1836.

————. "Historical Collections of the Indians in New England." In *Mass. Hist. Soc. Coll.,* 1 ser., I, 1792.

Harris, William. *A Rhode Islander Reports on King Philip's War. The Second William Harris Letter of August 1676.* Ed. and transcribed by Douglas Edward Leach. *Coll. R.I. Hist. Soc.,* Providence, 1963.

Hubbard, William. *A Narrative ...,* op. cit.

Hutchinson, Richard. "The Warr in New England Visibly Ended." In Lincoln, op. cit.

Mather, Cotton, and Mather, Increase. *The History of King Philip's War, By the Rev. Increase Mather, DD., Also A History of the Same War, By the Rev. Cotton Mather, DD.* Ed. S. G. Drake. Albany, 1862.

Rowlandson, Mary. "Narrative of the Captivity of Mrs. Mary Rowlandson." In Lincoln, op. cit.

Saltonstall, Nathaniel. "A Continuation of the State of New England." In Lincoln, op. cit.

Shepard, Thomas. "The Clear Sun-shine of the Gospel Breaking Forth upon the Indians in New-England." In *Mass. Hist. Soc. Coll.*, 3 ser., IV, 1834.

Shurtleff, Nathaniel E., and Pulsifer, David., eds. *Records of the Colony of New Plymouth.* Vols. 3 and 4. Boston, 1855–1861.

White, John. *The Planters Plea*, op. cit.

Williams, Roger. *Christenings make not Christians* (1645). Vol. 7 of *The Complete Writings of Roger Williams.* New York, 1963.

Winslow, Edward. "The Glorious Progress of the Gospel, amongst the Indians in New England." *Mass. Hist. Soc. Coll.*, 3 ser., IV, 1834.

B. Secondary Works

Adams, Charles Francis, Jr. *Three Episodes in Massachusetts History.* 2 vols. Boston, 1896.

Adams, James Truslow. *The Founding of New England.* Boston, 1921.

Arnold, Samuel Greene. *History of the State of Rhode Island and Providence Plantations.* Vol. I, 1636–1700. New York, 1859.

Bailyn, Bernard. *The New England Merchants in the Seventeenth Century.* Cambridge, Mass., 1955.

Bodge, George Madison. *Soldiers in King Philip's War.* Boston, 1906.

Bowen, Richard LeBaron. *Early Rehoboth: Documented Historical Studies of Families and Events in This Plymouth Colony Township.* 3 vols. Rehoboth, 1946.

Brockunier, Samuel Hugh. *The Irrepressible Democrat: Roger Williams.* New York, 1940.

Chapin, Howard M. *Sachems of the Narragansetts.* Providence, 1931.

Dorfman, Joseph. *The Economic Mind in America.* Vol. 1. New York, 1946.

Dorr, Henry C. "The Narragansetts." In *Collections of the Rhode Island Historical Society*, vol. VII, 1885.

Drake, Samuel G. *The Aboriginal Races of North America; Comprising Biographical Sketches of Eminent Individuals and An Historical Account of the Different Tribes from the First Discovery to the Present Period* ... 15th Ed. New York, 1880.

Ellis, George Edward. *The Red Man and the White Man in North America from Its Discovery to the Present Time.* Boston, 1882.

Ellis, George W., and Morris, John E. *King Philip's War*. New York, 1906.

Freeman, Frederick. *Civilization and Barbarism, Illustrated by Especial Reference to Metacomet and the Extinction of His Race*. Cambridge, Mass., 1878.

Gay, Peter. *A Loss of Mastery. Puritan Historians in Colonial America*. New York, 1966.

Greene, Lorenzo Johnston. *The Negro in Colonial New England*. New York, 1942.

Hagan, William T. *American Indians*. Chicago, 1960.

Hopkins, Stephen. "An Historical Account of the Planting and Growth of Providence." In *Coll. R.I. Hist. Soc.*, vol. VII, 1885.

Hutchinson, Thomas. *The History of the Colony and Province of Massachusetts Bay*. Vol. 1. Ed. L. S. Mayo. Cambridge, Mass., 1936.

Langdon, George D., Jr. *Pilgrim Colony: A History of New Plymouth, 1620–1691*. New Haven, 1966.

Leach, Douglas Edward. *Flintlock and Tomahawk: New England in King Philip's War*. New York, 1958.

McIntyre, Ruth A. *Debts Hopeful and Desperate: Financing the Plymouth Colony*. Plimouth Plantation, 1963.

MacLeod, William C. *The American Indian Frontier*. New York, 1928.

Miller, Perry. *Errand into the Wilderness*. Cambridge, Mass., 1956.

———. *Roger Williams: His Contribution to the American Tradition*. New York, 1962.

Moloney, Francis X. *The Fur Trade in New England 1620–1676*. Cambridge, Mass., 1931.

Morgan, Edmund. *The Puritan Dilemma: The Story of John Winthrop*. Boston, 1958.

Nash, Gary B. *Red, White, and Black: The Peoples of Early America*. Middletown, Conn., 1974.

Penhallow, Samuel. *The History of the Wars of New England with the Eastern Indians, 1726*. Cincinnati, 1859.

Potter, Elisha R., Jr. *The Early History of Narragansett*. In *Coll. R.I. Hist. Soc.*, vol. III, 1835.

Richman, Irving Berdine. *Rhode Island, Its Making and Its Meaning, 1636–1683*. New York, 1902.

Slotkin, Richard. *Regeneration Through Violence: The Mythology of the American Frontier, 1600–1860*. Middletown, 1973.

Smith, James M., ed. *Seventeenth Century America*. Chapel Hill, N.C., 1959.

Vaughan, Alden T. *New England Frontier: Puritans and Indians, 1620–1675*. Boston, 1965.

Ward, Harry M. *The United Colonies of New England, 1643–1690.* New York, 1961.

Washburn, Wilcomb E. "The Moral and Legal Justifications for Dispossessing the Indians." In Smith, op. cit.

——. *Red Man's Land/White Man's Law: A Study of the Past and Present Status of the American Indian.* New York, 1971.

Weeden, William B. *Economic and Social History of New England 1620–1789.* 2 vols. Boston, 1890.

Willison, George F. *Saints and Strangers.* New York, 1945.

Wright, Louis B. *Religion and Empire: The Alliance between Piety and Commerce in English Expansion, 1558–1625.* Chapel Hill, N.C., 1943.

PART II. DEMOCRACY IN VIRGINIA

A. Contemporary Sources

1. Seed of the Plantation

Arber, Edward, and Bradley, A. G., eds. *Travels and Works of Captain John Smith, President of Virginia, and Admiral of New England, 1580–1631.* 2 vols. Edinburgh, 1910.

Berkeley, Sir William. *A Discourse and View of Virginia* (1663). Norwalk, Conn., 1914.

Beverly, Robert. *History and Present State of Virginia* (1705). Ed. Louis B. Wright. Chapel Hill, N.C., 1947.

Hening, W. W., ed. *The Statutes at Large: Being a Collection of All the Laws of Virginia From the First Session of the Legislature in the Year 1619.* 13 vols. Richmond and Philadelphia, 1809–1823.

Kennedy, J. P., and McIlwaine, H. R., eds. *Journals of the House of Burgesses 1619–1776.* 13 vols. Richmond, 1905–1915.

Kingsbury, Susan M., ed. *Records of the Virginia Company of London.* 4 vols. Washington, D.C., 1906–1935. (Especially vols. 3 and 4.)

Percy, George. "Observations." In L. G. Tyler, ed., *Narratives of Early Virginia, 1606–1625.* New York, 1907.

——. "A Trewe Relacyon of the Procedeings and Occurentes of Momente which have hapned in Virginia from the Tyme Sir Thomas Gates was shippwrackte uppon the Bermudes anno 1609 until my departure outt of the Country which was anno Domini 1612." In *Tyler's Quarterly Historical and Genealogical Magazine* III (1922).

Quinn, David B., ed. *The Roanoke Voyages, 1584–1590.* London, 1955.

Rolfe, John. "Letter of John Rolfe, 1614." In Tyler, op. cit.

Tyler, L. G., ed. *Narratives of Early Virginia,* op. cit.
Virginia Assembly. "The Tragical Relation of the Virginia Assembly, 1624." In Tyler, op. cit.
Waterhouse, S. "State of the Colony." In Kingsbury, op. cit., vol. 3.

2. BACON'S REBELLION

Abernethy, Thomas P., ed. *More News From Virginia, A Further Account of Bacon's Rebellion* (1677). Charlottesville, 1943.
Andrews, Charles M. *Narratives of the Insurrections, 1675–1690.* New York, 1915.
"*Aspinwall Papers.*" In *Massachusetts Historical Society Collections,* 4 ser., IX, 1871.
Bacon, Nathaniel. "Manifesto." In *Virginia Magazine* I (1893).
Burwell Ms. "The History of Bacon's and Ingram's Rebellion." In Andrews, op. cit.
"Commissioners' Narrative" (1677). In Andrews, op. cit.
Cotton, Mrs. An. "An Account of Our Late Troubles in Virginia" (1676). In Force, *Tracts,* vol. 1, op. cit.
Eggelston Ms. "Bacon's Rebellion." *William and Mary Quarterly,* July 1960.
Hening W. W. *Statutes at Large,* vol. 2, op. cit.
Kennedy, J. P., and McIlwaine, H. R., eds. *Journals of the House of Burgesses,* op. cit.
Ludwell, Philip. "Letter to Secretary of State Sir Joseph Williamson, June 28, 1676." *Virginia Magazine* I (1893).
Mathew, Thomas. "The Beginning, Progress, and Conclusion of Bacon's Rebellion in Virginia, in the years 1675 and 1676." In Andrews, op. cit.
McIlwaine, H. R., ed. *Minutes of the Council and General Court of Colonial Virginia, 1622–1632, 1670–1676.* Richmond, 1924.
Sherwood, William. "Letter to Williamson, June 28, 1676." *Virginia Magazine* I (1893).
———. "Virginia's Deploured Condition." In *Mass. Hist. Soc. Coll.,* 4 ser., IX, 1871.
Smith, John. "Description of Virginia and Proceedings of the Colonie" (1612). In Tyler, op. cit.

3. DURANTE VITA

Adams, John. "A Dissertation on the Canon and the Feudal Law." In C. F. Adams, ed., *The Works of John Adams.* Boston, 1851.
Arber, Edward, and Bradley, A. G., eds. *Travels and Works of Captain John Smith,* vol. 2, op. cit.
Byrd, William. "Letters of the Byrd Family." In *Virginia Magazine of History and Biography* 36 (1928).

Donnan, Elizabeth, ed. *Documents Illustrative of the History of the Slave Trade to America.* 4 vols. Washington, D.C., 1930–1935.
Kennedy, J. P., and McIlwaine, H. R., eds. *Journals of the House of Burgesses,* op. cit.
Ruchames, Louis, ed. *Racial Thought in America.* New York, 1969.
Spotswood, Alexander. *The Official Letters of Alexander Spotswood, Lieutenant Governor of the Colony of Virginia, 1710–1722.* Ed. R. A. Brock. 2 vols. Richmond, 1882.

B. Secondary Works

Andrews, Mathew Page. *Virginia, The Old Dominion.* New York, 1937.
Bailyn, Bernard. "Politics and Social Structure in Virginia." In James M. Smith, ed., *Seventeenth Century America.* Chapel Hill, N.C., 1959.
Barbour, Philip L. *Pocahantas and Her World.* Boston, 1970.
Bruce, Philip A. *Economic History of Virginia in the Seventeenth Century.* 2 vols. New York, 1896.
———. *Institutional History of Virginia in the Seventeenth Century.* 2 vols. New York, 1910.
Craven, Wesley Frank. *Dissolution of the Virginia Company: The Failure of a Colonial Experiment.* New York, 1932.
———. *The Southern Colonies in the Seventeenth Century, 1607–1689.* Baton Rouge, 1949.
Franklin, John Hope. *From Slavery to Freedom: A History of Negro Americans.* New York, 1969.
Greene, Lorenzo J. *The Negro in Colonial New England.* New York, 1942.
Jennings, Francis. *The Invasion of America.* Chapel Hill, N.C., 1975.
Jernegan, Marcus W. *Laboring and Dependent Classes in Colonial America, 1607–1783.* Chicago, 1931.
Johnston, W. D. "Slavery in Rhode Island, 1755–1776." In *Collections of the Rhode Island Historical Society,* vol. II, 1894.
Jordan, Winthrop D. *White Over Black: American Attitudes Toward the Negro, 1550–1812.* Baltimore, 1969.
Mannix, Daniel P. *Black Cargoes: A History of the Atlantic Slave Trade.* New York, 1962.
Moore, George H. *Notes on the History of Slavery in Massachusetts.* New York, 1886.
Morgan, Edmund S. *American Slavery, American Freedom: The Ordeal of Colonial Virginia.* New York, 1975.
Morton, Richard L. *Colonial Virginia.* 2 vols. Chapel Hill, N.C., 1960.

Neill, Edward D. *Virginia Carolorum: The Colony Under the Rule of Charles the First and Second, 1625–1685.* Albany, 1886.
Robert, Joseph C. *The Story of Tobacco in America.* New York, 1949.
Rossiter, Clinton. *The First American Revolution.* New York, 1956.
Sauer, Carl Ortwin. *The Early Spanish Main.* Berkeley, Calif., 1969.
Smith, Abbot Emerson. *Colonists in Bondage: White Servitude and Convict Labor in America, 1607–1776.* Chapel Hill, N.C., 1947.
Taussig, Charles William. *Rum, Romance and Rebellion.* New York, 1928.
Vaughan, Alden T. *American Genesis: Captain John Smith and the Founding of Virginia.* Boston, 1975.
Washburn, Wilcomb E. "Governor Berkeley and King Philip's War." In *New England Quarterly* 30 (September 1957).
———. *The Governor and the Rebel: A History of Bacon's Rebellion in Virginia.* Chapel Hill, N.C., 1957.
Weeden, William B. "The Early African Slave-trade in New England." In *Proceedings of the American Antiquarian Society,* new series, vol. V. Worcester, 1889.
Wertenbaker, Thomas Jefferson. *Torchbearer of the Revolution: The Story of Bacon's Rebellion and Its Leader.* Gloucester, 1965.
Williamson, James A. *Sir John Hawkins: The Time and the Man.* Oxford, 1927.

PART III. THE CAUSE OF FREEDOM

A. CONTEMPORARY SOURCES

1. FOREST WARS

Boyd, Julian P., ed. *Indian Treaties Printed by Benjamin Franklin, 1736–1762.* Philadelphia, 1938.
Champlain, Samuel de. *Voyages of Samuel de Champlain.* Ed. W. L. Grant. New York, 1907.
Documents Relative to the Colonial History of the State of New York. Ed. E. B. O'Callaghan. Albany, 1855. (Vols. 3, 7, 9.)
Jameson, J. Franklin. *Narratives of New Netherland 1609–1664.* New York, 1909.
The Jesuit Relations and Allied Documents, Travels and Explorations of the Jesuit Missionaries in New France, 1610–1791. Ed. Reuben Gold Thwaites. Cleveland, 1907. (Vols. 22, 24, 26, 28, 35, 40.)

2. BATTLE FOR EMPIRE

Beverly, Robert. *The History and Present State of Virginia.* (1705). Chapel Hill, N.C., 1947.

Bond, Beverly W. "The Captivity of Charles Stuart." In *Mississippi Valley Historical Review*, June 1926.
Colden, Cadwallader. *The History of the Five Indian Nations of Canada, Which Are Dependent on the Province of New York, And Are a Barrier Between the English and the French in That Part of the World.* 2 vols. New York, 1904.
———. "The Letters and Papers of Cadwallader Colden," vol. 6, 1761–1764. In *Collections of the New York Historical Society*, 1922.
Crèvecoeur, Hector St. John. *Letters from An American Farmer.* New York, 1957.
Documents Relative to the Colonial History of the State of New York, op. cit., vols. 6 and 7.
Franklin, Benjamin. *The Papers of Benjamin Franklin.* Vol. 4. Ed. Leonard W. Labaree and Whitfield J. Bell, Jr. New Haven, 1916.
Jacobs, Wilbur R. *The Appalachian Indian Frontier: The Edmond Atkin Report and Plan of 1755.* Lincoln, Neb., 1967.
Johnson, Sir William. *The Papers of Sir William Johnson.* Vol. 4. Ed. Alexander C. Flick. Albany, 1925.
Morton, Thomas. *New English Canaan.* In Force, op. cit.
Pennsylvania Archives, 2nd series, vol. 7.
Pennsylvania Colonial Records, vols. 3, 6, 8. Philadelphia, 1852–1853.
Spotswood, Alexander. *The Official Letters of Alexander Spotswood.* Vol. 2, op. cit.
Washington, George. *The Writings of George Washington.* Ed. Worthington Chauncey Ford. Vols. 1 and 2. New York, 1889.
Wraxall, Peter. *An Abridgement of the Indian Affairs, Contained in Four Folio Volumes, Transacted In the Colony of New York, From the Year 1678 to the Year 1751.* Ed. Charles Howard McIlwain, Cambridge, Mass., 1915.

3. Declaring Independence

Adams, John. "What Do We Mean by the American Revolution?" In Daniel Boorstin, *An American Primer.* New York, 1968.
———. *The Works of John Adams.* Ed. C. F. Adams. Boston, 1851.
Boucher, Jonathan. *View of Causes and Consequences of American Revolution.* London, 1897.
Burke, Edmund. *Two Speeches on Conciliation with America.* London, 1886.
Franklin, Benjamin. *The Papers of Benjamin Franklin.* Vols. 4, 5 and 10. New Haven, 1916.
Jefferson, Thomas. *The Papers of Thomas Jefferson.* Ed. Julian Boyd. Princeton, 1950.
Kennedy, J. P., and McIlwaine, H. R., eds. *Journals of the House of Burgesses*, op. cit.

Morison, Samuel Eliot. *Sources and Documents Illustrating the American Revolution 1764-1788*. London, 1967.

Morris, Richard B., ed. *The American Revolution, 1763-1783: A Bicentennial Collection*. New York, 1970.

Oliver, Peter. *Peter Oliver's Origin & Progress of the American Rebellion. A Tory View*. Ed. Douglass Adair and John A. Schutz. Stanford, Calif., 1961.

Paine, Thomas. *Common Sense*. In Leonard Kriegel, ed., *Essential Works of the Founding Fathers*. New York, 1964.

Pennsylvania Colonial Records, vol. 6, op. cit.

Washington, George. *Writings*, vol. 2, op. cit.

B. SECONDARY WORKS

Abernethy, Thomas P. *Three Virginia Frontiers*. Baton Rouge, 1940.

———. *Western Lands and the American Revolution*. New York, 1937.

Adams, James Truslow. *Provincial Society, 1690-1763*. Chicago, 1970.

Alvord, Clarence. *First Explorations of the Trans-Allegheny Region by the Virginians 1650-1674*. Cleveland, 1912.

———. *The Mississippi Valley in British Politics*. 2 vols. Cleveland, 1917.

Ambler, Charles H. *George Washington and the West*. Chapel Hill, N.C., 1936.

Bailey, Kenneth P. *The Ohio Company of Virginia and the Westward Movement, 1748-1792*. Stanford, Calif., 1939.

Bailyn, Bernard. *The Ideological Origins of the American Revolution*. Cambridge, Mass., 1971.

———. *The Ordeal of Thomas Hutchinson*. Cambridge, Mass., 1974.

Becker, Carl L. *The Declaration of Independence*. New York, 1959.

Boorstin, Daniel. *The Genius of American Politics*. Chicago, 1967.

Christie, Ian R., and Labaree, Benjamin W. *Empire or Independence, 1760-1776*. New York, 1976.

Cook, Roy Bird. *Washington's Western Lands*. Strasburg, Va., 1930.

Davidson, Philip. *Propaganda and the American Revolution, 1763-1783*. Chapel Hill, N.C., 1941.

Davis, David Brion. *The Problem of Slavery in the Age of Revolution, 1770-1823*. Ithaca, N.Y., 1975.

Downes, Randolph C. *Council Fires on the Upper Ohio: A Narrative of Indian Affairs in the Upper Ohio Valley until 1795*. Pittsburgh, 1968.

Flexner, James. *George Washington*. Vol. 1. *The Forge of Experience, 1732-1775*. Boston, 1965.

Foner, Eric. *Thomas Paine and Revolutionary America,* New York, 1976.

Forbes, Allan, Jr. "Two and a Half Centuries of Conflict: The Iroquois and the Laurentian Wars." *Pennsylvania Archaeologist* 40 (December 1970).

Freeman, Douglas Southall. *George Washington: A Biography.* Vols. 1, 2, 3. New York, 1948.

Gipson, Lawrence Henry. *The British Empire Before the American Revolution.* 13 vols. New York, 1924.

———. *The Coming of the Revolution, 1763–1775.* New York, 1962.

Graymont, Barbara. *The Iroquois in the American Revolution.* Syracuse, 1972.

Hanna, C. A. *The Scotch-Irish.* New York, 1902.

Hawke, David Freeman. *A Transaction of Free Men: The Birth and Course of the Declaration of Independence.* New York, 1964.

———. *The Colonial Experience.* Indianapolis, 1966.

Heidenreich, Conrad. *Huronia: A History and Geography of the Huron Indians, 1600–1650.* Toronto, 1971.

Hofstadter, Richard. *America at 1750.* New York, 1971.

Hunt, George T. *The Wars of the Iroquois: A Study in Intertribal Trade Relations.* Madison, 1972.

Innis, Harold A. *The Fur Trade in Canada.* New Haven, 1930.

Jacobs, Wilbur R. *Wilderness Politics and Indian Gifts: The Northern Colonial Frontier, 1748–1763.* Lincoln, Neb., 1967.

Jennings, Francis. "The Indians' Revolution." In Alexander Young, ed., *The American Revolution: Explorations in the History of American Radicalism.* De Kalb, Ill., 1976.

Jordan, Winthrop. "Familial Politics—Thomas Paine and the Killing of the King, 1776," *Journal of American History* 60 (1973), pp. 294–308.

Kammen, Michael. *People of Paradox: An Inquiry Concerning the Origins of American Civilization.* New York, 1972.

Kellogg, Louise Phelps. *The French Regime in Wisconsin and the Northwest.* Madison, 1925.

Kercheval, Samuel. *History of the Valley of Virginia.* Strasburg, Va., 1925.

Knollenberg, Bernhard J. *Origins of the American Revolution, 1759–1766.* New York, 1960.

Leach, Douglas Edward. *Arms for Empire: A Military History of the British Colonies in America 1607–1763.* New York, 1973.

McIlwain, Charles Howard. "The Early Fur Trade" and "The New York Fur Trade and Its Regulation." In Peter Wraxall, *An Abridgement of the Indian Affairs.* Cambridge, Mass., 1915.

Morgan, Edmund S. *The Challenge of the American Revolution.* New York, 1976.

Morgan, Edmund S. and Helen M. *The Stamp Act Crisis.* New York, 1976.

Morison, Samuel E. *Samuel de Champlain, Father of New France.* Boston, 1972.

Morton, Richard L. *Colonial Virginia.* Vol. 2. *Westward Expansion and Prelude to Revolution, 1710–1763.* Chapel Hill, N.C., 1960.

Nammack, Georgiana C. *Fraud, Politics and the Dispossession of the Indians.* Norman, Okla., 1969.

Nettels, Curtis P. *The Roots of American Civilization.* New York, 1938.

———. *Washington and American Independence.* New York, 1951.

Parkman, Francis. *The Conspiracy of Pontiac.* New York, 1966.

———. *Montcalm and Wolfe.* New York, 1962.

Peckham, Howard. *The Colonial Wars, 1689–1762.* Chicago, 1964.

———. *Pontiac and the Indian Uprising.* Princeton, 1947.

Phillips, Paul Chrisler. *The Fur Trade.* Vol. 1. Norman, Okla., 1961.

Quarles, Benjamin. *The Negro in the American Revolution.* New York, 1973.

Robson, Eric. *The American Revolution.* London, 1955.

Rossiter, Clinton. *Seedtime of the Republic.* New York, 1953.

Semple, Ellen Churchill. *American History and Its Geographic Conditions.* Boston, 1933.

Silverman, Kenneth. *A Cultural History of the American Revolution.* New York, 1976.

Tooker, Elisabeth, *An Ethnography of the Huron Indians, 1615–1649.* Washington, D.C., 1964.

Wallace, Paul A. W. *Thirty Thousand Miles with John Heckewelder.* Pittsburgh, 1958.

Weslager, C. A. *The Delaware Indians: A History.* New Brunswick, N.J., 1972.

Wissler, Clark. *Indians of the United States.* Garden City, N.Y., 1966.

Index

Abnakis, 151
Adam and Eve, 114–115
Adams, John, 139, 192, 203–204, 219
Aix-la-Chapelle, Treaty of (1748), 164
Albany, 145, 151, 175, 176
Albany conference (1754), 169–171, 175, 204
Alexander, 58, 59–60
Algonquins, 18, 69, 94, 144, 145, 148, 150
Allen, Ethan, 216
Allerton, Isaac (Plymouth), 59
Allerton, Isaac (Virginia), 106, 115
American colonies:
  divine favor as seen in, 18, 23, 36, 38, 48, 73, 226–227
  fear of Indians in, 53, 69
  forces shaping governments of, 20, 44, 93, 97
  growth of, 157–159, 160, 162–163, 168, 175, 203–204, 206–207
  identity of, 139, 159–160, 203, 210, 227
  Indians as seen in, 18, 43–44, 45, 48, 55, 82, 85, 96, 225
  Iroquois and, 151–152, 153, 155–156, 168–171, 179–180, 225
  land acquisition by, 38, 43, 44–45, 63–64, 96, 110, 155, 225
  unity of, 46–47, 52–53, 66, 137, 171, 204, 210

American Revolution, 189–227
  British Indian policy and, 196
  colonial expansionists and, 195–197, 204, 205, 210–211, 213
  conciliation attempts before, 198–199, 207, 211–212, 215
  economic background of, 189–194
  Franklin's views on, 204–205, 206, 224
  Indians and deals of, 225
  opening hostilities in, 214–216
  parliamentary representation and, 198–199, 202
  principles of, 139, 192, 193; 198, 199, 202, 205–207, 217–220, 222–225
  slavery and, 213–214, 215–216, 222–224
  taxation issue in, 196–204, 207–209
American Whig, 206
Ames, Nathaniel, 182
Amherst, Jeffrey, 185–186, 188
Annawon, 82
Appomattocs, 94, 112
Archer, Gabrill, 86
Awashonks, 62, 79

Bacon, Elizabeth, 112, 113
Bacon, Nathaniel, 107, 111–112, 113, 114–116, 117–124, 125, 214

Bacon's Rebellion, 104–127
  in American tradition, 125
  Indian hostilities in, 111–113,
    115, 116, 118, 119–121, 123,
    125
  Jamestown and, 115, 117, 122, 123
  origins of, 102–103, 109–111, 119
Baltimore, George Calvert, Lord,
  99
Bay Colony, see Massachusetts
  Bay Colony
Baynton, Wharton and Morgan,
  196
Beauséjour, Fort, 176
Berkeley, Sir William, 91, 99, 100,
    101, 102, 103, 106, 107–110, 111,
    112, 126–127, 161
  Bacon's Rebellion and, 112, 113–
    116, 117–118, 119, 120, 121–122,
    123, 124–125
Bernard, Francis, 200
Beverwyck, 145, 151
Blainville, Pierre Céleron de, 164–
  165
Bland, Giles, 120, 121
Bland, Richard, 205
Block Island Indians, 41
Bloody Creek, 69
Borden, John, 60
Boston, 36, 70, 156, 200–201, 208–
  210, 212
Boston Evening Post, 208
Boston Port Act (1774), 209–210,
  212
Boston Tea Party, 209, 213
Boston Town Meeting, 208–209
Boucher, Jonathan, 221
Bouquet, Henry, 185–186, 187
Braddock, Edward, 172, 173, 191
Bradford, William, 19, 23, 26, 31,
    32, 52, 59
  Merrymount and, 33–34, 35
  Pequot War and, 46
  Wessagusset and, 29
Bradford William (son), 59, 79
Brookfield, 67, 68

Bunker Hill, 216
Burke, Edmund, 139, 211–212, 224
"Bushy Run," 187
Byles, Rev. Mather, 211
Byrd, William, 107, 111, 124
Byrd, William (son), 136–137, 194

Cadillac, Antoine de la Mothe, 162
Canada, 175, 189, 216, 217
Canesetego, 155
Canonchet, 57, 65, 71, 73, 74–75,
  76–77
Canonicus, 41, 44, 54
Carolinas, 109, 131, 133, 134, 136,
  154
Cartier, Jacques, 144
Carver, John, 20, 22, 23
Carver, William, 120, 121
Cayugas, 144, 147, 175
Cedar Swamp, 67
Champlain, Samuel de, 144, 145
Charles I, King, 100
Charles II, King, 101
Cherokees, 143–144
Chesapeake Bay, 86, 87, 109
Chippewas, 173, 183, 184, 185, 188
Christian Island, 149
Church, Benjamin, 79–80, 81
Coercive Acts (1774), 209–210, 212,
  213, 215
Cole's Hill, 21
Columbus, Christopher, 90, 128–
  129
Common Sense (Paine), 217–218,
  219–220
Concord, 212, 214
Connecticut, 39, 40, 51, 134
  General Court of, 39, 46
  King Philip's War and, 71, 73,
    74, 76–77, 79
  Pequot War and, 39, 46, 47–48,
    51
Connecticut Gazette, 217
Conoys, 154
Continental Congress, First, 210,
  211

Continental Congress, Second, 212, 214–215, 216, 220
Corbitant, 25–26, 58
Crèvecoeur, Hector St. John, 159
Croghan, George, 174, 183, 196
Cromwell, Oliver, 100, 101
Cushman, Deacon, 27–28

Dartmouth, 66–67
Davies, Rev. Samuel, 178–179
Declaration of Independence, 220, 222, 223–224, 225
Declaration of Rights (1774), 210
"Declaration of the People" (Bacon), 119
Declaratory Act (1766), 207
Deerfield, 69
Deer Island, 70
Delaware, 134
Delawares, 143, 155, 160, 163, 164, 167, 188
    French and Indian War and, 173–174, 175, 179
    Pontiac's Rebellion and, 183, 185, 187
Desire, 51, 130
Detroit, 162, 183, 185, 187, 188
Dinwiddie, Robert, 164, 165, 166, 177–178
Doegs, 104–105
Dragon Swamp, 121
Drake, Sir Francis, 90
Dryden, John, 221
Dunmore, John Murray, Earl of, 212, 213–214, 215–216
Duquesne, Fort, 166–167, 176, 179, 182, 185
Duquesne, Marquis of, 165
Dutch colonists, 40, 61, 134, 145–146, 147, 151
    see also Holland

East India Company, 209
Easton, John, 63
Easton Treaty, 179–182
Edward, Fort, 175–176

Egmont, John Perceval, Earl of, 136
Eliot, John, 56, 57, 70
Endicott, John, 41, 46
England, 18, 196–197, 207
    slavery and, 129–130, 134, 158, 223
    Virginia and, 100–101, 102, 125
    see also American Revolution; Parliament, English
Eries, 143, 149, 150, 152
"Ethiopian Regiment," 216

Five Nations, *see* Iroquois League
Florida, 136, 189
Franklin, Benjamin, 157–158, 171, 189, 195–196, 198, 199, 204, 207
    American revolt defended by, 204–205, 206, 224
Franklin, William, 196
Franks, David, 196
French, 56, 61, 162, 188, 189
    in French and Indian War, 167, 171–172, 175–176, 178
    initial influence of, 144–145, 148
    Iroquois League and, 150, 152–153, 154, 175, 179
    Ohio Valley and, 162, 164–165, 166, 167
    as threat to English, 151–152, 153–154, 162, 164–165, 204
    see also New France
French and Indian War, 163–188
    American Revolution and, 204–205, 213
    British successes in, 182, 204
    colonial evasion of regulations in, 190–191
    defeat of Braddock's army in, 172–173
    Delawares and, 173–174, 175, 179
    dimensions of, 167
    economic effects of, 189–190, 195–197, 204
    Indian terror in, 173–175, 185, 187

French and Indian War (*cont.*)
   initial hostilities in, 165–167
   Iroquois League and, 167–171,
      175, 179, 187
   trade rivalry and, 163–164
   Washington's role in, 165–167,
      171–173, 177–178
Frontenac, Fort, 152, 182
Frontenac, Louis de Baude, Comte
   de, 152
fur trade, 28, 39, 152, 161, 162, 164,
   196
   Dutch and, 145–146
   Iroquois wars and, 146–147, 148,
      150–151

Gage, Thomas, 202, 209–210, 212,
   216
Gardiner, Lion, 46
George, Fort, 168, 169
George III, King, 209, 211, 215, 217,
   219
Georgia, 136
Gist, Christopher, 165, 166
Goochland, 162
Gookin, Daniel, 70
Great Dismal Swamp, 213
Grenville, George, 197, 198–199

Hancock, John, 212
Hansford, Thomas, 125
Hawkins, John, 129–130
Hendrick, 168–169, 175–176
Henry, Patrick, 193, 194, 195, 199–
   200, 210, 212, 214, 215
Hispaniola, 128–129
Hobomok, 25–26, 30
Holland, 18, 97, 100, 102, 190
   see also Dutch colonists
Hooker, Thomas, 39, 43
Hopkins, Stephen, 23–24, 53
Hubbard, Rev. William, 73
Hudson, Henry, 145
Hurons, 143, 144, 145, 147, 148–149,
   150, 163

Hutchinson, Thomas, 200, 201, 206,
   207, 222

indentured servants, 19, 33, 93, 99–
   100, 102, 103, 122, 123, 158–
   159
Indians:
   American Revolution and, 225
   Christianization of, 55–57, 63, 69,
      70
   colonists as seen by, 29, 31, 42, 51,
      52, 60–61, 63–64
   conflicts among (see also
      Iroquois League), 37, 40, 52,
      113, 145
   European supporters of, 43, 53–
      54, 72, 125–126, 128–129, 187
   firearms and, 26, 35, 146–147
   precolonial, 14, 146, 148
   smallpox and, 17–18, 24, 37, 147,
      185–187
Intolerable Acts, *see* Coercive
   Acts
Iroquois, 105–106, 143, 148, 160, 225
Iroquois League, 144, 145, 150, 154–
   155, 164, 167–169, 175, 187
   Covenant Chain of, 155–156, 168,
      169, 179–182
   English and, 151–152, 153, 156,
      169, 175, 179, 187
   European conflicts and, 151–152,
      153, 154, 156, 175, 179
   French and, 143–145, 150, 152–
      153, 154, 175, 179
   French and Indian War and,
      167–171, 175, 179, 187
   in wars for fur trade, 146–150,
      151, 154
   see also Cayugas; Mohawks;
      Oneidas; Onondagas; Senecas;
      Tuscaroras

James, Fort, 87, 114
James I, King, 18, 86, 91, 97
Jamestown, 87–88, 91, 95

Bacon's Rebillion and, 115, 117, 122, 123
disease in, 87–88, 93, 97
founding of, 86–87
population of, 88
"Starving Time" of, 88
Jefferson, Peter, 195
Jefferson, Thomas, 195, 212, 220, 223, 224, 225, 226
Johnson, Sir William, 179, 187

Kames, Henry Home, Lord, 206
King George's War, 164
King Philip's War, 61–82
origins of, 61, 62, 63–64
King William's War, 153–154

"Lake of the Iroquois," 39, 145
La Salle, Robert Cavelier, Sieur de, 152, 156
Las Casas, Bartolomé de, 128–129
Lawes Divine, Morall and Martial, 89, 93
Lee, Richard Henry, 194, 195, 210, 212, 220
Lee, Thomas, 163
Leonard, Daniel, 221
Leverett, John, 79
Lexington, 214
Liberty Tree, 200
Livingston, Robert R., 206–207
Locke, John, 137
Logstown conference, 164
Lost Colony, 85
Loudoun, John Campbell, Earl of, 178
Louisburg, Fort, 179
Louisiana, 162
Ludwell, Philip, 116
Lyons, Peter, 193

Manhattan, 135, 145
Maryland, 99, 105, 106, 131, 154, 174, 186, 220
Mason, John, 47, 48

Massachusetts, American Revolution and, 191–192, 198, 200–203, 208–210, 212, 214, 216
Massachusetts Assembly, 192, 198, 212
Massachusetts Bay Colony, 36, 37, 43, 52
Charter of, 55
expansion of, 37, 38, 39
founding of, 36, 37
General Court of, 40, 43, 48
Indian opposition to, 37, 38
King Philip's War and, 65–66, 67, 69, 71, 73, 75
Pequot War and, 39, 40–41, 42, 45, 46–47, 48
power of, 36, 40, 46, 51, 54
Massachusetts Bay Company, 36, 38
Massachusetts Indians, 17–18, 29, 30, 31, 37
Massachusetts Spy, 209
Massasoit, 43–44, 57, 58, 60–61
as Pilgrims' ally, 22–23, 24–25, 26, 27, 57, 60–61
Mather, Cotton, 43, 55
Mather, Richard, 56
Mathews, Thomas, 104
Matoonas, 67, 79
Mattapoisett, 25, 64
Mattaponis, 94
Mayflower, 19, 27
Medfield, 74
Merrymount, 31–32, 33–35
Metacomet, *see* Philip, King
Miamis, 152, 154, 163–164, 165, 185
Miantonomo, 41, 44, 45, 46, 51, 52, 53–54
Middleborough, 66
Miles, Rev. John, 64
Mingos, 163, 164, 173, 174, 175, 185
Mississippi Company, 195
Mohawks, 50, 73, 78, 144, 145, 147, 148–149, 168–169, 175
Mohegans, 47, 50, 65, 68, 71
Mohicans, 39, 145

Molasses Act (1733), 197–198
Montreal, 144, 182
Morton, Thomas, 17, 31, 32, 33, 34–35, 170
"Mother of Nations," 144
Mount Hope, 24, 60, 62, 65

Nanticokes, 154
Narragansetts, 24, 25, 37, 40, 52, 57, 61
   King Philip's War and, 65–66, 70–71, 72–75, 76, 77, 79
   Pequot War and, 41, 42, 45–46, 47, 50
   Roger Williams and, 42–43, 44
Nashaways, 69, 77, 79
Natick, 57, 62, 65, 70
Nausets, 20, 24
Navigation Act (1660), 101–102, 190
Necessity, Fort, 167, 171–172
Nemascheuks, 24, 26
New Amsterdam, 145, 146
New England, 75–76, 82, 86, 130–131, 176, 190
   first Europeans in, 17, 18, 21
   population of, 36, 37, 52
   slavery and, 130–131, 134
New English Canaan, The (Morton), 34, 170
New France, 151, 152, 153, 154, 165, 175, 182, 189
New Haven, 51
New Jersey, 134, 220
New Netherland, *see* Dutch colonists
New Orleans, 164, 189
New York, 134, 135, 151, 154, 157, 168–169, 172, 195, 220
Niagara, 152, 153, 176, 182
Nipmucs, 37, 67, 68, 69, 74, 79
Nonatums, 56, 57
North, Frederick, Lord, 212

Occaneechees, 112–113
Ohio Company of Virigina, 163, 164, 165, 166, 195, 205

Ohio River, 160, 163
Ohio Valley, 156, 160–161, 163, 176, 182–183, 185, 189, 205
   American revolt and, 195–196, 210–211, 213
   French and Indian War and, 175, 176, 182
   strategic importance of, 161, 162, 163, 165, 175
Old Briton, 164, 165
Oldham, John, 39, 40–41
"Olive Branch Petition," 215, 217
Oliver, Andrew, 200
Oliver, Peter, 221
Oneco, 68, 77
Oneidas, 144, 147
Onondaga Council, 144, 175
Onondagas, 144, 147
Opechancanough, 95, 96, 98–99
Oswego, Fort, 178
Otis, James, 192
Ottawas, 147, 149, 150, 151, 152, 165, 172–173, 183, 184, 185, 188

Paine, Thomas, 211, 217–218, 219–220, 223, 227
Pamunkeys, 94, 121, 122–123
Paris, Treaty of (1763), 195
Parliament, English, 100, 137, 179, 190, 207
   American resentment of, 192, 198, 208, 210, 211, 215, 218–219
   American taxation by, 196–198, 204, 207–208, 209
"Parsons' Cause," 193
Paspaheghs, 94
Passonagessit, 32–33
Patuxet, 21
Peace of Utrecht (1713), 154, 156, 157
Pecksuot, 30
Penn, William, 154
Penns Creek massacre, 173–174
Pennsylvania, 134, 143, 154, 155, 159, 160, 186, 187, 194, 220
   French and Indian War and, 172, 174, 176, 191

Pequots, 37, 39, 40, 41–42, 45, 46,
    47–50, 51, 71, 145
Pequot War, 41–42, 45, 46–50
    origins of, 38–40, 41
Percy, George, 87, 94
Peskeompscut, 77–78
Pessacus, 74
Petonowowett, 65
Petuns, 147, 149–150
Philip, King, 57, 58, 60–61, 62–64
    war of, 65, 66, 67–68, 69, 73–74,
    79–80, 81
Pickawillany, 164, 165
Pierce, Michael, 74
Pilgrims, 19, 31, 202
    divine favor and, 18, 23
    financial backing of, 19, 27, 28
    indentured servants of, 19, 34
    Indian accord with, 21–23, 24–25
    Indian opposition to, 25–26, 29–30
    internal conflicts of, 20, 27–28
    Massasoit as ally of, 22–23, 24–25,
    26, 27, 57, 60–61
    military stance of, 21, 22, 23, 31
Pitt, Fort, 185, 187
Plymouth, 21, 22, 31, 32, 36, 57–58
    expansion of, 39, 57–58
    fear of Indians in, 29, 35, 58
    founding of, 18, 19, 21
    King Philip and, 60–61, 62, 63–
    64
    King Philip's War and, 64, 66, 67,
    71, 74–75, 82
    Massachusetts Bay Colony and,
    36, 46–47
    Merrymount and, 33, 34–35
    Pequot war and, 46–47
    power of, 26, 27, 29, 30, 31, 34, 36
    Wessagusset and, 28, 29–30, 31
Pocahontas, 94–95
Pocasset, 65
Pocassets, 25, 63, 67, 68, 70, 80
Pocumtooks, 69
Pokanoket, 24, 25, 60, 81
Pomham, 71, 74
Pontiac, 184–185, 187, 188
Pontiac's Rebellion, 182–188

Potawatomis, 150, 152, 183, 184,
    185, 188
Powhatan, 87, 94, 95
Powhatans, 94, 95, 98–99
Proclamation of 1763, 194, 196
Prohibitory Act, 217
Providence, 44, 45, 75, 82
Provincial Congress, 212
Puritans, 34, 211
    in Europe, 18, 19, 27, 31
    Indians as seen by, 18, 55–56
    Virginia and, 88, 100, 101, 108

Quaiapen ("Old Queen"), 72, 79
Quakers, 135, 154, 172, 176, 187
Quebec, 144, 182, 204, 210, 217
Quebec Act (1774), 210–211
Queen Anne's War, 154
Quinnapin, 74, 82

Raleigh, Sir Walter, 90
Rappahannocks, 86
Rehoboth, 66
Revolution of 1688, 137
Rhode Island, 44, 45, 52, 63, 66
Roanoke Island, 85, 90
Robinson, John, 18, 31
Rolfe, John, 91, 93, 94–95
rum, 130–131, 170, 171, 184, 188
Rutledge, Edward, 216

Sachem Head, 50
Sagamore John, 79
Sakonnets, 63, 79
Samoset, 21–22
San Salvador, 90
Sassacus, 41, 50, 145
Sassamon, John, 60, 62
Sauks, 150, 185
Saybrook, 46, 47
Senecas, 106, 144, 147, 149, 153, 175,
    183, 185
Shawnees, 143, 155, 160, 163, 164,
    173, 174, 175, 179, 183, 185,
    187, 188
Shingas, 173, 174
Shirley, William, 176–177

Sidney, Algernon, 137
slavery, 128–139
  American Revolution and, 213–
    214, 215–216, 222–224
  Indians and, 23, 50–51, 67, 82, 95,
    116, 132–133
  liberation from, 123, 135, 215–
    216
  opposition to, 135–136
  paradox of, 222–224
  as threat to colonies, 113–135,
    136–137, 176–177
  trade in, 51, 128, 129–131, 134,
    158, 223
smallpox, 17–18, 23, 37–38, 147
  early settlements and, 18, 21, 29,
    37–38
  English view of, 18, 38
  Indian view of, 25
  as weapon, 185–186
Smith, John, 88–89, 105
Sons of Liberty, 201–202, 213
Spain, 85, 90, 136, 189
  slavery and, 23, 129
Spotswood, Alexander, 138, 161, 162
Squakheags, 69
Squando, 69–70
Squanto, 23–24, 25, 26
Stamp Act (1765), 198, 199–203,
  204
  repeal of, 207
Stamp Act Congress, 202, 208
Standish, Miles, 22, 26, 29–30, 31,
  35, 59
"Starving Time," 88, 94
Stiles, Ezra, 203
Stone, John, 39–40
Sudbury, 77
Susquehannocks, 105–108, 112, 115,
  121, 166
Swansea, 62, 64–65, 66

Talcott, John, 79
Tarrantines, 37, 69, 77
Taunton, 66, 80
Taunton Treaty, 61–62, 68

Tea Act (1773), 209
Teft, Joshua, 72
Thanksgiving, 26–27
Ticonderoga, Fort, 179, 182, 216
tobacco, 22, 90–91, 192–193
  taxes on, 91, 96, 97, 102
  trade restrictions on, 100, 101
Townshend Acts (1767), 207, 208,
  209
Trois Rivières, 144
Turner, Frederick Jackson, 13
Tuscaroras, 143–144, 154, 174
Tutelos, 154
"Twopenny Act," 193

Uncas, 47, 51, 53, 145
Underhill, John, 47, 48
United Colonies, 171, 176, 215, 220
United Colonies of New England,
  52–53, 56, 71–72
Unkompowin, 60, 79

Venango, Fort, 185
Virginia, 33, 85, 86, 89, 90, 100, 103,
  131, 162, 186
  aspirations in, 88–89, 93, 101, 137,
    161
  Bacon's Rebellion in, 112, 113–
    116, 117–125, 126
  conflict with England in, 192–
    194, 199, 212–214, 215–216
  early hardships in, 87–90, 97, 100
  early Indian conflicts with, 86,
    94, 95–96, 98–99
  Europe and, 85, 90, 100, 101, 102,
    137
  expansion of, 93, 96, 98, 99, 110,
    161, 162–163
  freedmen in, 102, 103, 110–111,
    112, 114, 122, 137
  French and Indian War and, 167,
    172–174, 177–178
  government of, 93, 97, 98, 100,
    101, 103, 109, 137–138
  indentured servants in, 93, 97,
    99–100, 102, 122, 123

Indians as seen in, 96, 105, 108,
    110
internal tensions in, 102–103,
    110–111, 122
Ohio Company of, 163, 164, 165,
    166, 195, 205
Ohio Valley and, 161, 162–163,
    166, 186
population of, 91–93, 97, 100, 109
slavery in, 128, 131–134, 136–137,
    138–139
strategic value of, 85, 90
Susquehannocks and, 105–108,
    115, 121
tobacco's importance in, 91, 97,
    102, 110, 192–193
see also Jamestown
Virginia Assembly, 97, 100, 101,
    108, 109, 125, 126, 137, 162, 166,
    172, 193, 199, 210, 212, 215
Bacon's Rebellion and, 114, 115–
    116, 117, 118
slavery regulated by, 131, 132–134,
    138
Virginia Company, 19, 89, 93, 96–
    97

Waban, 56, 57, 70, 79
Wampanoags, 18, 21, 22, 42, 57, 61

King Philip's War and, 64–65, 66,
    68, 74, 77, 80, 82
Roger Williams and, 43–44, 82
Washington, Augustine, 165
Washington, George, 165, 166, 194,
    195, 196, 226
in American Revolution, 213,
    214–217, 224–225
in French and Indian War, 165–
    167, 171–173, 177–178
Washington, John, 106, 115, 166
Washington, Lawrence, 165
Weetamoo, 58, 62
King Philip's War and, 65, 66, 68,
    70, 73, 74, 80–81
Wessagusset, 28–30, 31
Weston, Thomas, 19, 27, 28
Williams, Roger, 43, 50–51, 55, 61,
    82
King Philip's War and, 65–66, 75
Pequot War and, 42–43, 45–46, 50
Winslow, Edward, 22, 23–24, 27,
    30, 31, 39, 44, 59
Winslow, Josiah, 59, 71–72, 73
Winthrop, John, 36, 38, 41, 46–47,
    53, 55, 88
writs of assistance, 191–192
Wyandots, 183, 184, 185, 188

About the Author

David Horowitz graduated from Columbia University and the University of California at Berkeley. A former editor of *Ramparts* Magazine, he is the author of *Student, The Free World Colossus, Empire and Revolution* and *The Fate of Midas* and co-author of *The Rockefellers: An American Dynasty*. He is married and has four children.

CON-fidence

TODD STRASSER

Holiday House / New York

Library of Congress Cataloging-in-Publication Data

Strasser, Todd
Con-fidence / Todd Strasser.—1st ed.
p. cm.
Summary: Lauren would love to be part of the popular crowd at school,
and when an attractive new girl seems to befriend her and offers a chance
at popularity, Lauren does not recognize how she is being manipulated.
ISBN 0-8234-1394-2 (hardcover)
[1. Self-confidence—Fiction. 2. Friendship—Fiction.
3. Schools—Fiction.] I. Title.

PZ7.S899 Cr 2002
[Fic]—dc21

2001039236

ISBN-13: 978-0-8234-1394-2 (hardcover)
ISBN-13: 978-0-8234-2061-2 (paperback)

ISBN-10: 0-8234-1394-2 (hardcover)
ISBN-10: 0-8234-2061-2 (paperback)

To Regina, John, Kate, and the crew at Holiday House,
thanks for letting me do this.

chapter
one

Lunchtime in the cafeteria. In your hands is the sandwich your mom packed. Two pieces of yellow American cheese between two plain white slices of Wonder Bread. You gaze off across the noisy room, ripe with the scent of sour milk and the sickly sweet odor of rotting apple cores. Kids squeeze together at tables and devour their lunches. Pressed so closely their elbows are pinned to their sides, sitting like rows of squirrels, chattering and laughing, happy to be with their friends.

You are not happy, nor are you sitting where you want to be.

The center of the cafeteria is Krista Rice's realm. Her table is jammed so tightly with girls that, if one of them sneezed, the wanna-bes at the ends would fall off their seats and tumble to the floor. Queen Krista sits in the middle of these girls. She is small and dainty with straight dark brown hair, big brown eyes, a cute upturned nose, and a light sprinkle of freckles. She is certainly one of the prettiest girls in your grade, but there is something extra about her that the other pretty girls don't have. It's a sheen that radiates from her hair, eyes, and lips, from her clothes. It is the glow of confidence. The special knowledge that every other girl in the grade secretly wishes she were her. Krista is the ultimate "Don't-You-Wish-You-Were-Me" girl.

"Stop it, Lauren." Your best friend, Tara Snead, places her plump elbows on the lunch table and leans forward.

A warm flush crosses your face. "What?"

"Don't pretend you don't know." Tara points a black-nailed finger toward the middle of the cafeteria. "You were staring at Krista again."

You look down and take a bite of the cheese sandwich your mom packed. The girls at the Don't-You-Wish-You-Were-Me table buy school lunches. They wouldn't be caught dead bringing a wrinkled brown paper bag from home. Hunger is a powerful sensation, especially here on the outskirts of the cafeteria. Out here at an almost empty table near the door with the red exit sign above it. Out here where a cold draft wafts in from the hall and there is elbowroom to spare. You could stretch out along the seats and take a nap if you wanted. Here in the realm of the socially inferior.

You chew slowly on your plain-tasting sandwich the way your mind chews slowly over every thought. Oddly enough, Krista Rice was once your best friend. Back in grade school. Back before she moved to a nicer neighbor-hood and became snotty and backstabbing and boy crazy. Back before she turned on you.

And you turned to Tara, a chubby raven-haired girl with a pretty face and black fingernails. All soft corners except her sharp tongue. She writes poems about death, and brings three teriyaki beef jerkies from home every day. She always finishes the first two quickly, then slowly savors the third, as if painfully aware that it will be her last nourishment until the school day ends.

"Who's the new girl?" she asks.

You swivel around and look across the cafeteria. A girl you've never seen before has just come out of the lunch line carrying a tray. She is tall and pretty, with a petite nose and straight blond hair that hangs down to the tops of her shoulders. Wispy bangs cover her fore-head and fall into her eyes. She is wearing jeans and a light blue turtleneck sweater. Holding the tray, she looks around and her half-hidden eyes seem to fix on the DYWYWM table where Queen Krista holds court.

Strangely, the DYWYWM table has gone quiet. The A-list girls pause from their gab and gossip to study this new arrival. The rest of the kids in the cafeteria carry on with their normal everyday jabber, but you hardly notice. Instead, you are acutely aware of the silent spot in the center of the otherwise noisy universe.

The new girl turns to an empty table near the

windows and sits by herself. The girls at the DYWYWM table start to chatter once more. You gaze a moment longer at the new girl. Through the windows the red, yellow, and orange leaves drop from tree branches and float lazily to the ground. It is mid October—a strange time of year for someone to start school.

"She looks like a sheepdog with that hair in her eyes," Tara observes. "How can she see?"

"Same way a sheepdog does," you answer.

Tara chews sullenly on her last jerky. "I think we're going to hate her."

"Why?"

"Oh, *come on,* Lauren." Tara has no patience when you pretend to act dumb. "You *know* why. Just look at her. She's pretty and has nice clothes. Unless she's a total spaz, she'll be sitting with Krista by Christmas."

"Looks aren't everything," you reply, and take another bite of your utterly uninteresting sandwich.

Tara pinches her nostrils with her fingertips and speaks in a nasal voice: "Yes, Mrs. Walsh."

Your name is Lauren Walsh, and *Mrs. Walsh* is your mom. And Tara is right. What you just said is exactly what your mother would say.

And she would be severely wrong.

Because here, at Woodville Middle School, with very few exceptions, looks mean just about everything.

two

"You happen to be very pretty, Lauren." Mom stands behind you at the little white makeup table in your room. You sit, looking at yourself in the small mirror outlined with smoky white bulbs. Is she telling the truth? She's your mother. She'd probably say you were pretty even if you had a wart the size of a golf ball in the middle of your forehead. She lifts your hair, giving it some bounce and body. "You just have to do a little more with your hair."

"I'm plain."

"You're not plain. You're fair skinned and pale. Why don't you try a little makeup?"

Only the DYWYWM girls wear makeup. If you tried that, someone at school would be sure to notice. They'd snigger and say you were trying to be an A-list girl. It's safer not to try.

The new girl's name is Celeste Van Warner. She has what teachers call "a lively personality and a winning smile." She wears eye shadow and lip gloss and can always think of something clever to say. By the first week of November,

Tara's prediction has come true. Celeste has a regular seat at the DYWYWM table.

But Celeste isn't entirely like Krista and her snotty friends. Where Krista will never begin a conversation with anyone who isn't "A-list," Celeste seems nice to everyone. You and she have gym and math together, and you have seen her chat and laugh with girls who Krista Rice wouldn't be caught dead speaking to.

Lunch in the land of the socially inferior. Today your mother has packed sliced turkey on whole wheat. Through the windows, the few leaves that remain on the trees have turned brown and wrinkled. Most have fallen to the ground.

"Want to go to the mall after school and Christmas shop?" Tara asks. "Lauren? Are you staring again? Yoo-hoo, Earth to Lauren."

You look back at her. "The weirdest thing just happened."

"Krista choked to death on a meatball?" Tara guesses hopefully.

"You wish."

"No, Lauren. *You* wish."

"That girl, Celeste, just smiled at me."

Tara makes her eyes wide with pretend disbelief. *"No!"*

"I'm serious."

"Seriously psycho."

"Why do you always have to be sarcastic?"

Tara sticks out her tongue at you. "It's my defense mechanism. So she smiled at you. What's the big deal?"

"It was a *nice* smile. I mean, she's sitting with Krista, but she still acts nice."

"So?"

You can't explain it. Tara's too sarcastic and defensive. It's a shame because she really does have a pretty face, but she's heavy, and sometimes the other girls say mean things about her behind her back. And not *so* far behind her back that she is completely unaware. Tara knows what they say. She's decided that she will never be popular, and now she doesn't even try. In fact, she goes out of her way to make them think she doesn't care.

But you were once Krista Rice's best friend.

And why you aren't sitting at the DYWYWM table right now is the greatest mystery of your life.

three

"You have to stand up and defend yourself when they pick on you."

"I know, Mom, but it's hard."

"What does Tara do when they pick on her?"

"They don't dare. She's too quick. They know if they cut her down, she'll come right back with something even nastier. But I'm not like that. I can never think of what to say."

In math you settle down at your desk and open your book. When you look up, Stephanie Eisley is standing over you.

Stephanie is a skinny girl with long streaked blond hair. Her eyes are too little and her mouth is too big. She sits with the wanna-bes at the end of the DYWYWM table and would be the first to fall off if someone sneezed. You've heard that the only reason she gets to sit at the table at all is that her father owns Carmen's, the nicest restaurant in town. Twice a year he lets her have a pizza party there with a deejay, and all the pizza and soda anyone could ever want.

Now, looming over you, Stephanie has a cruel smirk on her oversize lips. The room has gone quiet. You don't have to look around to know that everyone is watching.

"Hey, Lauren," she says, "I hear your mom's so fat there's a sign on her back that says, 'To be continued.'"

Your mom isn't fat. But it doesn't matter. Around the room, kids chuckle. Stephanie waits to see if you'll reply. You've heard a million comebacks, but suddenly your mind is as blank as the chalkboard.

"Your mom's so dumb she took half an hour to cook minute rice." Stephanie hits you with another one.

You freeze in panicked terror, afraid that whatever you say will come out wrong and the other kids will laugh even more. But out of the corner of your eye you see Celeste, two rows over. Her eyes are hidden behind those bangs; her lips are pressed into a hard, flat line. She is not smiling.

"Your mom's so ugly they tried to put a paper bag on her *shadow!*" goes Stephanie.

Tears start to well up in your eyes. *Oh, no!* You blink hard to force them back.

Mr. Youngstrom, your math teacher, comes in. "Seats, everyone."

Stephanie returns to her desk. With brimming eyes,

you stare straight ahead, not daring to move or blink for fear that giant tears will spill down your cheeks.

Mr. Youngstrom starts to write on the board. You wait as long as you can, and then dab the tears away with the cuff of your shirt. At the same time you carefully glance around. They're all watching Mr. Youngstrom. *Except* Celeste, who is watching *you*. Feeling embarrassed, you quickly yank your sleeve away from your face. But Celeste does not wrinkle her nose or sneer. Instead she purses her lips in a sympathetic way, and nods as if she understands.

You can't wait for school to end. Still feeling the raw burn of Stephanie's cut downs, you want to get away as fast as you possibly can. At the end of the day, you pause at your locker to grab your jacket.

"Hi," a voice says behind you. You turn. It's Celeste.

"Oh, hi." You nervously brush a few strands of hair off your face. Celeste parts her blond bangs with her fingers as if to get a better look. Her eyes are grayish green.

"Hair." She rolls those eyes as if it's a big pain.

"Yeah." You roll yours.

You both giggle.

"Don't let Stephanie get to you," Celeste says. "She's a jerk. Severely insecure."

"I guess." Feel the color rise on your cheeks. You don't know Celeste. This could be a trap. You must be careful about what you say, lest Celeste goes running back to Stephanie to tell her.

But Celeste changes the subject. "You really understand that stuff about equivalent fractions?"

"Well . . . yeah."

"Wish I did. I don't know whether it's me or Mr. Youngstrom. But I'm just not getting it."

The pace in the hall quickens as kids hurry to their buses. "I could help you."

"Really?" Celeste asks.

"Sure." This is like one of those medieval torture racks that stretch people in two directions at once. You have to get to your bus, but how can you leave this A-lister who's acting so friendly?

"Maybe you should give me your number," you suggest. "I could call you later."

"I wish." Celeste sighs. "Our phone's been all messed up ever since we moved. The phone company keeps coming back to fix it, but they never get it right. It's such a pain."

Two kids run past you, their backpacks bouncing behind their shoulders. "I really have to go."

"Catch your bus?" Celeste realizes. "Why didn't you tell me? Come on, girl."

You both start to run. Ahead through the doors you see the last kids climbing onto the buses.

"You can come to my house now if you want," you offer at a gallop.

"Cool."

You're out the doors and running for the bus, both of you laughing for no reason. It all happens so quickly. Celeste Van Warner is coming to your house!

four

You and Celeste sit together on the creaky, squeaky bus. You're feeling queasy, but it's not motion sickness. The brief thrill of her coming to your house has turned to dread. This could still be some kind of trick, although with every passing second it seems less likely. Celeste's friendliness feels genuine. But what will she think when she sees the little one-story houses in your neighborhood? Most have yards no bigger than throw rugs. Even the trees, with their skinny, dark branches, seem small. You've ridden your bike through Hillside, the neighborhood where Krista and some of the other DYWYWM girls live in large two-story houses, some with three-car garages and lawns big enough to play touch football.

"You mustn't think that way," you imagine your mother saying. *"Having more money doesn't make anyone better than you."* Judy Knight and Rob Carlucci both live near you in little houses like yours, and they're A-listers. And Sean Evans, whose father owns a company that builds malls, is mean and conceited and despised. But

the girls whose parents have more money wear nicer clothes and throw nicer parties. Some of their parents go away together for summer vacations. Having more money doesn't automatically put anyone on the A-list, but it doesn't hurt, either.

You and Celeste get off at your stop. In your neighborhood the sidewalk only runs along one side of the street. As if it doesn't deserve a second sidewalk like the nicer neighborhoods have.

Your house is dark reddish brick with gray shingles and black shutters. Walking with Celeste you see things you wouldn't normally notice. The gutters overflow with dull brown leaves and bare twigs. A rolled-up dark gray, soggy, week-old newspaper lies on the walk.

"I know it's not much." You let Celeste in your house. "But it's okay for my mom and me."

"Don't be dumb." Once inside, Celeste looks around. "It's great. And look at these." She picks up one of the blue bottles that line the windowsills. "They're cool."

"Mom collects them," you tell her. "Mostly at yard sales. Hungry?"

"Starved."

She isn't kidding. In the kitchen you make her a box of macaroni and cheese, then a bowl of chunky chicken soup. When she's still hungry, you share some chocolate chip cookies.

"That was great." Celeste licks cookie crumbs off her fingertips.

"Want anything else?" You're joking, of course.

"What have you got?" She's serious.

"Uh, ice cream?"

"Sure."

You look in the freezer. "Vanilla okay?"

"With hot fudge sauce?"

"How's chocolate syrup?"

"Good enough."

You prepare two bowls, but give more of the ice cream to Celeste. She floods her bowl with chocolate syrup, then starts to wolf down the sundae in heaping spoonfuls.

"How do you stay thin?"

"My mom says I have a superfast metabolism," she answers. "I just burn up calories."

The wall phone rings. You jump up and answer. "Hello?"

"Ready?" It's Tara.

The phone cord is extra long. You stretch it out of the kitchen and into the living room where you hope Celeste won't hear. "For what?"

"We're going to the mall, remember? Christmas shopping."

"Oh, uh, I can't." You shoot a hasty glance back

through the kitchen doorway. Celeste's still spooning up vanilla ice cream with chocolate sauce.

"How come?" Tara asks.

You lower your voice to a whisper. "Know Celeste Van Warner?"

"Never heard of her," Tara deadpans.

"She's here."

"So?"

"She needs help with math."

"And you can't go to the mall," Tara says. "How sad. Poor helpless Celeste."

"Be serious. Can't we go tomorrow?"

"But what about poor helpless Celeste? Tomorrow she might need help with Spanish. Or archery. Or tying her shoes." Tara hangs up.

You start to dial Tara back but then glance into the kitchen. A spoon in an empty bowl sits on the table. Where's Celeste? You hang up the phone, go looking, and find her in your room sorting through the clothes in your closet. You catch your breath and feel humiliated. The room is a wreck—clothes all over the floor and bed. Magazines, books, CDs, and candy wrappers scattered everywhere. What a dump!

Meanwhile, from the closet Celeste pulls out a tight, low-cut black top with a gold star on the front.

"Have I seen you wear this?" she asks.

"No way." A nervous laugh bursts from your lungs. "My crazy aunt Sarah gave it to me for my birthday. She lives in Los Angeles. You know. La-la land."

Celeste holds it up to herself in the mirror. "I'd wear it."

You get the funniest feeling. Almost as if she's asking for it. "Borrow it if you like."

"Could I?" Celeste gasps.

"Sure. I mean, that's better than if it just hangs there."

"That's sooo nice," Celeste says. "Maybe you'll come over to my house and find something you'd like."

You feel your pulse jump. This is like candy to your ears. Girlfriends sharing clothes. Like they do in books and on TV shows. The A-list girls must spend hours trying on one another's things. They all have such nice clothes. You don't have much. Some jeans, a few skirts, and a bunch of tops. But no one to share them with. You're a size six and Tara is a size twelve. About the only things you can share are sweatshirts.

Celeste reaches into your closet again, this time pulling out your turquoise skating outfit with the glitter finish and flared skirt. She gives it an uncertain look.

"It's a skating outfit," you explain.

"Oh." She glances around the room, now taking in the skating posters, the little silver trophies you won when you were younger, and your first pair of skates, scuffed white, which hang from a nail on your wall.

"Been skating since I was three," you tell her. "One summer I even went to skating camp at Lake Placid."

Celeste brings a finger to her lips and chews on a fingernail. For the first time you notice that her nails are all bitten down to the nubs.

"Do you skate?" you ask.

"Not really."

Disappointment creeps under your skin. There's a new skating rink in town and you're dying to go. But Tara doesn't skate and you don't want to go alone.

Celeste looks down and, with her shoe, sorts through the magazines and clothes on your floor. She bends down and picks up a CD. "Oh, wow, I love her. Isn't she great?"

"My fav," you reply, aware that if Tara ever heard you say "fav" instead of "favorite" she'd probably drive a stake through your heart.

"Mine, too." Celeste loads the disc into your boom box. The room fills with music, and she spins on her toes and dances over to the big green ceramic piggy bank on your dresser. It's shaped like a barrel and is more than a foot tall.

She slides her arms around it and lifts slightly, almost as if she wants to dance with it. The change inside clatters.

"Careful!" you yelp, picturing the barrel slipping through her arms and smashing apart on the floor.

Leaving the piggy bank, she waltzes over to the little makeup table. She seems to need to touch everything—every piece of clothing, every CD, every eyeliner and compact. "We're going to have so much fun together," she sings to you as she twists the top off a lip gloss.

You sit on your bed and watch as if in a dream, not quite believing that this A-lister likes your clothes and taste in music and wants to be your friend. "We are?" you answer in dazed uncertainty.

Celeste stops abruptly and turns to you. The music is still playing. She crosses her arms and beneath her bangs her eyebrows dip into seriousness. The abruptness of the change catches you by surprise.

"What?" you stammer warily as if worried you just said the wrong thing and she will now vanish from your life as quickly as she appeared.

"Have I ever seen you wear makeup?" she asks.

"Huh? Uh, no."

"Why not?"

A warm shiver crawls over your skin. Dare you speak the truth? That you're dying to wear makeup but terrified someone like Krista or Stephanie will make fun of you?

"I never have time in the morning."

"Well, come on." She pats the chair at the makeup table. "Let's do it now."

"What about equivalent fractions?"

Celeste makes a face. "Oh, please." She waves the idea away. "We'll do that later."

chapter
five

"We'll go to California and find sugar daddies." Celeste kneels beside you painting fantasies in your mind and blue eye shadow on your eyelids.

"Why?"

"They'll give us money."

"Why?"

"Because they're yucky, old, wrinkly rich guys who give pretty girls like us money to hang around and make them feel good."

"We won't have to kiss them, will we?"

"Maybe on the cheek."

"Gross!"

"Oh, come on, you kiss your grandfather on his cheek, don't you?"

"I guess."

"Hold still." She adds eyeliner. "And then, when we have enough money, we'll open a boutique and get all our clothes wholesale."

"How do you know about all this stuff?"

"My mom."

"Your . . . mom?"

"Yeah. She told me she once had a sugar daddy when she was younger. But that was a long time ago. She's really different now."

"Oh."

"Hold it." She applies mascara to your lashes. No one except your mom has ever put makeup on you before. No one except your mom has ever fussed over you and made you feel so special. You imagine Celeste and you becoming the world's tightest, bestest friends. You feel like you're in a magic, Cinderella-type dream. Only here, Celeste is the prince who's discovered you.

"I'd kill for your cheekbones," she says, the mascara stick wedged between her lips, as she brushes blush on your cheeks, then gets up and stands behind you. "So what do you think?"

You stare at yourself. "I look like I'm twenty-five!" This is only a slight exaggeration.

Behind you, Celeste winks. "That's the whole idea, right?"

You can't get used to the two people in the mirror. You, looking like someone completely new, and Celeste, who is completely new. The two of you framed like a painting. A portrait of friends forever? Is this the beginning of a new life? Truth be told, that is your greatest single wish.

"I hate to say it." Celeste glances at her Swatch. "We better do our homework."

Now? Disappointment weighs down your shoulders. The fun can't end now. The music, the makeup, the hair and girl talk. It's too enjoyable to stop. You can't remember having a friend who made you feel this good. Not since Krista Rice lived across the street, back when you both were little. Back before she moved and left you behind in every way. . . .

You and Celeste sit on the floor with open notebooks. She wasn't kidding about not getting the math. You wind up doing almost all the homework yourself. Celeste plays more CDs and thumbs through magazines. Finally she looks up from the *Teen People* she's been reading. "Oh, my gosh! It's dark!"

"So?"

"I'll have to call a cab. What's the address here?"

After you tell her, she picks up her books and the low-cut black top with the gold star, and heads for the kitchen. You follow and wait while she uses the phone.

"That's lucky. There's a cab in the neighborhood." She hangs up and glances at the kitchen clock. "Won't your mom be home soon?"

"No. She works late."

"What does she do?"

You hate when people ask. "She's a waitress . . . at Carmen's. I know it doesn't sound like much, but you'd be amazed at how much she makes with tips and every-thing."

"Isn't that the place Stephanie Eisley's father owns?" Celeste asks.

You nod, wincing inside at the sound of Stephanie's name.

Celeste narrows her eyes. "So *that's* why you didn't fight back today when Stephanie cut you down. How could you? Your mother works for her father."

It's nice of her to say that, but deep down you know that even if your mom didn't work at Carmen's, you wouldn't have fought back.

You and Celeste walk through the living room. "What's with this school anyway?" she asks by the front door.

"What do you mean?"

"Some of the girls are so cruel."

"Aren't they?" You're incredibly glad that she said that. Only, aren't some of the cruelest girls also Celeste's friends? "Maybe it's just when they're with their crowd and they feel like they have to show off."

"You don't have to make excuses for them," Celeste says. "Maybe they're just bad people." A car honks out-side. It's the cab. Celeste sticks her hand in her bag and searches around. "Oh, no, where's my money?"

The cab beeps again. Celeste bites her lip and gives you a "What am I going to do?" look.

"I've got money." You race back to your room and take five dollars out of your wallet. When you return, the front door is wide open and cold air is blowing in. Celeste is down at the curb getting into the cab. You run down the front walk and hand her the money through the window.

She smiles up at you. "Well, I'm just glad I met one of the *good* people. Thanks for everything, Lauren."

"No prob, Celeste. Thank *you.*"

The cab goes down the street, around the corner, and disappears into the dark. Back inside the house, your room feels empty. As if Celeste sucked the life out of it when she left. To bring back the memory of the fun you just had, you decide to put on that first CD she played. The one you both like so much. You look for a moment and can't find it. Must be buried somewhere beneath the clothes and junk.

You put on a different CD. The throbbing music helps fill the emptiness. Celeste is unlike anyone you've ever been friends with before. You can't say that you understand her completely, but you are very, very glad she came over today. You slip into the chair in front of the mirror. Once again that new, unfamiliar girl with makeup looks back at you. She is definitely prettier than you. You would like to be that girl, and you don't understand this sudden urge to run into the bathroom and scrub off every bit of makeup. Who are you afraid will see? There's no one here except you. Can't you be a little bit brave? Yes. You decide to be that pretty girl, just for tonight, and not wash off the makeup until you go to bed.

chapter
SIX

"You need more confidence in yourself, hon."

"I know, Mom."

"You're smart and attractive and likeable. There's no reason why you should feel this way."

"I know. It's just . . . I don't know how you get confidence. I mean, it's not like going to a gym and getting more muscles, or just waiting until I grow more hair."

"You get it by believing in yourself."

You are waiting at Tara's locker the next morning to make sure she is still your friend, when you spot Krista Rice coming down the hall with Stephanie Eisley and Judy Knight. While Krista is the ultimate DYWYWM girl, and Stephanie is the ultimate DYWYWM wanna-be, Judy is altogether different. She wears her curly black hair short and dresses plainly without a touch of makeup. The smartest person in the grade, she floats freely above the cliques, admired by, and friendly to, almost everyone.

Always invited to parties, but more likely to spend Saturday night doing homework than hanging out.

And while Krista and Stephanie must carry the latest handbags, Judy lugs a backpack heavy with books. She lives a block away from you and has a brother with muscular dystrophy who goes to a special school and needs a lot of expensive medical treatment.

As usual when the A-listers pass, you avert your eyes and pretend to be immersed in your planner. So you're caught totally off guard when Krista breaks away from the others and comes toward you.

"Lauren?"

You look up, surprised and wary. It's been years since you've heard her utter your name. "Oh, hi."

Krista's brown eyes are made darker by her makeup and tight brown shirt. She looks right into yours as she steps close and whispers, "I saw Celeste Van Warner get on the bus with you yesterday."

You're not sure how to answer. Judy and Stephanie have stopped nearby, but a polite distance away—not so close that they can hear.

"I'd be careful if I were you," Krista continues in a low voice. "There's something about her that isn't right."

"Uh, okay, thanks."

Krista's eyes have not left yours, as if she's looking for something inside you. Finally she angles back to Stephanie and Judy and those three continue down the hall. You're totally not sure what to make of this. The first time in a thousand years Krista decides to talk to you, and it turns out to be a warning about this new girl who sits at the DYWYWM table and yet wants to be your friend?

"Well, look who's here." Tara arrives with a smirk and pulls off her dull black parka with the white stitching where her mom has sewn up rips in the nylon material. Hard to believe she still wears that jacket, since it's at least two sizes too small. "That must have been a pretty short friendship."

"What are you talking about?" you ask.

"You and Celeste."

"We're still friends."

"Then how come you're waiting for me?" Tara asks.

You decide to give her a dose of her own medicine. "Oh, right, how could I be so stupid? I forgot I can only have one friend at a time. Well, see ya."

Of course, you don't leave. Tara starts to do the combination on her lock.

"Did you go to the mall?" you ask.

"No."

"How come?"

"What do you care?"

You can't believe how seriously she's taking this. "Tara, come on. You're my best friend."

She straightens up and faces you, the lines between her eyebrows deepening. "When Celeste isn't around."

"No, even when she *is* around. Yesterday was an exception. I just wanted to get to know her."

"Why couldn't you get to know her on another day?" Tara sniffs.

"I don't know. It wasn't like that. She needed help with math."

"And what if she needs help again today?" Tara asks. "What if she needs homework help every day?"

"She won't," you answer, although now that Tara's mentioned it, you do wish that every afternoon could be like yesterday. "Anyway I want to go to the mall with you. That is, if you still want to go."

"I'll think about it," Tara replies.

It doesn't take Tara long. By lunchtime you and she are back at your regular table in the land of the socially inferior. Celeste, wearing your black top with the gold star, is sitting at the DYWYWM table, halfway between Queen Krista in the middle and the wanna-bes at the ends.

"Isn't that your top?" Tara asks.

"She borrowed it."

"Uh-huh." Tara nods slowly.

"Uh-huh what?"

"Guess I'm just wondering. If you're such good buddies, how come you're not sitting with her?"

Funny she should ask. You've been dreaming all morning that Celeste would suggest it. "I don't know."

"Wrong answer," Tara says. "You're supposed to say, because you want to sit with me."

"Maybe someday we'll *both* sit over there."

Tara snorts. "When pigs fly."

At the DYWYWM table, Celeste looks up and catches your eye. You feel yourself start to flush with embarrassment that she caught you staring, but she gives you a little wave.

And even though you're not sitting with her, it almost feels like you are.

chapter

seven

"It really makes me mad," Celeste says about a week later at the food court in the mall. You've finally gotten up the nerve to ask her about the DYWYWM crowd. "It's so not fair. I mean, why shouldn't you sit at that table with us? Why weren't you invited to Shelby Kirk's party over the weekend?"

"Shelby had a party?" You hadn't even *heard* about it. "Who was there?"

"Oh, you know, the same old crowd." Celeste reels off the names of all the guys and girls you'd imagine would be invited. They may have been the same old crowd to her, but you are completely envious.

"I just don't understand why it has to be this way," she says.

"You mean, the way the whole grade is divided into cliques?"

She nods and reaches up to the counter to get the paper plate with her slice of pizza. It's still hard to believe you're at the mall with her. You were supposed to go home after school and do the laundry, but then Celeste came by your locker and asked if you wanted to go to the mall. So you'll do the laundry later. Your mom will understand.

"Seven fifty," says the counter man with the stained T-shirt.

Celeste searches her bag, then frowns and looks back down the corridor at the stores you've just visited.

"Forget your money again?" you ask.

"No, I can't find my wallet."

"You lost it?" This is cause for serious concern.

Celeste begins to gnaw on a fingernail. Her eyes are wide with panic. "I don't know."

"Okay, when did you last see it?" You take charge the way your mom does in an emergency.

"I don't know! I don't remember!" Completely forgetting the slices and Cokes you've just ordered, she turns toward the corridor.

"Wait!" You grab her arm. "I don't remember you taking it out since we got here. Are you sure you even brought it?"

Celeste stares at you uncertainly. She blinks twice. "I did switch bags at home today."

"So it's probably in the other bag," you conclude.

"No, I wouldn't have forgotten it."

"You sure?"

She goes limp and puts a hand on your shoulder, not

so much for support as in appreciation. "No, I'm not sure . . . Oh, Laur, I'm sorry."

"It's no problem."

She smiles weakly. "Thanks, Laur. And thanks for being so calm. That was totally freaky."

"Let's just sit down, okay?" Crisis averted, you pay for the slices and Cokes and lead her to a table. Recently she's started calling you Laur, especially when she wants to talk about something serious and personal. She's the only person who's ever called you that. As if she knows a different you than everyone else.

"I'll pay you back tomorrow," she says as you both settle into metal chairs bolted to the floor.

"Oh, stop. It's nothing. I'm just glad we know where your wallet is."

You both bite into your slices and sip your sodas. It feels good to know that in some ways she needs you as much as you need her.

After a moment, Celeste parts her bangs and looks straight at you. "How do you always have money?"

"Baby-sitting. While you were at Shelby Kirk's party on Saturday, I was watching the McGuire twins."

"Not fun." Celeste shakes her head.

"It's not so bad. I'm in demand. So if a kid gives me a hard time I just don't baby-sit him anymore. There's always someone else who wants me."

"How much do you get?"

You tell her, and she wrinkles her brow. "That's *all?*"

Her comment stings. You thought it was pretty good for a kid your age. "Don't forget. Three or four times a week adds up."

Celeste leans toward you, dropping her voice. "How much do you have?"

You're caught off guard by this awfully personal question. Even Tara has never asked. Then you think about all the other private things you and Celeste have shared over the past week. Things that feel way more personal than money.

Across the table, Celeste shakes her head. "I shouldn't have asked. It's none of my business."

"I don't care," you tell her. "If you want to know the truth, I have more money than I know what to do with. You know that big piggy jar? It must have four hundred dollars in it."

"No way," Celeste says. "I picked it up. It didn't weigh that much."

You grin proudly. "That's because it's not in change. It's mostly fives, tens, and twenties."

chapter
eight

"Why don't you run for student government?" Mom asks.

"Why would I do that?"

"You're smart and capable. I think you'd be good at it."

"It's just a popularity contest, Mom."

"There has to be more to it than that, hon. It's about responsibility."

"Right. You get to pick themes for the spirit days and organize the holiday party and the spring dance. You'll see. I'll bet anything no one even dares to run against Krista for president."

"Don't you just love it?" Celeste gazes at a choker made of four strands of dark silverish beads in the display counter at Silverstone's Accessories. You're at the mall again. For you it's fun. But for Celeste it seems to be more than that. It's almost as if she *has* to go.

"I could never wear that," you say.

"Of course you could."

"No way."

"Why not?"

"Because . . ."

"Because you're afraid of what someone might say?"

You feel your face turn red with shame.

Celeste clamps her hands on her hips. "You can't be like that, Laur. You're pretty and smart and just as good as anyone else." She waves at a saleslady who's standing down at the other end of the counter. "Excuse me."

You're gripped by sudden panic. *"What are you doing?"*

"I'm buying it for you."

The saleslady is coming. "Can I help you?"

"You can't!" You whisper under your breath.

"Try and stop me." Celeste turns to the saleslady. "I'd like to see this choker."

"No!" you blurt.

The saleslady scowls.

"Don't listen to her," Celeste says.

"No! Don't listen to *her!*" You grab Celeste by the arm and start to drag her away from the counter. "She doesn't know what she's talking about. She must be on drugs."

"I am not!" Celeste cries, and pulls back. "I just want to do something for a friend."

"Well, not that!" You pull harder.

The saleslady crosses her arms and gives you both an impatient, annoyed look. You're just a couple of kids fooling around and wasting her time. She turns to help someone else.

Outside Silverstone's, you and Celeste are red-faced and giggling.

"Did you see the look she gave us?" You chortle.

"She wouldn't have, if you'd let me buy you that stupid choker," Celeste answers.

"You're not buying me anything. If I want something, I can buy it myself."

"The only thing you'd buy is a nun's habit," she teases, slipping her arm through yours. Arm in arm you stroll down the corridor. "Come on, prude, when are you going to loosen up?"

"Probably when I run away from this dumb town," you mutter.

"No!" Celeste stops and puts her hands on your shoulders and stares sternly into your eyes. "Never say that! That's just what they *want* you to do. You're going to stay and fight, Laur. Promise?"

You nod, surprised, but delighted that she feels so strongly. "Promise."

Next stop is Baskin-Robbins for ice cream. Celeste tries to treat you, but they don't accept credit cards.

"Know what we should do?" she asks between licks of her pink bubble-gum ice-cream cone. "Run for student government."

"*You* could."

"You, too," she goes.

"Not a chance."

"Uh-oh, is this like the choker?"

You stare down at your French vanilla cone and feel your face start to heat up.

"You have to believe in yourself, Laur."

That's weird. It's the same thing your mom said. "I do. I believe that if I ran . . . I wouldn't get five votes."

"What if we run together?" Celeste asks. "Walsh and Van Warner for president and vice president."

"Against Krista and Judy? Are you out of your mind?"

Celeste slides a fingernail between her lips. "What about secretary and treasurer?"

Before you can answer, she changes her mind. "No, forget about secretary. All you do is take notes at the meetings. And then you're supposed to type them up and read them back before the next meeting."

"Too much work?"

"*Way* too much work." Celeste licks her bright pink ice-cream cone. "Hey, why don't we *both* run for treasurer?"

"Against each other?"

"No, silly, like co-treasurers. You're good at math and I'm good at—"

You fill in the blank: "Being liked."

chapter
nine

"Mom?"

"Yes, hon?"

"There's, uh, something I need to tell you."

"Don't be shy."

"I've decided to run for class treasurer."

"That's wonderful! Why do you look so worried? Are you afraid you'll lose?"

"Well, it's not that. I mean, I guess I should be worried about that, too. But it's something else."

"I'm listening."

"I'm running against Stephanie."

"Mr. Eisley's daughter?"

"Yeah, Mom. I'm sorry."

"You don't have to be sorry, hon. I'm sure Mr. Eisley will understand. It's a free country. Anyone who wants to can run for office."

"Sure, but . . ."

"It's not your concern. You do whatever you want."

"Thanks, Mom."

You're standing on a chair in the hall, taping one of the posters you've made to the wall above your locker.

"Good for you," someone says.

You look down at a head of short, curly light brown hair. It's Rob Carlucci, a thin boy who wears glasses, preppy khakis, and light blue shirts with collars.

"You think?"

"Sure, why not?"

"I've never done anything like this."

"Then it's about time." Rob lives across the street from you in the house where Krista once lived. Rob always has a smile and something nice to say. He's one of the few popular boys who isn't a big jock or a big jerk. He's just friendly to everyone and seems very sure of himself.

"You don't think Stephanie will be mad?"

"No madder than I am at Shelby Kirk since she decided to run for secretary."

"How mad's that?"

Rob shoves his hands into his pockets. "Zero mad. Whoever wins, wins. There's no hard feelings. So what made you decide to do it?"

"It was Celeste's idea, really. She'll shake hands and I'll crunch numbers."

"Sounds like a plan." Rob grins. "I hope you win, Lauren. I really do."

There's something in his voice you've never heard before. You're not sure what it means, but it makes your ears feel warm.

"Thanks, Rob."

He lingers in the hall a moment more, gazing up at you. "Well, guess I better go. Let me know if I can help, okay?"

"Okay."

He heads off down the hall and you watch, wondering what that was about. But then the tape comes off on the upper corner of the poster and you have to restick it before the whole thing falls. With your back to the hall, you are uncomfortably aware that kids are stopping to look.

"Walsh and Van Warner for co-treasurers?" You know the voice. It's Tara.

"Hi." You twist around, feeling guilty. It's been days since you two spoke. Instead of going to the cafeteria at lunch, you've been making posters in the art room.

"What is this?" Tara asks.

"It's what I've been doing at lunch instead of eating in the cafeteria," you explain.

"Oh. I thought you didn't want to be seen with me anymore." The sharp, perceptive words jab into you. "Why didn't you just tell me?"

"Celeste wanted it to be a surprise." You step down from the chair.

"Well, you can definitely forget about being invited to Stephanie's next pizza party." This is a joke, since you've never been invited anyway.

"Guess that's a price I'll have to pay."

"Seriously, Lauren. You're sure you want to do it?"

"Why not?"

"Maybe because it's totally obvious you're riding on Celeste's coattails."

That hurts. You know Tara is just calling it the way she sees it. But still, she's supposed to be your friend. You lower your voice. "Can I tell you a secret?"

"Why not?"

"I'm only doing it because Celeste needs someone who's good at math."

"Uh-huh." Tara gives you an exaggerated, disbelieving nod.

"It's true!" you insist.

"You are too much, Lauren."

She's angry and hurt. She's always been a good friend. Until recently, the only one you had. "What are you doing after school today?" you ask.

"Uh, let me guess. Helping you make more posters?"

"If you want."

"What about your co-treasurer?"

"She has a doctor's appointment."

Tara chuckles. "Why am I not surprised?"

chapter
ten

By week's end you've put up three times as many posters as Stephanie. So many that one teacher teases that you could have a career in wallpapering. Back in the cafeteria for the first time in a week, you gaze at the DYWYWM table. Celeste is deep in conversation with Judy Knight. The only person who meets your gaze is Krista.

"Lauren!" Tara grunts irritably.

"Sorry." You look down at today's lunch. Mom packed a tuna fish sandwich. The oil has seeped out and stained the brown paper bag, leaving your backpack and books smelling fishy.

"I thought for sure you'd be sitting over there by now," Tara says.

"Not without you."

"Gee, I didn't know you cared."

Tara's nonstop sarcasm grates, but still, she's your best friend. Carefully using the tips of your fingers, you unwrap the tuna sandwich. The fishy scent grows stronger. The DYWYWM girls don't smell of fish. Tomorrow, you decide, you will buy lunch.

"Lauren?" Tara says.

"Hmmm?"

"This is just a suggestion, but you might want to tell Celeste to be a little less obvious about copying homework out of your notebook in the library."

You feel your face start to glow.

"If she gets caught, you'll get in trouble, too," Tara says. "Why do you let her?"

"I didn't actually know."

"You didn't know she had your notebook?"

"Well, yes, she asked to borrow it. I just . . . didn't ask why."

Tara gives you a truly scathing look. You shrug meekly. It's hard to explain this to her. "It's just . . . we're getting friendly, you know?"

"If you're getting so friendly, how come she never sits with us?"

You look up from your smelly sandwich and across the table at Tara. She's wearing a white sweatshirt with a light brown stain on the front. Not a new stain that she's just gotten that day, but an old washed-a-hundred-times stain. How can you tell her that you know *exactly* why Celeste doesn't sit at your table? For the same reason you wouldn't sit there either, if you had the choice.

"Can I give you some advice?" Tara asks.

"Okay."

"Be careful with her. There's something about her I don't trust."

That's odd, because it's the same thing Krista said. But you don't mention that because you know they're both wrong. The truth is, neither of them really knows Celeste. Not the way you do.

eleven

"How's the campaign going?" Mom asks.

"Good. I have to tell you the funniest thing. I got a 98 on a math quiz, and Mr. Youngstrom told the whole class that if they vote for me they won't have to worry about the class bank account."

"That's great, hon."

"And Stephanie was sitting right there!"

"Oops!" Mom smiles.

Something has changed. You can feel it. Yesterday Judy Knight, who's running for vice-president, stopped you in the hall and said she liked your posters. A-list girls like Shelby Kirk, who never even looked in your direction before, now smile at you. Even the hot boys, like Reed Palmer, seem to notice you.

You hardly sleep the night before the election. At school you see Celeste in the girls' locker room before gym.

"Did you write up the science lab?" she asks in a low voice.

"Here. I made you a copy." You pull the lab write-up from your science folder and hand it to her. You're not in the same science class, but you both have the same teacher, Ms. Dillsen, and she gives the same homework. "I changed the numbers a little, but the results are still the same, okay?"

"Thanks, Laur, you're a real friend. So, think we have a chance today?"

"Who knows?"

"Two girls told me this morning they're going to vote for us because they don't want Stephanie to win."

"Great! The 'We-Hate-Stephanie' vote!"

You both giggle and start to change for gym. Secretly you estimate that if half the popular kids vote for Celeste and a lot of the social outcasts vote for you, you have a shot at winning.

The vote is held at lunchtime. They make everyone line up in the hall outside the cafeteria and cast ballots before they can go in. Otherwise, the only kids who'd vote would be the candidates and their friends.

Waiting in line with Tara, you look around for Celeste. You don't see her or the other A-list girls, but once again the kids you do see act differently. Those who once looked away now smile or nod.

Rob Carlucci strolls up, hands in the pockets of his khaki slacks, a relaxed expression on his face. "Hey, Tara. Hey, Lauren. Who're you guys gonna vote for?"

"Don't know," Tara answers. "Just can't make up my mind."

"How can you be so calm?" you ask him. "Aren't you just a little nervous?"

"That Shelby Kirk might beat me for secretary and then she'll get stuck taking all the notes and typing them up?" Rob chuckles. "Do me a favor, vote for her, okay?"

He's kidding, of course. But you're struck by how relaxed he is. He could lose and it really wouldn't bother him.

"So, Lauren," he says. "If elected, just what do you plan to do for our grade?"

"I intend . . ." you begin in a whisper, "to throw the biggest party this school has ever seen!"

"Sounds good to me." Tara lifts her hand as if to share a hi-five, but then sees something and stops abruptly. You turn and see Stephanie Eisley coming down the line toward you, her long streaked blond hair parted in the middle and flapping slightly like a pair of wings.

Expecting a nasty cut down, you feel yourself start to freeze.

Stephanie stops. "Hi, Rob, Lauren, Tara."

"Uh-oh!" Rob grins. "Fight fair, girls. No eye gouging or hair pulling."

"Lauren." Stephanie focuses on you. "I just hope that no matter which of us wins, there'll be no hard feelings, okay?"

You nod mutely, still bracing for the nastiness that's sure to follow. But it doesn't come.

"You mean, no fight?" Rob pretends to be disappointed.

"Sorry, Rob." Stephanie turns around and heads toward the back of the line.

"Guess I better get on line, too," Rob says. "Otherwise I'll never get to eat. See ya later."

He follows Stephanie. You're still in shock. Is it possible that Stephanie Eisley, the girl who only a few weeks ago had no problem cutting you down to tears in front of everyone, is now making sure you two won't be enemies?

"Now I've seen everything," Tara mutters.

"Running for class government sure changes things," you observe.

"Not quite," Tara whispers. "Running with Celeste Van Warner is what changes things."

chapter
twelve

You and Tara vote, then go into the cafeteria and sit at your usual spot among the undesirables. But when you look over at the DYWYWM table, Celeste flashes a hopeful thumbs-up sign. Even Krista smiles.

"Don't let me stop you," Tara grumbles as she peels the wrapper off the first beef jerky of the day.

She's right. The A-list girls have made it more obvious than ever that it will be okay if you sit with them. All you have to do is get up and go.

"Would you go, too?" you ask Tara.

"Give me a break," she replies. "Don't make this a big deal, Lauren, just go."

You are dying to go but also frightened. What if Shelby Kirk and Stephanie decide to get mean? What if all the other kids in the cafeteria see? And what about Tara? Can you really get up and leave her there alone? Inside you are torn by what you know you want, what still scares you, and what you know is right. It's the golden rule. You would hate it if Tara were to leave you sitting by yourself. Is that what it takes to be a DYWYWM girl? The ability to think only of yourself? But look at Celeste. She thinks of you.

"Attention, students, for an announcement from Principal Hansen." Toward period's end, the cafeteria loud-speaker crackles, then your principal comes on. "I have the results of the student government election. Krista Rice, president. Judy Knight, vice president. Rob Carlucci, secretary. And for treasurer . . . Lauren Walsh and Celeste Van Warner."

The bell rings. The announcement always comes just before the end of the period so that the losers can disappear into the crowd of kids moving to their next class. All around the cafeteria kids rise and strap on their backpacks.

"Well, congratulations, Lauren." Tara starts to get up. "Aren't you coming?"

"In a moment." You're still sitting.

Tara follows your eyes to the DYWYWM table. "Right. See you later." She heads out.

A moment later you do get up, but you time it so that you join Celeste and the others near the exit as they leave the cafeteria.

"Congratulations," Celeste says.

"Congratulations to *you,* co-treasurer," you reply.

"Congratulations, Lauren," adds Krista. "We're going to meet in the band room after school today. See you then?"

"Definitely." *You're in! You've done it!*

After school, you're the first to arrive in the band room. Since this meeting isn't a class one has to be on time for, the A-listers will arrive "fashionably late." You even know precisely where they are—in the girls' room fixing their hair and makeup.

Celeste is the next to arrive. With broad smiles you congratulate each other again.

"Can you believe how lucky we are?" she asks. "We only beat Stephanie by five votes."

"Really?" That's a lot closer than you expected.

"Guess she still has a lot of friends," Celeste says. "But, hey, we won, and that's all that counts, right?"

"Right!"

Krista comes in with Judy and Rob. You all move chairs into a circle. Rob opens his laptop computer. You all wait for Krista to speak, but Krista also waits.

"Ready," Rob says.

"I just thought it would be a good idea if we got down to business right away," Krista says, very businesslike. Her words are echoed by the rapid clicking of Rob's fingers on his laptop. "The last Friday of every month is a spirit day. We already know that everybody loves pajama day, hippie day, school color day, and dress-up day. But that still leaves four months. Any other suggestions?"

"Underwear day?" Rob suggests.

"You'd just love that," Krista says with a smirk.

"What about bathing-suit day?" Celeste suggests.

Krista and Judy exchange approving looks. You wish you could have thought of that.

"Let's do it in February," Rob says.

"The last Friday in May." Krista jots it down on her Palm Pilot. She, Judy, Celeste, and Rob bat around a few more possibilities. You remain quiet. Not that you're being shy. If you had a good idea you'd suggest it. But everything you think of seems dumb.

The rest of the spirit days are finally decided and Krista moves on to the holiday party.

"Any suggestions?" she asks.

"I know one thing," Judy says. "It's not going to be another swimming party."

"Why not?" Celeste asks.

"You weren't here last year, so you don't know what a disaster it was," Krista says. She looks around and her gaze settles on you. Her brow furrows slightly. "Were you there, Lauren?"

You shake your head.

"Smart," Krista says, although you both know that the reason you weren't there had nothing to do with being smart. Tara, being heavy, refuses to be seen in a bathing suit. And without your closest friend, you couldn't see yourself going to the party either.

"Not only was it freezing," Krista explains to Celeste, "but the boys decided it would be fun to throw the girls in, whether they wanted to go in or not."

"A lot of wet hair?" Celeste guesses.

Judy pretends to shiver at the memory. "What a nightmare."

"So," Krista says, twirling her brown hair on her finger thoughtfully, "any *other* ideas?"

"That don't involve dancing," Rob adds.

You have an idea. "How about an ice-skating party?"

Krista shows a raised eyebrow's worth of interest.

Inspired, you continue. "They just opened that new rink in town. So it should be nice."

"Sounds like fun," says Judy.

"*If* you like to skate," Rob points out.

"They also have a video arcade," you quickly add.

"Cool." Rob instantly brightens.

Judy turns to Krista. "Doesn't Peter play hockey? Maybe you could get him to come."

Krista's face goes blank. "You're joking, right?" she replies in a chilly monotone.

Nothing more is said about the mysterious Peter.

"Won't it be expensive?" Celeste asks in her new role as co-treasurer.

"Do you know what it costs, Lauren?" Krista asks.

"No," you answer. "But since the rink's brand new I

bet the owners would give us a good deal, because once the kids go there they'll want to come back."

"Hey, *someone's* thinking," Rob says, and you feel yourself flush with pride at the compliment.

"Does anyone know what's in the class fund?" Krista asks.

Judy flips through a notebook. "A little over five hundred dollars."

"Good." Krista turns to Celeste and you. "As our new co-treasurers, your first job will be to find out how much it will cost to rent the skating rink. Try to get them to give you a good price."

chapter
thirteen

"Congratulations on winning, hon."

"Wait, Mom, it gets better. They needed an idea for the class party. I suggested skating and they liked it."

"That's wonderful. And all that time you thought they didn't like you."

"Well, I'm just a co-treasurer."

"You're the one who said it was a popularity contest. Have they ever seen you skate?"

"I don't think so."

"I think they're going to be very impressed."

"Laur." In the middle of a math test, Celeste's whisper sends a startled shiver down your spine. As much as you enjoy the attention she gives you, this is one time when you wish she'd leave you alone. When she first came to the class in October, Celeste sat at a desk two rows over. But recently she moved to the desk next to yours.

You glance nervously at Mr. Youngstrom, sitting at his desk, his head bent as he marks tests from another class. You turn slightly and give Celeste a quick look. Just as you feared, she motions you to move your test to the right side of your desk, where she can see it.

You feel your stomach tighten. Your heart starts to pound uncomfortably. You've never cheated on a test, nor helped anyone else cheat. Maybe you've helped Celeste with her homework. Maybe you've even done her homework for her. But this is different. If you get caught, you'll be in megatrouble.

Mr. Youngstrom's head stays bowed as he concentrates on marking.

"*Laur?*" Celeste whispers again. You're not just worried about getting caught. You know this is really wrong. You should say no. But how do you say no to someone you owe so much to?

With a sour, uneasy feeling in your stomach, you slide your test to the side of your desk. Not daring to look at Celeste, you can't help hearing the feverish scratching of her pencil as she copies your answers.

And that's when the loudspeaker over the door crackles: "Lauren Walsh and Celeste Van Warner, please come to Principal Hansen's office at the end of the period."

For a moment, you can't breathe. Your heart may have been banging before, but now it booms in your chest, each beat like the thunderous blast of a cannon. It feels like it will burst and your life will end right there in math class. You grab your test and slide it back to the center of your desk, just as Mr. Youngstrom raises his head and nods at you and Celeste.

The rest of the class continues taking the test. Mr. Youngstrom goes back to marking. You steal another glance at Celeste. She widens her eyes for a second, then shakes her head as if to say, "That was freaky, but it's okay, nothing happened."

She's right. The announcement was a coincidence. Gradually your heart slows down and stops banging.

Math ends. You hand in your test and walk with a quickened step out into the hall. It's not that you're so eager to see Principal Hansen. It's just that you *have* to get out of Mr. Youngstrom's room and away from the crime you've just committed. Celeste comes out with a guilty grin on her lips. You start to feel a little better. You got away with it, and Celeste is still your friend.

"Can you believe that?" you gasp. "For a second I was sure we'd been caught!"

Celeste presses a finger to her lips. "Shush!" She doesn't seem nearly as rattled as you.

"So what do you think Principal Hansen wants?" you ask as you both start down the hall toward the office. "I mean, we can't really be in trouble, right?" Even now you can't quite shake the guilt.

Celeste shrugs. "We'll see."

"Every year I give this speech to the new treasurer," Principal Hansen begins a few minutes later, in her office. She is a tall, stern-looking woman with black hair that curls under her chin, framing her face in an oval shape. Her black eyebrows are tweezed into thin crescents over each eye. Everything about her is serious, including her serious gray suit. But you've always suspected that behind that stern outside is a nicer, softer inside that she tries to keep hidden. Once, when you saw her catch some boys plugging up a water fountain with gum, it almost looked like she was going to laugh, but she got control of herself and acted somber and principal-like instead.

The principal slides a large index-size card across the desk toward you and Celeste. "You are taking over the most responsible job in student government. You'll be in charge of the money. I hope you'll take this job seriously."

You and Celeste lean forward and look at the card. On the top the words FIRST NATIONAL BANK are printed in large fancy letters. Then come two paragraphs of single-spaced small print.

"This is a signature card," Principal Hansen explains. "Each year the new treasurer signs it and I send it to the bank. Before you can take out any money, the teller will compare the signatures on the withdrawal slip to the signatures on this card to make sure you're really who you say you are. Since you're co-treasurers, you'll *both* have to sign each time you withdraw money. If there's ever a problem, you can always talk to my husband. He's an officer of the bank. Any questions?"

You and Celeste shake your heads. Principal Hansen hands you a pen. You both sign the signature card. You are now official.

chapter
fourteen

"Isn't it weird that Principal Hansen's husband is a police-man?" you ask Celeste. School is over and you're back at the mall. You've never known anyone who loved to shop as much as Celeste. Every time you two go, she finds something to fall in love with, but never buys anything. At least, not when she's with you. The only thing she's ever come close to buying was that choker.

Celeste gives you a puzzled look. "No, he isn't."

"She said he's an officer at the bank."

"That just means he works there. The officers are the ones who sit at the desks." She studies you for a moment. "Have you ever been inside a bank, Laur?"

You have to think about this. "Depends on what you mean."

Celeste parts her bangs and gives you a close look.

"I mean," you go on, "I've been inside the front door. Like where the ATMs are. But not *really* inside."

"Okay, here's how it works," Celeste explains. "The tellers are the ones who sit behind the plastic windows.

When you want to put money in the bank, you give it to them. And when you want to take it out, they give it back to you. The officers usually sit at desks. They're in charge of more important things, like making loans and opening accounts, and they're the only ones who can get into the vault."

"Where they keep the money?"

"Right—Ohmygod!" She stops and stares into a display window outside a boutique called Sherman's. A mannequin there is wearing a long brown coat and the cutest maroon knit cap. "Don't you just love it?" She grabs your hand and pulls you inside.

"Why don't you get it?" you ask a few moments later while she tries it on in front of a mirror.

"I really should." But then she stops, and for a long moment she is no longer looking at herself in the cap, but at something else . . . something in the mirror that you can't see. She takes the cap off. "No."

"I don't get it," you go. "How come you never buy anything for yourself?"

"I'm always afraid I'll get home and hate it," she answers.

"So? You'll just return it. Any anyway, why would you hate this? It looks great on you."

"You think?" She tries it on again, studying herself in the mirror for a long time. You truly do not understand what the problem is.

"Laur?"

"Yes?" you answer.

"Do people ever talk about me?"

"Like how?"

"You know what I mean. Like, what do they say?"

"Well, nothing *bad.*" Except Tara, you think to yourself. But that's just jealousy. And what Krista said a few weeks ago—that there was something about Celeste that wasn't right.

"You sure?" Celeste asks.

"Uh-huh. I mean, why would they?"

"Who knows? I guess because I'm new, and people always talk about the new girl."

"Well, I'll let you know if I hear anything," you joke.

Once again Celeste takes off the cap.

"You're not going to get it?" you ask, disappointed.

"I'll think about it," she replies. The mood has changed and grown heavier. The lighthearted gleefulness is gone. You leave Sherman's together.

"What's bothering you, Celeste?"

She gives you a reluctant look and then sighs. "It's that crowd. Krista and Stephanie and the rest of them. I know some of the girls are jealous of me. I mean, especially the ones who aren't really popular. Like, they've been around here forever and they're still not really in that crowd. They'll probably never be in it. But I'm here for less than two months and I am. Know what I mean?"

Do you ever.

"There are bound to be people who are jealous of you," you answer. "But no one says anything mean. Really, Celeste." Did you ever think you'd find yourself consoling someone else for being popular?

Out in the corridor Celeste stops and turns to you with the most serious expression. "You'll tell me if anyone does say anything?"

"Uh, sure."

"Promise?" She's *really* serious.

"Promise."

chapter
fifteen

"Mom, I just called the skating rink and made an appointment to talk to the owner about the party."

"Did he sound interested?"

"Totally. I said we'd have two hundred kids."

"That's great, hon. Talking to the owner is a very grown-up thing to do."

"I know, but I'm a little scared, Mom. I've never discussed 'business' before."

"You'll do fine, hon."

On the day of the appointment, you get to school early and wait at Celeste's locker. You spot her coming down the hall with Krista and Reed Palmer. Reed is a "hottie," tall and slim with black hair and dark eyes and a dreamy smile that makes girls melt and giggle. He, Krista, and Celeste are talking and laughing.

So much for Krista's warning that there was something "not right" about Celeste. It's clear that she was just jealous and wanted Celeste for herself.

Then you notice that Celeste is wearing the maroon knit cap from Sherman's.

"So you bought it," you say.

"Bought what?" Celeste stops. Her eyes follow yours and she reaches up and touches the cap. "Oh, right, I . . . I went back and got it. So, what's up?"

"We have to go to the skating rink after school and talk to the owner about the party."

"A skating party?" Reed raises a thick dark eyebrow. "Sounds cool."

Krista's eyes dart toward Celeste. She takes Reed by the arm. "We better go."

She leads him away. Meanwhile, Celeste slides a finger between her lips and starts to gnaw. "You're going to kill me, Laur. I totally forgot that I have a doctor's appointment after school today. Think you could go without me?"

That's the last thing you want to do. "Uh, sure. Don't worry about it."

Celeste puts her hand on your shoulder. "You're great, Laur."

The bell rings and you head for homeroom in a terrible mood. It's not Celeste's fault. Everyone forgets things.

At lunch you ask Tara if she'll go with you to the skating rink.

"What happened to your co-treasurer?" she asks,

glancing over at the DYWYWM table where Celeste and the others are chatting away.

"Doctor's appointment."

Tara chews thoughtfully on a beef jerky. "I heard Stephanie's thinking of inviting you to her next pizza party."

"Liar. Celeste and I beat her for treasurer. Stephanie must hate me. She's the *last* person who'd invite me to anything."

"I don't think that's the way she looks at it," Tara replies. "If you beat her in the election it means she almost *has* to invite you to the party."

"Why?" you ask, honestly puzzled.

"Because if you beat her, then you must be somebody," Tara explains, like it's incredibly obvious. "I mean, do you think Stephanie Eisley could bear the thought of being beaten by a nobody?"

In the weird, twisted logic of popularity, this apparently makes sense. You pretend to shrug the news off. Partly because you're not sure you believe it. And partly because, if it's true, you don't want Tara to see how excited you are.

After school it's one of those strange, unseasonably warm, sunny winter days. Your brain has a hard time matching the bare tree branches and dull brown grass with the balmy air and people wearing their sleeves rolled up. As you and Tara walk toward the new skating rink with your jackets tucked into your backpacks, you explain what you pray will happen. "I'm really hoping the owner will give us a discount on the party in exchange for bringing so many kids."

"Sounds good to me," Tara responds.

"Think you could do it?"

"Do what?"

"Talk to him."

Tara stops walking. "Wait a minute. I don't skate. I wouldn't go to this stupid party if you paid me."

"I know, Tar, but it would be a really big help. I mean, you *always* know what to say."

"Oh, okay." Tara gives in easily. She doesn't mind talking to grown-ups. And maybe she likes being needed.

The new skating rink is in a building with blue walls and a silver roof made out of wavy metal like Ruffles potato chips. Inside, the skating rink office is cold and bare. The owner, Mr. Johnson, sits behind a plain brown desk and wears a heavy white-and-brown Norwegian sweater and a gray wool cap. He has a thick gray beard and a round, friendly face. A small space heater sits on the floor, aimed at his chair. The coils inside it glow bright reddish orange, but the room is still chilly enough to make you and Tara put your jackets on before you sit down in the wooden chairs. Today you didn't need your jackets outside, but you sure do in here.

When "talking business," Tara puts on an amazing performance. She seems to know all the right things to say: "It's not just when the kids come to the party. It's all the times they'll come back and bring their friends. A party like this will jump-start word of mouth. It'll really help increase your business."

"I'm very impressed with your argument," Mr. Johnson replies with a bemused smile as if he is also charmed by this young lady who uses words like *jump-start* and phrases like *word of mouth*. "And I would be delighted to have your party here. My only problem is that I can't close the skating rink for a whole evening just for your party. Even if it means a lot of business, I can't afford to turn away other people who might want to use the rink."

A wave of disappointment crashes down on you. First, because the skating party was your idea and now no one will know that you thought of it. And second, because you wanted everyone to see you skate. Of course you know both reasons sound selfish, but you sincerely believe that everyone else would have enjoyed the skating party, too. Only now it's not going to happen.

Mr. Johnson pulls open the top drawer of his desk and takes out two thin red-and-white coupon books. "To show you how much I appreciate you wanting to have your party here, why don't you take some discount passes for you and your families."

He slides the coupon books across the desk. You give Tara a miserable look. It's not the coupon books you want. It's the party. Now, as your second official act as school co-treasurer, you'll have to go back to Krista and tell her you've failed. You take one of the coupon books and start to get up.

"Suppose we only rent *half* the rink?" Tara suddenly asks. "You can put some plastic cones right through the middle. Then we can have our party on one side and the public can still use the other. Not only that, but when they see the party, they'll think of having parties here, too."

Mr. Johnson blinks. "Why . . . that is a fantastic idea! And since you'll only be renting half the rink, you can have it for a better price."

With Tara negotiating, Mr. Johnson agrees on three hundred dollars, including skate rentals and some tokens for the arcade games and coupons for the snack bar.

A few minutes later, outside the rink, you hug Tara. "You are a genius! What would I do without you?"

"Think we could stop at the mall?" she asks.

Oh, no . . . Of all the things she could have suggested, why that? You've been there *way* too many times lately and you have things to do at home. But how can you say no? It's simple: You can't.

Luckily the bus from the skating rink to the mall takes only a few minutes and in almost no time you're helping Tara with her Christmas shopping. It's so weird. Before you got friendly with Celeste, you probably came here once a month. Now you're here so often you're surprised the salespeople don't wave and call out your name as you pass.

Tara is looking in the window of the Toy Express for gifts for her cousins when you hear familiar voices. In the mirror behind a tall Lego display, you spot a group on the other side of the broad corridor—Krista, Celeste, Reed Palmer, and his best friend Jason Buckley.

"I thought she had a doctor's appointment," Tara says when she sees who you're staring at in the mirror.

"Tara, turn around," you whisper almost frantically.

"You don't want them to see us?"

"Please, Tara."

She lets out a big sigh and turns. You both stand there, watching in the mirror until the others are far down the corridor.

"I want to go home," you announce.

"We just got here," Tara protests.

"You can stay if you like."

"Lauren . . ."

You're already walking away.

Behind you Tara calls, "What's *wrong* with you?"

You feel like crying. But maybe you shouldn't be so upset. Maybe Celeste did have a doctor's appointment and came to the mall after it was over. Or maybe the appointment was canceled. But inside you know that's not what happened. It all seems so clear now. Why Krista had acted so awkwardly and had pulled Reed away that morning in the hallway.

"You're crying," Tara says on the bus home.

"Thanks, I hadn't noticed."

"Hey, don't be mad at me."

"Sorry."

You don't say another word for the rest of the ride home. Tara gets off first.

"See you tomorrow?" she asks.

"Sure." If you don't kill yourself first.

chapter
sixteen

You're too old to be called a latchkey kid, but not too old to feel like one. You wish you could call Mom at Carmen's, but it's not like she has a job at a desk and can chat on the phone. It's dinnertime and you know she's hustling around taking orders and carrying heavy trays.

Should you call Celeste and ask her why she lied? No, that would only make her angry with you. Instead, you lose yourself in television and homework. Then the phone rings. Heave yourself up. It's either Mom calling to check up or Tara. Or possibly a kid from school who isn't sure what the homework is.

"Laur?" It's Celeste and instantly you are thrown into a thick soup of confusion and speechlessness.

"Hello? Laur?"

"Uh, I'm here."

"Was that you at the mall today?"

"I guess."

"I thought so! Krista said she didn't think so, but I did."

"What happened to your doctor's appointment?"

"Would you believe I had the wrong date written down? So you know me. A free afternoon and—"

"You just had to go to the mall." You end the sentence for her and suddenly feel a rush of relief. She didn't lie!

"And I ran into Krista and those guys. So, did you find anything good?"

"No, I was just tagging along with Tara. What about you?"

"You know. Always looking, never buying."

"Except the cap."

"Right. So what happened with the skating rink?"

"Celeste, you won't believe it. The owner really loved the idea of the party, but he said he couldn't close the rink to the public."

"Oh, no! What did you do?"

"Well, I didn't know what to do . . ." you begin. "And then I . . . had . . . this idea. Like, what if we only rented *half* the rink? So we could have the party and the public could still use the other half."

"And?"

"Well, I also figured that renting half the rink wouldn't be as expensive as renting the whole rink."

"And?"

"He agreed. And he's going to throw in the skate rentals and some other stuff, too."

"Laur, that's great! You're a genius!"

seventeen

"What's wrong, hon?"

"Nothing."

"How did it go at the ice-skating rink?"

"Good. We can use it for the party."

"That's wonderful. You must be very proud of yourself."

"Whatever."

Another meeting in the band room after school. You all sit in a circle with notebooks on your laps. Except Rob, who has his laptop computer, and Krista with her Palm Pilot.

"Celeste and Lauren," Krista begins, "can you give us an update on the skating party?"

"We've got the rink," Celeste reports, and then goes on to tell them how you made this great deal with the owner. "I hate to say it, but I had nothing to do with it. Lauren handled the whole thing herself."

"Way to go, Lauren," cheers Judy Knight.

Krista also nods appreciatively.

"Good thinking, Lauren," Rob chimes in. "Renting half the rink was a stroke of genius."

You force a weak smile onto your lips. Both Celeste and Rob have now called you a genius. And it's all based on a lie. You can't believe you didn't just tell them the truth. Well, that itself is a lie. You can believe it. But really, it's not the worst lie, is it? It's not like Tara would have ever gotten the credit. Or done anything with it. This way you'll get the credit. And once you're really comfortable with this crowd, you'll bring Tara in.

"Judy, you're good at decorations," Krista says. "Can I put you in charge of them for the skating party?"

"Sure." Judy agrees.

"Could I do the decorations, too?" Celeste suddenly asks.

"Think you'll need help?" Krista asks Judy.

"All the help I can get," Judy answers.

"Can I help, too?" you ask.

"No way, Lauren," Krista says. "We all saw the posters you made for treasurer. We'll need you to do a whole bunch for the party."

You feel both disappointed and flattered. It's nice that Krista thinks you're so good at making posters. But the meeting ends and Krista, Celeste, and Judy immediately start talking about the decorations. Once again you feel left out. Not knowing what else to do, you pick up your backpack and go out into the hall.

"Lauren?" Rob comes out behind you, his black computer bag slung over his shoulder. "That really was good thinking. I *never* would have thought of dividing the rink in half."

"Oh, uh, thanks." What a bittersweet feeling—accepting a compliment you don't deserve.

Together you walk down the hall. Rob checks his watch. "It's gonna be awhile till the late bus leaves. I know it's kind of far, but you feel like walking?"

You pause by a classroom door and look through it and out the classroom windows. Except for a few puffy white clouds the sky is blue and some kids are outside with unzipped jackets and their hats and gloves stuffed into their pockets. "Okay, sure."

You and Rob go to your lockers and get your jackets. The memory of that day a week ago in the hall when he complimented you on your posters comes back. You recall the way he looked at you and start to wonder if it meant anything different than usual.

"Ready?" The nearness of his voice catches you by surprise. You spin around and there he is in a navy blue baseball jacket, the strap of his backpack slung over one shoulder, the computer bag now tucked under his arm. The jacket makes him look huskier than he really is.

And while you would not call him handsome, he is definitely cute.

You accidentally swing your locker door closed a little too hard. *Clang!* The sound is jarringly loud. Rob gives you a funny look. Together you leave school and start down the sidewalk. The air is cool, but not uncomfortable. The trees are dark and bare.

"Know what's so great about that skating rink idea?" he says. "We really don't need the whole rink anyway. And this way we won't have to pay for it."

"It wasn't my idea." The words just pop out, but you're not surprised. You've always been severely uncomfortable with lies. Sooner or later the truth always claws its way to the surface. "It was Tara's."

"But Celeste said—"

"She thinks it was my idea, too." Strangely, you don't mind admitting the truth to Rob. You know he's the kind of person who'll keep it to himself. As you walk together, the orange winter sun begins to drop toward the tree line and the chilly shadows grow long. You zip your jacket up to your chin and secretly wish you'd waited for the late bus.

"It doesn't really matter," goes Rob.

"It does to me."

"Well, it's brave of you to tell me," he says. It's his habit to always try to find something nice to say.

"I should have told everyone."

"Why?" Rob says. "You're smart, Lauren. You could have thought of it, too."

"Maybe." Now you begin to feel ashamed and embarrassed. Maybe you shouldn't have told him the truth. Not if you really do want him to like you.

As if he senses how uncomfortable you feel, he changes the subject. "So, did you check out what video games they have?"

"Sure, Rob, I tried out every one of them." You grin.

"Seriously."

"You can go check them out if you want. You don't have to wait for the party to do that."

"Aw, guess I'll wait." From there the conversation veers off into school and teachers and tests. Before long, you've reached the block where you both live. You stop on the sidewalk in front of your little house. The sun has dropped out of sight and with it the temperature. It's cold enough for your breath to come out in a small cloud of white.

"So, uh . . ." Rob scuffs his shoe against the sidewalk and seems uncertain of what to say. "See you tomorrow, okay?"

"You won't tell anyone, will you?" you ask.

He shakes his head. "Like I said, Lauren, as far as I'm concerned, you could have thought of it yourself."

"Thank you, Rob." You say this as softly and sweetly

as you can. Hoping he'll stay and say something. Something sincere that might indicate that he likes you more than just a friend.

"Well . . ." He pauses uncertainly. "See you tomorrow." He turns and heads toward his house.

Just friends, you think, feeling disappointed.

chapter
eighteen

"I'm coming to your house after school today," Celeste announces in the hall on the way to lunch the next day.

This catches you by surprise. Of course, you're delighted, but puzzled, too. "Well, great, but . . . why?"

"It's a surprise."

You feel a smile grow on your face, but it promptly vanishes when you and Celeste step into the cafeteria. Out in the land of the socially inferior, Tara is already sitting by herself at your regular table. Meanwhile, at the red-hot center of the social universe, the DYWYWM girls are crowded around theirs.

"You want to sit with Tara and me?" you ask Celeste.

"Oh, uh, I would, but I told Judy I'd plan decorations with her. Another time, okay?"

"Sure." You and she part ways. Everywhere else in school you're the co-treasurers and you almost feel like you are part of the A-list crowd. But here in the cafeteria, life is the way it's always been.

Later, Celeste takes the bus home with you. You are dying to know why she wants to come to your house, but she refuses to tell. This time there is no major chow down in the kitchen. She marches straight to your room and points at your vanity. "I want you there, now!"

"Why?" you giggle.

"Because it's time you got hip, girl." She takes a small makeup kit out of her bag. "Look what I got you."

It's a sample makeup kit. A week ago they were giving them away at JC Penney's.

"I don't need makeup," you protest.

"Oh, really? Every *other* girl on earth does. Why not you?"

"Because I'll never wear it."

"Tomorrow you will."

"Why?"

"Because it's dress-up day, remember?"

You'd totally forgotten. "Oh, okay. It's just that . . ."

"Just what?"

Just nothing except that you're still afraid people will think you're trying to be one of the DYWYWM girls. *"Can you believe Lauren? Just because she's co-treasurer she thinks she's suddenly popular."*

"Mom doesn't let me wear makeup," you lie. "Except on special occasions."

"Isn't dress-up day a special occasion?" Celeste asks

as she applies eye shadow over your eyes. "Besides, why does she have to know? First thing tomorrow morning, we'll do you up in the girls' room. And another thing. Tomorrow after school you're going to the bank."

"To get the money for the skating rink?"

"Uh . . ." In the mirror the lines between Celeste's eyes deepen. "No, we've got time for that."

"Then why?"

"Haven't you ever heard of robbers?" She points at the green ceramic barrel on your dresser. "What do you think would happen if a robber broke into this house and found that?"

"I—I guess he'd take it."

"Duh. So tomorrow after school you're putting it in the bank where it will be safe."

"I can do that?"

"Of course, silly, why not?"

"I thought you had to be a certain age."

"Nope. Anyone can open a bank account. And when you do, you'll get interest." One thing about Celeste: she's smart. Right away she picks up on your silence. "Okay, here's the deal on interest. When your money is in the bank, not only is it safe, but it grows."

"The nickels and dimes get bigger?" you joke.

"When you give your money to the bank, they add a little more each day. It's not a lot, but at least it's something. Suppose they give you five percent interest. On five hundred dollars that's twenty-five extra dollars a year."

How is it that Celeste is totally helpless in math class but can figure out how banking works? Probably because she doesn't care about math class. Anyway, twenty-five dollars for doing nothing sure beats a long night of baby-sitting.

"You'll come with me, won't you?" you ask.

"I would, but remember that doctor's appointment I messed up? Tomorrow's the day I really go."

"Suppose I wait till the day after and then you come with me?" you ask as she pats blush onto your cheeks.

"The day after is Saturday," Celeste says. "Serious, Laur, it's easy. You ask for Mr. Hansen and tell him you're from school. He'll help you do everything."

You know she's right. You're too old to have a piggy bank. There's still one big question in your mind, but it feels too dumb to ask. Only Celeste is so smart it's almost like she can read your thoughts. "Okay, Laur, now what?"

"Promise you won't laugh?" you ask.

"I'll try."

"Well, you know my mom works during the after-noons and evenings? So she can't take me. So . . . I'm not exactly sure how . . . I'm supposed to get the money to the bank."

Celeste scowls. "Come again."

"I can't see myself getting on the bus with *that.*" You point at the piggy bank.

"Of course not. You put it in a bag or something." She goes over to your closet and starts to rummage through it. Not finding anything she likes, she puts her hands on her hips and looks around the room, tapping her foot. Finally, she focuses on your backpack. She picks it up and dumps out the books. "Here you go."

"You really think I can walk into the bank with a backpack filled with money?"

"Believe me, Laur, they'll take it any way they can get it." She drops your backpack on the floor and returns to the makeup table. "Now hold still, I'm going to try the mascara."

Celeste applies the mascara to your eyelashes. There is certainty and assurance in the way she handles the mascara stick. If there's one thing Celeste has a lot of, it's confidence. And gradually, as you spend more time with her, you are beginning to feel more confident, too. When you are around her, it just seems to go on like makeup.

"Ta-da!" She steps back and you see yourself in the mirror. Once again you look like you're twenty-five years old.

"What do you think?" she asks proudly.

You stare at the person in the mirror. It's weird how much older you look, but fun and exciting, too. It would be so cool if you could really be that person. Maybe Celeste is right. For dress-up day tomorrow you can. And Rob will see you. Celeste puts a CD on the boom box and pulls some blank sheets of paper off your desk. "Let's draw."

"Uh, okay." Another thing about Celeste—she's full of surprises. *Draw?* You've never seen her even doodle in her notebook. Still, a few moments later you two lay side by side on your stomachs on the floor with pencils, drawing and gossiping.

"Remember when Judy kidded Krista about a boy named Peter coming to the skating party?" Celeste goes. "I found out he used to be Krista's boyfriend . . . until he dumped her."

You feel your jaw fall. "Krista Rice has been dumped?"

"Hard to believe, right?"

"Try impossible."

"He goes to Portswell across town. They went together almost all of last year. Judy doesn't know why he dumped her, but Krista goes ballistic when anyone brings him up."

"Except Judy," you point out.

"There's not much Krista can do about that."

"What do you mean?"

Celeste leans close. "When Judy and I work on decorations for the party we talk about the way Krista tries to control everything. Keep everyone in their place, you know? Judy would love to see Krista get knocked down a few rungs. And to tell you the truth, so would I."

You are fascinated and thrilled. This is it! The secrets you've been dying to hear. The inside story. The juicy tidbits the A-list girls share only with one another. Celeste seems lost in thought for a moment.

"Know what?" she suddenly says. "You're right. It'll look really dumb if you walk into the bank and just dump a backpack full of money on a desk. They might even think *you* were a robber."

Huh? How did she go from secrets about Krista's love life back to money so fast? Who cares about the money? You want to hear more secrets.

"I think you should organize it," Celeste decides. "Like put all the bills in order and put all the coins in rolls."

"Rolls?"

"You know. The paper tubes the lunch ladies are always banging open into the cash registers."

"Oh, right."

"I'll get some for you tomorrow. Now let's practice our signatures."

"Why?"

"It's fun. Haven't you ever done it?"

"No."

"Look." Celeste signs her name once with regular-size letters and once with big loopy letters. "This is how I normally do it. But maybe I should do it this way. What do you think?"

You point at the loopy signature. "That looks like the way a movie star would do it."

"Cool. We're going to Hollywood, remember? Now how about yours?"

You sign your name the normal way, then try it with big loopy letters, too. You both spend another half an hour practicing different ways of signing your names. Meanwhile, Celeste tells you how the A-list girls really can't stand Stephanie, but they tolerate her not just because her dad throws those parties at Carmen's, but because Stephanie's house has a pool and a hot tub that are total boy magnets in the summer.

"I feel kind of bad for her," Celeste says. "I mean, deep inside she has to know."

Then it's time for Celeste to go. Once again she doesn't have money for a cab, but you don't mind lending her some. It's just so much fun having her around.

chapter
nineteen

"Mom, I can't wear this scarf to school."

"Come on, hon, have some fun. You could wear this pearl necklace doubled over like a choker. And let's try a little makeup."

"I can't, Mom."

"But it's dress-up day."

"Why did I open my big mouth and tell you?"

"I honestly don't understand you, Lauren. Who'll care?"

"The other girls."

"But they'll all be dressed up, too."

"I know. I'm sorry, Mom. I can't explain it."

In typical Lauren Walsh style you leave for school dressed as Ms. Totally Plain in your nicest skirt, blouse, and sweater. You're dressed up—for church. What happened to the confidence you felt yesterday? It seems to have left with Celeste. Half the kids at the bus stop are dressed up. A few have decided that *dress up* means "dress crazy." Rob shows up wearing a tie and jacket . . .

and a white clown face with a red nose and a bright orange clown wig.

"You look nice, Lauren," he says.

"Thanks, Rob. You look . . ." You almost say "ridiculous," but catch yourself just in time. "Uh, funny."

He grins. "Hey, I'm dressed up, aren't I?"

It's hard to believe that Rob, who is usually so reserved and preppy, would do something so outrageous. Isn't he worried about calling attention to himself? Doesn't it bother him that people might laugh at him?

Yours is the first stop so the bus is always empty when you get on. You settle into your seat and glance out the window to see if any late kids are running down the block.

"May I join you?" Clown Rob is standing in the aisle.

"Sure." You are, of course, surprised. He's never sat with you before.

"So let me guess," he says after he slides into the seat beside you. "You're supposed to be, uh . . . not a business woman. Not a college student . . . I know! A spy."

"How'd you guess?"

"Couldn't think of anything else."

The bus begins to bump along. You think of something and smile.

"What's so funny?" he asks.

"When I saw you dressed like that, I wondered why you weren't afraid that kids would laugh at you. Then I realized you're dressed like a clown! People are *supposed* to laugh at you."

"Like, duh."

"I know. It's just . . . Oh, forget it."

At the next stop more kids get on, including Shelby Kirk, a long-time member of the DYWYWM crowd, and the girl Rob defeated for class secretary. Shelby has bright red hair and blue eyes that lock on you and Rob sitting together. You feel yourself begin to blush, then realize Rob is looking at you, too.

"Seriously, Lauren," he says in a low voice, "why do you care so much about what other people think?"

You just shrug. "Don't *you* care?"

"Not really."

"Then why'd you run for class secretary?"

Rob's red clown lips widen until you see his small white teeth. "Because if you want to get a scholarship to a good college, it really helps to show that you're a well-rounded student who held an office in student government in high school. And if you want to get elected in high school, it helps to show you did a good job in middle school."

"So it's all about getting a college scholarship?" you ask.

"It's that or community college."

Hardly anyone you know really thinks much about college yet. But even at Woodville Middle School everyone knows the local community college is a joke unless you plan to be a computer technician, electrician, or beautician. Anyway, as far as caring what people think about you, maybe it's just that Rob is a boy and boys don't worry as much about things like that.

At school you expect Celeste to be waiting at your locker. So you're disappointed when she isn't there. You even dawdle in the hallway longer than usual, hoping that she will show up, but she doesn't. Finally, you go down the hall and peek into her homeroom, but she isn't there, either. That leaves only one other place—the girls' room.

You place a trembling hand against the girls' room door and push. Inside it's just as you imagined. In the perfumed mist the A-list girls are lined up at the mirrors, dressed in their fanciest clothes, busy fixing their makeup, and primping their hair. Right in the middle is Celeste, wearing the black low-cut top you loaned her and a black satin choker with a single pearl in the center.

As soon as they hear the door hinges squeak, everyone looks in your direction. An icy chill of fear freezes you, but no one frowns or wrinkles her nose. Most just go back to their makeup and hair.

Except Celeste, who winks first, *then* goes back to her hair.

Briiinnnggg! The bell rings and the girls' room starts to clear out. You leave with Celeste.

"We never got to do your makeup," she says as you walk together quickly down the hall to your homerooms.

"It's okay."

"You sure?" she asks.

"Totally."

"Oh, here." She digs into her bag and pulls out a handful of paper tubes for coins. They are all white, but some have thin green stripes, others red or yellow stripes. And they're different widths for different-size coins. "Looks like you'll be having fun this weekend."

"Yeah, right." You groan at the thought of counting all your coins and stuffing them into rolls.

"Doing any baby-sitting?"

"Three jobs. Tonight, tomorrow night, and Sunday afternoon."

"Busy girl. Okay, catch you later." She veers off. You're secretly relieved that she didn't insist on making you up. But you also wish she would have tried harder.

twenty

"You hear about Reed and Krista?" Tara asks at lunch.

You could have worn makeup. You could have dressed much cooler. After the way they all accepted you in the girls' room, you feel more certain than ever that you could be sitting at the DYWYWM table right now, wearing makeup because it's dress-up day, and sharing A-list gossip and secrets.

"Hello?" goes Tara. "Yoo-hoo. Earth to Lauren."

"Huh?"

"I asked if you heard about Reed and Krista."

"What about them?"

"I don't understand, Lauren. Now that you're popular, I thought you knew about *everything*."

"Give it a rest, Tara. What's the story?"

Chewing on one of her beef jerkies, Tara leans close. "Reed asked Jason to ask Stephanie if Krista would skate with him at the skating party."

"Oh, that."

Tara eyes you. "You *knew?*"

"Everybody knows Reed and Krista like each other."

"Oh, excu-u-use me." Tara crosses her arms and pretends to pout. "I thought it was fresh gossip."

Sometimes her sarcasm can be really annoying. It may be dress-up day, but she's wearing old jeans that are rubbed shiny on the thighs, and the white sweatshirt with the washed-out stains.

You finish lunch in silence. Celeste and some of the other A-list girls get up and go outside. Through the cafeteria windows you see that the sky is blue except for a few powder-puff clouds. Boys in shirtsleeves are throwing a football around. Girls in sweaters and unzipped jackets stand in groups talking. It's another unusually warm and sunny day for this time of year.

"Looks nice outside." You stand up.

Tara glances out the window and sees Celeste and the others. Then she gazes up at you. "Lauren?"

You freeze, expecting more sarcasm. "Yes?"

"You look nice."

"Thanks, Tara." The stress drains out of you. Tara's your friend. She wouldn't hurt your feelings on purpose. Maybe she told you that stuff about Krista and Reed because she wants to be in the crowd, too. Maybe she's simply afraid of losing you.

Outside, you spot Celeste standing beside a big tree with her back to you. The trunk is so wide that three kids can easily fit around it with their arms spread. When you're close enough to reach out and touch her, you realize she's talking to someone on the other side of the tree.

"You can't tell anyone I told you this," she's saying in a low voice. "But Krista's really hoping her old boyfriend, Peter, will skate with her."

"Peter Sandifer?" That's Jason Buckley's voice. "He goes to Portswell."

"That doesn't mean he can't come to the skating party," Celeste goes. "And I hear he's a really good skater."

"Yeah, he is," Jason says. "They skate against us in hockey. Think I should warn Reed?"

"I don't know," Celeste says. "I'm just telling you what I heard."

"I better let Reed know." Jason makes up his mind.

"Make sure you tell him it's only a rumor," goes Celeste. "I mean, even if it's true, just because Krista's *hoping* Peter will come doesn't mean he will."

"I know," Jason says. "But Reed would still want to know."

As he starts to come around the tree you duck around the other side. "Celeste?"

She turns, and looks surprised. "Oh, hi, Laur. What's up?"

"I heard what you just said to Jason. Didn't Krista say

that she never wants to talk to Peter again for as long as she lives?"

Celeste lowers her forehead and her eyes almost disappear behind her bangs. "Okay, I'm going to tell you something you can't tell anyone else, understand?"

"Yes."

"You're right. Krista's not waiting for Peter to ask her to the skating party. She's waiting for Reed to ask her."

"But you told Jason—"

"Wouldn't it be nice if just for once Krista didn't get what she wanted?" Celeste cuts in. "Wouldn't it be totally great if she got to the skating party and didn't have anyone to skate with?"

You don't know what to say. You're stunned that Celeste made up the story about Krista wanting Peter to take her to the skating party. Celeste puts her hands on her hips and leans toward you, dropping her voice. "Judy feels the same way I do. And so do a lot of the other girls. Only they're afraid to say so. Don't you get it, Laur? I did it for *you*. Aren't you tired of Krista deciding who's in and who's out? Don't you think it's time someone knocked her off her throne?"

"Yes, but—"

"Aren't you sick of her deciding who sits at *her* table? Like she owns it? I mean, who gave Krista Rice the right to rule the rest of us?"

It's as if she's read your innermost thoughts.

"It could be totally different, Laur. And not just for you. For everyone. Even Tara. Wouldn't it be great if we were all equal? If we all sat wherever we wanted and had whatever friends we wanted? If we completely got rid of all the stupid cliquey garbage?"

"But . . . *you're* popular."

"So?" Celeste frowns as if she doesn't understand. Then she gets it. "Oh, Laur, I like everyone. I don't care who's popular and who isn't. What I care about is that everyone is equal. Wouldn't that be great?"

"Absolutely."

"Well, that's what's going to happen. But *only* if you can keep a secret."

Now you understand. "And you want it to happen at the skating party because the whole grade will be there?"

"Can you think of a better place?" Celeste asks, smiling.

chapter
twenty-one

"So the skating party is next Friday, hon?"

"I can't wait."

"You should be proud. It was your idea and you made it happen. Is Tara going?"

"Probably not, Mom. She doesn't skate."

"But she's your best friend. And not everyone who goes skates, do they?"

"No."

"Don't you think you should see if you can get her to go?"

You spend the weekend baby-sitting, sorting and counting coins, and flattening out bills. At school on Monday you see Celeste.

"Ready to go to the bank after school?" she asks.

"Sure am . . . Only, don't banks close at three?"

"First National is open till five on Mondays. Also, I've been thinking. You know all those rolls of coins?"

"Do I ever." You groan at the memory of sorting, counting, and sealing them.

"You're probably better off turning them in to a teller first and getting bills. It'll just make everything easier."

"What would make it easier is if you came with me."

"Can't. Doctor's appointment, remember?"

"I thought you said it was Friday."

"Oh, right. I meant dentist."

At home after school you put the bills and rolls of coins into your backpack and climb on your bike. It feels so strange. On your bike you must look like any other kid with a backpack, but you're scared. What if some robber has X-ray vision and can see into your pack? What if you fall and all the money spills out? If only Celeste were with you.

Of course you ride all the way without being robbed or falling down. You get to the bank just as a blue-and-yellow town bus pulls away from a bus stop in front. Glancing in the windows you thought you caught a glimpse of maroon knit cap just like Celeste's.

A moment later, the bus is halfway down the block and you begin to wonder if you just have a bad case of Celeste on the brain.

Inside, the bank is set up like some kind of techno living room. To your left, a row of tellers sits behind a counter, but there are no Plexiglas windows to separate them from the public. In the center are some comfortable-looking gray chairs, a large television, and a few children's toys on an orange-and-pink rug on the floor. The bank officers sit at curving gray desks to the right.

Following Celeste's instructions, you go up to one of the tellers and turn in all the rolls of coins for bills. Then you go over to the desks where the officers sit.

A red-haired woman in a navy blue suit looks up from her desk. "Can I help you?"

"I'm here to see Mr. Hansen."

The woman turns her head toward another desk where a man with short gray hair sits speaking to another man who is mostly bald. Both wear dark suits, white shirts, and ties. The man with the short gray hair has bushy black eyebrows. "He's speaking to someone right now," the red-haired woman reports. "Please have a seat."

You sit down on one of the cushiony gray chairs. On the TV a woman is talking about the stock market. Charts and graphs fill the space behind her, and rows of mysterious letters and numbers crawl across the screen beneath her. It amazes you that there are television channels devoted twenty-four hours a day to money. Who could possibly care that much?

Back at the desk, both men rise and shake hands. The bald man leaves and the gray-haired man turns to you. "Can I help you?" He gestures to the chair where the bald man was just sitting and smiles reassuringly. "Please, have a seat. I'm Jay Hansen. Your name is?" He extends his hand.

"Lauren Walsh." You shake his hand.

"Pleased to meet you, Lauren."

You sit down. The seat feels warm. "Well, I go to Woodville and—"

"Oh, yes. Carol told me you'd be coming in. The new school treasurer."

"Right. Anyway I want to put some money in the bank."

"Excellent. Is this your first time here?"

You nod.

"Well, it's very simple." Mr. Hansen pulls open a desk drawer and takes out a slip of paper. "We'll fill out this deposit slip and then you'll take it over to the teller." He turns to his computer and begins to type. "Now let's see the number on the class account."

"It's not for the class account."

Mr. Hansen stops typing. "Sorry?"

"I want to start my own account."

"Oh." He smiles. "We can do that, too." He opens his desk drawer again and takes out a letter-size form, then tells you about the kinds of savings accounts you can have. You pick the one that sounds the best, and then sign the form. Once again he reaches for the deposit slip. "And how much would you like to deposit?"

"Four hundred and twenty-eight dollars."

Mr. Hansen's eyes widen and his black eyebrows rise. "Wow, that's a lot for a young lady like you."

"It's from years of baby-sitting." You open your back-pack and take out the neatly stacked bills.

"You must be one very busy young lady."

"I guess."

"Well, it's good. Someday there'll be something you'll really want and you'll be glad you saved."

It's funny that he says that. You know what you want, but it's not something money can buy.

chapter
twenty-two

"It's late. Shouldn't you go to bed?"

"Soon as I finish, Mom."

"More posters?"

"For the skating party."

"Hon, isn't this last year's Spanish book?"

"Oh, yeah. My friend Celeste left it here by accident."

"This homework has her name, but it looks like your handwriting."

"Oh, I, er, just helped her with it."

"You're sure you didn't do it for her?"

"Mom!"

Four days until the skating party. Halfway through English, the last period of the day, the loudspeaker crackles. "Lauren Walsh and Celeste Van Warner, please come to the office right away."

Everyone stares at you. It's unusual for Principal Hansen to call kids down to her office in the middle of class. Out in the hall you see Celeste step out of a class-room a few doors down.

"What's going on?" you ask.

"You got me." Celeste shrugs, then starts to bite one of her fingernails. "Probably something to do with the skating party. Have you decided if you're going to wear your skating outfit?"

"I still can't decide." Together you start down the hall.

"I really think you'll look great in it, Laur."

"You don't think it'll look a little corny?" you ask. "I just know everyone else will be wearing jeans and sweaters."

"It'll make you look unique," Celeste answers. "Besides, when they see how good you skate they'll understand."

"Thanks, you always know how to make me feel good."

Celeste laughs. "Believe me, Laur, you're easy."

You get to the main office.

"Go right in, girls." The secretary points at the door to Principal Hansen's private office. Inside, Principal Hansen is sitting at her desk, a pen in one hand, looking down at some papers. Two buttons on her phone blink, but she hasn't taken either call. She looks up. "Have a seat, girls."

No smile. No "hello." Celeste gives you a puzzled glance as you both sit down in the chairs facing the desk.

"I just received a call from Dick Johnson, the owner of the skating rink," Principal Hansen says. "Are you aware that he hasn't gotten the money for the party yet?"

"We're going to the bank today to get the money," Celeste says.

Principal Hansen cups her hands on the desk in front of her. "I'm confused, girls. According to my husband, you closed the class account a week ago Monday."

"Closed the account? What does that mean?" Celeste asks.

Principal Hansen raises a carefully tweezed eyebrow. "When you close an account, it means you take out all the money."

"But—we didn't," you sputter.

"I didn't," says Celeste.

Principal Hansen's thin crescent eyebrows dip in toward each other. "Well, someone did. And without that money you can't pay the skating rink and there can't be a skating party."

A fog of numb shock envelops you. Something's wrong.

"Can't we find out who took the money?" Celeste asks.

"We'll have to," Principal Hansen replies. "Until now I assumed it was you two, but you say you didn't."

A flashing red warning light slashes through the fog around you. It's something in her voice. Something that suspects this isn't just about some missing money.

"Both of you go back to class," Principal Hansen says. "I'll let you know if I find out anything else."

Back out in the hall, Celeste says, "I don't get it."

"Neither do I," you agree. "I hope it's just the bank's mistake. I remember my mom once saying they accidentally put a bunch of money that belonged to someone else in her account."

"It *better* be the bank's mistake," Celeste says grimly. "Because you know what's going to happen if they can't find that money?"

"You don't think we'd *really* have to cancel the party, do you?"

"What choice would we have?" Celeste answers. "If there's no money, we can't rent the skating rink."

twenty-three

The next morning you go straight to the office when school starts. Principal Hansen is standing at the counter reading through some papers. When she looks up and sees you, her eyebrows tilt down and almost touch. Like a bird with wide, arcing wings.

"Did you find out about the money?" you ask.

"It's not even nine o'clock, Lauren. The bank hasn't opened yet."

"Oh." You didn't think of that.

"Get along to your class," Principal Hansen says.

"Would you tell me as soon as you hear anything?" you beg.

"Yes, Lauren, I certainly will."

For the next few periods, you can't concentrate in class. All you can think about is how the party just can't be canceled. Now that you know Celeste's plan, it has to happen! And not just for you, but also for everyone who's ever been scorned by Krista and the other A-list girls.

No matter where your next class is, you make a point of going past the office in the hope that Principal Hansen will see you and have some news. She sees you twice, but both times just gives you a funny scowl and shakes her head.

Right before lunch Principal Hansen's expression changes. When she sees you in the hall she waves you into the office.

"Let's go into my room," she says, gesturing down the short narrow hall inside the main office. You go in and sit in the same chair you sat in the day before. Principal Hansen sits down on the other side of the desk. Interlacing her fingers, she leans forward on both elbows. "My husband just called. He found the withdrawal slip that was used to close the account. It has both your name and Celeste's on it."

"That's not possible!" you gasp. "I didn't sign any withdrawal slips and Celeste couldn't have done it without me."

"There's always the unfortunate possibility that someone forged your signatures," Principal Hansen says.

"But if they did that and took the money, it's not our fault."

"The money's still gone, Lauren. And without it, Mr. Johnson won't let you have the party."

From Principal Hansen's office you go straight to the cafeteria. It's lunchtime now and Celeste is sitting at the

DYWYWM table, chatting happily with the other girls as if she doesn't have a care in the world. You touch her on the shoulder and whisper in her ear. "We have to talk."

The conversation stops. Everyone looks at you. You feel a shiver of self-consciousness and wish you weren't doing this. But what's really strange is that you are doing it—standing right there in front of all the A-list girls, and interrupting them. And that's something you never could have done before.

"Talk about what?" Celeste asks.

"You *know.*"

Celeste makes sure everyone sees her frown as she gets up. Why is she acting as if she has no idea what this is about? You both step away from the table to get some privacy.

"You won't believe this," you whisper. "Principal Hansen spoke to her husband. Someone forged our names on the withdrawal slip and took the money."

Celeste puts her hand on your shoulder. "Oh, Laur, that's totally not fair."

Tears unexpectedly flood into your eyes, and you quickly turn away and start out of the cafeteria. The last thing in the world you want is to let the A-list table see you cry. On the way past the land of the socially inferior, you catch a glimpse of Tara sitting alone at your usual table. She gives you a concerned look and places her hands flat on the table, as if to get up. You shake your head and gesture for her not to follow. Out in the hallway you lean against a cold tile wall, press your face into your hands, and let the tears spill out.

Celeste comes out into the hall. "Laur?"

"It's not fair," you sob, wiping the tears from your cheeks.

She gives you a hug. "You're right. It was going to be your night. More than anyone else's, your star was going to shine."

"I'll do anything to go to that party. *Anything!*"

"But there's nothing you can do . . . unless you want to pay for it yourself."

You pull back and stare at her through watery eyes. She's right! It would be that easy! "Then that's what we'll do," you announce, straightening up with determination. "I've got the money in my account. We'll use it to pay for the party."

Celeste raises her hands as if to stop you. "Wait, Laur, I wasn't serious. There's no way you're going to use the money you worked so hard for to pay for the stupid skating party."

"All I'll do is *lend* the money," you explain. "Then, when this whole thing is straightened out, I'll get it back." You grab her hand and pull. "Come on, let's go tell Principal Hansen that's what we're going to do."

"Whoa." Celeste pulls back and doesn't budge. "I don't know if I want to go see her so fast, Laur. I kind of feel like a jerk. I mean, we took this job and she gave us that lecture about responsibility and the first thing we did was blow it big time."

"But it's not our fault."

"I know, but . . . look, let's think for a second. Who else do we know? I mean, maybe someone whose parents would have the money."

"Krista?"

"Oh, right." Celeste rolls her eyes. "We get her to put up the money and then she goes to the party and we shoot her down. That's really nice."

"What about Stephanie?"

"I couldn't ask her," Celeste says. "Could you?"

"No. What about your parents?"

"Forget it. I'm already in trouble for the credit-card bill I ran up this month. What about your mom?"

"No way."

Celeste crosses her arms and gazes off down the hall. "There has to be someone."

"There is. Me. And I just remembered something else Principal Hansen said. Mr. Johnson has to have the money *tomorrow*. Face it, Celeste. We don't have the time to figure out where else to get the money. I have it, and all we have to do is go to the bank after school and take it out of my account and give it to him."

Celeste places her hands on your shoulders again, and looks straight into your eyes. "Know what, Laur? You are a really good person to even *volunteer* to do that. An *incredibly* good person. But I still don't want you to do it. Let's wait and think. I bet before school is over we'll come up with another way to save the party."

"Don't be so sure," you warn her.

"Let's just think about it, okay?" she asks. "We'll meet at your locker at the end of school and see if we haven't come up with a better idea."

"Sure," you answer. "Whatever."

chapter
twenty-four

At the end of school you meet Celeste at your locker. "Think of anything?"

She purses her lips and shakes her head, frustrated. "Have you?"

"The only thing I can think of is using my money. Really, Celeste, it's okay. I'm sure the bank will find the school's money, and when they do, we'll just pay me back with it."

"I still don't like it," she argues.

"Look, Celeste, I really don't want the skating party to get canceled, okay? It's really, really important to me. So you're just going to do this with me and not argue." It's hard to believe that you spoke those words so firmly and with such assurance. But for once you are sure, and completely confident that you're doing the right thing.

Celeste hesitates. She's still unsure. Somehow that makes you feel even more certain that this is the right thing to do. "Come on, we have to go to the bank." You take her hand. "Now."

But she pulls her hand out of yours. "I can't, Laur. I promised my mom I'd help her with some Christmas shopping."

"Why don't you call her and tell her to meet us at the mall after we drop the money off at the skating rink?"

"Uh, she wants to go someplace else." Celeste seems suddenly distracted. Her eyes dart this way and that and you sense she's thinking about other things.

"You okay?" you ask.

"Huh? Oh, yeah."

"What about tomorrow?" you ask.

"We're going to go shopping tomorrow, too," she answers. She wants to leave. You know you should let her, but it's hard to let go.

"Want to come over after school on Friday and help me get ready for the party?" you ask.

"Yeah, definitely," Celeste says. "Let's do that."

"Great, see you then." You watch her go off down the hall, and then you head for the bank. You get there just before closing time and withdraw the three hundred dollars out of your account. From there you go to the skating rink and give it to Mr. Johnson.

There. It's done, and you did it all by yourself. Outside the skating rink, the afternoon sky is graying toward evening, and people are bundled in coats, hats, and scarves. The wind has picked up and their scarves flap behind them as they walk. A white paper cup skitters along the road. You feel so good you decide to walk home despite the cold and the wind and the approaching darkness. Nothing's going to stop the skating party now.

chapter
twenty-five

For the past few weeks you have bought a school lunch every day. It is costly, considering it means pitching the lunch your mother makes for you and then paying for the new lunch yourself. But it's worth it. Only today there's no point in buying a whole lunch. You barely have an appetite. Tonight is the skating party and you're so excited you could get away without eating anything. But you get in line for some fries just because you're afraid you'll be hungry later.

Someone taps you on the shoulder and you turn to find Krista and Rob.

"Everything ready for tonight?" Krista asks.

"Oh, yeah." You feel a strange pang of guilt. Krista was once your friend and now you are planning to do something mean to her. Even if she'd never been your friend, is it ever right to be mean to anyone?

"Can't wait to check out those video games," Rob chimes in.

You force a smile on your face and move closer to the food counter.

"You've done a great job, Lauren," Krista says, then lowers her voice. "And everyone knows you did most of the work."

"Oh, that's not true," you answer. "Just wait till you see the decorations."

Krista doesn't say anything. You go up to the counter and get your fries. "Well, see you later."

"Wait, Lauren," Krista says. "Why don't you ever sit with us?"

You know you heard her clearly, but you still can't believe your ears. "Oh, well, I'd love to, but, you know—" You tilt your head toward the land of the socially inferior— "Tara."

"She can sit with us, too," Krista goes.

This results in temporary brain freeze. You're totally not sure what to make of it. It is so out of the blue. So not the way you thought things were. You look over at the DYWYWM table. It is already crowded with girls. Celeste and Judy are shoulder to shoulder, their heads tilted toward each other, talking. "Doesn't look like there's room."

Krista nods. "But another time, okay?"

"Sure. Thanks."

On dazed autopilot you head for the table where

Tara sits. What just happened? What does it mean? Is it possible that Krista knows Celeste is up to something and is being nice to you to find out what it is? Or, is it possible that Krista is just plain being nice?

"What did Krista want?" Tara asks as you join her.

"Just making sure everything's ready for tonight."

"Bet you'll get brownie points for this," Tara quips.

You force a weak smile. Suddenly you're uncertain. Now that Krista's being nice to you, you don't know what you'll get. "Sure you don't want to come tonight?" Given how confused you are, it would be nice if Tara were around to help you think straight.

"Thanks, but I'd rather watch dust balls grow under my couch."

Lunch ends and you really need to speak to Celeste, but she leaves the cafeteria still talking to Judy. As the day continues, you look for her in the hall between classes. Finally, when school ends, you wait for her at her locker. You spot her with Judy, but the hall is crowded and they don't see you yet.

"I'll go home and get the streamers and tablecloths," Judy's saying. "When's your mom taking you to get the balloons?"

"Soon as I get home," Celeste replies.

Not expecting to hear this, you blurt, "Celeste?"

She looks up, surprised to see you. "Oh, hey, Laur."

"I thought. . ." You don't want to continue while Judy's there.

Celeste gives you a puzzled look. Then her jaw drops as if she's just remembered why you're waiting by her locker. "Oh, uh, I just have a couple of things to do first for the party. So I'll come over to your house later, okay?"

"Okay." You're a little disappointed, but you wouldn't say anything in front of Judy. Meanwhile, the pace in the hall begins to pick up as kids head toward the bus circle.

"Lauren, I hear you're a really good skater," Judy says with a sincere smile.

"I'm okay."

"Guess we'll see tonight," she says.

"I guess."

"Oh, Judy, there's something else I forgot." Celeste pulls the focus back to herself. It's odd, the way she needs Judy's full attention, but you don't have time to dwell on it. Lockers are slamming shut and kids are starting to run. If you don't hurry, you're going to miss your bus.

"See you later!" you call to Celeste as you start down the hall. If she answers you, you don't hear it.

twenty-six

"Aren't you late for the party, hon?"

"I guess."

"Who do you keep trying to call? What's wrong?"

"Nothing, Mom."

"Come on, hon. You should be excited. This is your big night. Do you know what you want to wear?"

"The turquoise outfit."

"I have some eye shadow that would go great with it."

"I don't know, Mom."

"Come on, I see all the girls your age wearing makeup. You don't have to wear a lot. Just enough to bring out your features. This would be the perfect night for it."

"Oh, okay."

"That a girl."

You're almost finished getting ready when the phone rings. You quickly reach for the receiver. *It must be Celeste calling to explain why she couldn't come to your house to help you get ready.*

"Hello?"

"Hey." It's Tara.

"Oh, hi."

"Who were you expecting to call?" She's so quick.

"Doesn't matter."

"Getting ready?"

"Trying. I'm already late."

"What time does it start?"

"Like fifteen minutes ago. Why? Are you thinking about going?"

"Dream on."

"Then?"

"I just wanted to wish you good luck. I hope you have a good time tonight."

"Oh, Tara, you're so sweet. Seriously, why don't you come?"

"And miss a rerun of *Star Trek: Insurrection*? Have you lost your mind?"

"I guess."

"I want a full report, okay?"

"On what?" you ask. "I thought you didn't care."

"Oh, yeah. Almost forgot. So just let me know how it goes, okay? For you."

"You got it." You hang up.

"Ready, hon?" Mom calls from the front door.

"Just a second!" You hurry back to your room to get your skates. The light is off and when you switch it on, you catch your reflection in the makeup table mirror—a girl in a turquoise skating outfit, her hair in a French braid, a touch of makeup. You stand motionless, knowing you'll be the only girl at the party tonight in an outfit like this. The rest of the kids will be wearing jeans and sweaters. Suddenly you feel an intense urge to get out of this costume and into clothes that will make you look like everyone else. Clothes that will let you blend in and be like everyone else. You know this urge is driven by fear. Fear that you will walk into the party and people will point at you behind your back and say mean things. You reach behind your neck and start to unzip the outfit.

Then you stop.

Why do you have to be like everyone else?

Why do you have to look like everyone else?

That's all you've been doing for years, and it hasn't changed a thing. What makes you think you're so important that anyone would even care what you wore? And so what if they say mean things behind your back? You don't have to wear this skating outfit to get them to do that. And why would you want mean girls for friends anyway? Tara may be heavy, and she may wear yucky clothes, but she's a good person and close friend and she's not afraid to say nice things.

"Hon?" your mom calls through the house. "By the time you get there you'll be half an hour late."

You go to your closet and get the skates, but on the way out you stop and look at the girl in the mirror again. You feel a smile creep onto your lips. Suppose they do point? Suppose they do say mean things behind your back? At least they'll notice you.

twenty-seven

You get to the ice rink and hurry into the concession and rental room. The tangy aroma of hot dogs mixes with the heavy scent of damp wool. Ice-skate blades click against the floor as groups of chattering kids bang through the swinging doors from the ice rink and head for the food stand. *Whizz-bang!* sounds burst from the video games lining the hall just past the rental stand. Rob is bent over one of the machines, his face illuminated by the yellows, reds, and blues flashing off the screen. You're tempted to go say hello, to let him see you wearing makeup and your turquoise skating outfit, but the pull of the scene out on the ice is much greater right now. You sit down on a wooden bench and start to lace up your skates. You're dying to see if Celeste's "plot" has worked.

Before you finish lacing, the double doors to the ice rink swing open and Krista clamps through on her skates. She's wearing the most adorable pink-and-white snowflake Polartec jacket, jeans, and white skates that look so new you suspect she bought them just for this party. But her face is blotched red and streaked with tears as she heads directly for the girls' room. The ice rink doors swing open again and Stephanie Eisley follows, walking on her skates. Not crying herself. Definitely following Krista to lend support. You're sure neither of them noticed you.

This can only mean one thing: *Celeste's plan worked!* The DYWYWM crowd has been torn apart! You race to lace up the other skate, impatient that your fingers can't move any faster. Then you're up on your feet, clumping as fast as you can toward the swinging doors.

You push through. The loud music invades your ears and that first blast of cold air slaps your face. The left side of the rink is all little kids and parents, but on the other side of the bright orange cones is your grade. Skating in a slow circle around the perimeter, laughing, falling, standing around in groups on the inside ice, gabbing.

You eagerly look around for Celeste and spot her out on the ice. The sight stops you cold. Celeste is wearing the most gorgeous and sexy pink skating outfit with spaghetti straps, a handkerchief front skirt, mesh midriff, and flesh-colored tights. Where did she get that outfit? How? Why is she wearing it?

It takes a moment to shake off your surprise. Then you get it. Celeste is wearing that outfit so that you won't be the only one in a skating dress. It's her way of making sure you won't be singled out and scorned.

You feel a wave of warm relief, and a smile creeps onto your face. Celeste is standing on the ice with Shelby Kirk. From the way Celeste's ankles bend in and her knees wobble and she holds out her hands for balance, you can see that she's hardly ever been on skates before.

You step onto the ice and glide effortlessly. Skating to you is as natural as breathing. You head toward Celeste and Shelby.

But before you reach them, Reed Palmer and Jason Buckley cut across the ice and get there first. Jason stops beside Shelby, and Reed circles around behind Celeste, taking her by the elbow to help steady her. You feel a strange chill. It's the unexpectedly relaxed way that Reed holds Celeste's arm, and the way she allows him. As if this isn't the first time they've touched. Or even the sixth.

Something tells you to make a quick detour into the crowd of slowly circling skaters. You weave through the crowd and watch the two couples on the middle ice. Even with Reed there for support, Celeste can hardly keep her skates from sliding out from beneath her. Reed is busy trying to keep her from falling. Laughing and crying out in fake fear, she throws an arm around his neck and hangs on to him.

No wonder Krista ran into the girls' room crying.

The four of them stay in the middle of the ice and talk and laugh as if they're the only ones there. As if it's the DYWYWM table moved to the rink. You repeatedly catch Celeste's eye, but she only looks away and doesn't wave. Why is she ignoring you?

Finally, you give up and get off the ice. You stand by the skating rink rail feeling miserable and confused. Is Celeste so swept away by Reed that she's forgotten the plan? Or has she been plotting this all along? You can't help thinking back to that day by the big tree, overhearing her tell that lie to Jason about Krista wanting Peter Sandifer to come to the skating party.

Out on the ice the two couples begin to skate. Celeste with Reed practically holding her up. Shelby and Jason. As they join the counterclockwise flow of skaters, they pass the rail where you're standing. You give Celeste a little wave. She looks away and smiles warmly at Reed.

You feel a heavy sensation on your shoulders. Sadness. Anger. Regret. It's obvious now, isn't it? You were fooled. It was never about everyone becoming equal. It was only about Celeste replacing Krista as queen of the DYWYWM girls. Oddly, you're not taken entirely by surprise. It's as if somewhere deep inside you had a feeling this might be the case. The lies Celeste told. Her not showing up at your house earlier tonight. You just didn't want to see the signs. Now you have no choice.

The four of them circle around and pass you again. Celeste still refuses to look in your direction, and you start to feel useless and silly just standing there by the rail. You're dying to go out and skate, but you don't want to skate alone.

The endless circle of kids in pairs, threesomes, and quartets skates past you. The music plays amid laughter and shouts. Everyone seems happy, and despite the hurt of Celeste's betrayal, you do feel an unexpected sense of pride and accomplishment. The party was your idea, and thanks to you it has happened.

The kids who aren't skating sit on benches or walk around outside the rail. Out of the corner of your eye you see Rob with a group of his friends. He glances in your direction. You smile and he smiles back. You turn and look back at the skaters again, praying hard that he'll decide to come over and talk.

Nothing happens. After a few more moments, you look in his direction again, but he and his friends have gone. You let out a deep disappointed sigh. Celeste is still totally focused on Reed. Except for the dethroning of Krista, the world of the A-list girls is still intact. Nothing's going to change tonight. No magic wand or surprise prince will turn you into Cinderella. You might as well go home.

You go back through the concession and rental room, take off your skates, and get your coat. You call a cab from the pay phone, and step outside into the dark. A fine, cold, wet mist floats down through the outdoor lights. Your breath comes out in a damp cloud of white. Someone is standing in a shadow to your right, staying under an overhang to keep out of the drizzle. This person sees you, too, and backs deeper into the shadow as if not wanting to be recognized. But it's too late. You know it's Krista. She must be waiting for a ride, too.

Here you both stand, separated by the cold mist that glitters in the light. How strange. In a way you're both leaving the skating party for the same reason—because of Celeste. Can you go over and talk to Krista? Why can't she come over and talk to you?

It's odd, but you feel bad for her. Maybe because you also know how it feels to be tricked and used. But could you say that to her? Would she ever admit it? Maybe she's not in the mood to talk. Maybe you're not either.

She steps out of the shadow and looks straight at you. "Do you need a ride, Lauren?"

Caught by surprise, you hardly know what to say. "It's . . . in the other direction."

Krista smiles ever so slightly. Ever so sadly. "I know where you live, silly."

And she does, of course, because she used to live across the street.

"I'm kind of waiting for a cab," you explain.

Krista pulls a small black phone out of her bag. "I can tell them not to come."

"Well, then sure, thanks. That's really nice of you."

Krista calls the taxi company and informs them that you no longer need the cab. You cannot help being a little in awe of how mature and confident she sounds when speaking to that unseen grown-up at the cab company switchboard. Then she turns off the phone and drops it back into her bag. Once again you look at each other. The wet mist is cool and chilly against your face. It collects on the roof and drips off the eaves to the ground.

"Remember weeks ago you told me to be careful with Celeste?" you ask. "That something wasn't right with her? How did you know?"

Krista shrugs. "It was just a feeling."

"Then why were you friendly to her?"

The soft lines around Krista's mouth deepen slightly. As if the answer is painfully obvious. "I had no choice."

"I . . . I don't get it," you admit.

"Celeste was going to be popular whether I liked it or not. Everyone knew it the second they saw her."

"So you had to be her friend?" you realize.

The little smile on Krista's lips is wrinkled and bitter, like a crabapple. "Stupid, isn't it?"

A large dark car coated with a dull film of moisture pulls up and Krista steps completely out of the shadow. You also start toward the car. Just then, someone behind you says, "Lauren?"

You turn to find Rob standing in the doorway of the skating rink, backlit by the lights from inside. His hands jammed into his pockets, he asks, "You're not going home, are you?"

You don't know how to answer.

"I, uh, thought maybe you'd like to stay and do something," he says.

You look back at Krista, waiting by the car. Won't she be angry? But she smiles. "What are you waiting for? Go, girl."

"But . . ."

Krista waves at you. "We'll talk, okay? Later." She gets into the car and pulls the door closed.

You turn back toward Rob. "That's a really nice-looking outfit, Lauren."

"Thank you, Rob." Maybe something *has* changed after all.

chapter
twenty-eight

Back inside, Rob waits while you hang up your coat again. "So, want to play some video games?"

"Why don't we skate?" you ask.

"Uh, because I'm the worst skater ever?" He grins.

"Worse than me at video games?" You grin back.

"How about, first we play some video games, then we skate?"

"Sounds like a plan."

You prove to be as bad at video games as you promised, and it's not long before Rob agrees to go skating.

"You weren't that bad for a beginner," he says while he laces up his scuffed black rental skates.

"Then how come I used up four times as many tokens as you?" you ask.

"Don't worry, it will all even out on the ice."

You soon see that Rob wasn't joking about not being a good skater. He might be even worse than Celeste. Once you're on the ice, it's not a question of trying to hold him up. He clings to the rail and refuses to let go.

"You won't learn to skate if you don't let go," you tell him.

"I won't learn if I do let go," he answers. "All I'll do is learn to fall."

"What are you afraid of?" You laugh.

"How about breaking every bone in my body?"

"I've fallen a million times. It doesn't hurt as much as you think."

"Yeah, right." Rob rolls his eyes as if to let you know he thinks you're certifiably insane.

In one of the boldest moves you've ever made, you slide your arm through his. "Okay, look. I promise one of two things will happen. Either you won't fall, or I'll fall with you."

Rob finally lets go and you help him around the rink. His skates keep slipping out from under him and you almost do fall several times. But at least it's late and most of the kids have stopped skating. Few are around to witness what clods you are together. Each time the double doors swing open, you catch a glimpse of Celeste, Reed, Shelby, and Jason in the snack bar. It makes you feel bad.

So you try not to look.

Finally, Rob actually does begin to skate a little.

And you forget to look.

Then the skating rink lights blink on and off and a voice on the loudspeaker announces that the rink is closing for the night. You realize that you and Rob are just about the only ones left on the ice.

"Aw, darn," Rob complains. "I was just getting ready to do a triple axel into a quadruple toeloop."

"Guess you'll just have to wait until next time."

He grins. "That was fun, Lauren. Thanks for teaching me."

"No prob."

You leave the ice together. And clop on your skates into the snack bar/rental area. Hardly anyone's around. Celeste and the others are gone. The music has been turned off. It's quiet. In the snack bar they're scraping the grill and washing out the fryers.

You and Rob quietly untie your skates. "Guess it really is time to go," Rob says after he returns his skates to the rental counter. "You need a ride?"

"Okay, thanks."

Rob calls his parents and a little while later Mr. Carlucci arrives. You and Rob sit together in the back. Mr. Carlucci asks if you had fun and you both say yes, but aside from that, most of the ride home is quiet. At your house, Rob hops out and holds the door open for you. You step out into the night. The neighborhood is quiet. The houses are dark and the air is chilly. The street is still glistening wet, but the mist has passed, and between the dark shadows of clouds the sky is filled with twinkling stars. Rob walks with you to your front door and you actually feel nervous that he may try to kiss you. But he wouldn't with his father watching from the car, would he?

"That was fun," he says, standing near you while you unlock your front door.

"Yes."

He shoves his hands into his pockets. "So, uh, see you in school Monday?"

"Where else?"

"Yeah." He shrugs. "Guess you're right."

You get the door open and turn to him. "Thanks, Rob." And then, in an impulse that comes from you don't know where, you lean forward and kiss him on the cheek.

chapter
twenty-nine

"You must have gotten in awful late last night, hon."

"Pretty late."

"Have fun?" (Why must every adult ask this? you wonder.)

"Of course."

And it's strange because it was both the best and worst night of your life, and you're still really not sure how you feel. Rob is nice, and he's the first boy who's ever really paid any attention to you. But every time you think of Celeste, you feel like crying.

The weekend passes slowly. You do homework, watch TV, and baby-sit. Hardly a minute passes that you don't think of picking up the phone and calling Celeste. You want to ask her why she led you along, why she lied to you. Why'd she even bother with you?

You are proud that you manage not to call her. What would be the point? No matter what she said you probably wouldn't believe her. The few times the phone rings, you let your mom answer it. You're slightly afraid it will be Celeste with a new story, a new explanation, a new lie.

"Hon, it's for you," Mom says around eight o'clock on Sunday night after she answers the phone.

"Who is it?" you ask warily.

"A boy."

You pick up. "Hello?"

"Hi." It's Rob. "So what's up?"

"Just doing homework. You?"

"Same." And it's obvious that he really has no reason for calling. Except to talk.

thirty

At school on Monday morning, you don't even look for Celeste in the hall. It's strange, but you feel a different kind of confidence. The confidence not to need her anymore.

You've barely gotten seated in Spanish class when you're called down to the office. You can't imagine what the problem is this time. After all, you've already paid for the skating party. As you reach the office, you're surprised to find Celeste coming out and into the hallway. That's strange because you didn't hear any announcement calling her down to see the principal.

Neither of you smiles or says anything about the skating party.

"What's going on?" you ask.

Celeste tips her head down and her eyes practically vanish behind her bangs. "You better go in. There's still some kind of problem."

For a moment neither of you moves. You just look at each other. You're dying to tell her that she's a liar and a phony, but you know it won't change anything. Besides, you never say things like that. You're always too scared. You'll just stand there and let Celeste think she's won Reed for herself and taken over Queen Krista's throne. You doubt anyone will ever be able to sink her ship.

Celeste turns to go, but as she does, you feel your lips begin to move as if they have a mind of their own. "Have fun at the skating party?"

Celeste stops and slowly turns back to you. She parts her bangs with a finger and her eyes narrow. You catch a glimpse of something you never saw in her before. Something fierce and determined. Something that knows it must fight and win to survive. "You wouldn't understand."

"I think I might."

Then, unexpectedly, Celeste's lips twist into a hard little smile. "You'd better go in. Principal Hansen is waiting."

In her office Principal Hansen has a stern look on her face. The eyebrows dip. She taps the eraser end of a black pencil against a manila folder on her desk. "Have a seat, Lauren."

You feel a deep and uncomfortable chill. Goose bumps rise on your skin and your heart begins to bang. Either the air just became really heavy or you're suddenly having trouble breathing. Principal Hansen opens the manila folder. Inside are photocopies of deposit and withdrawal slips.

"I have some very disturbing news, Lauren," she says. "It appears that on the same day the class account was closed, you opened a bank account and deposited a large amount of money."

It takes a moment to understand what she is implying. "But . . . that was my money."

"What does that mean to you?" Principal Hansen asks.

"It means I earned it. Every penny. It took almost two years."

"How?"

"Baby-sitting."

Principal Hansen slides one of the sheets of paper toward you. "Then why did you withdraw the money from your account and use it to pay for the skating party?"

You stare down at the sheet of paper. It's a photocopy of the withdrawal slip you filled out to get the money for the party.

"Because the party was going to be canceled if I didn't," you explain.

"Why would you use your hard-earned money for that?" Principal Hansen asks. "It was just a class party."

You stare at her dumfounded. How can you explain what that party was supposed to mean? What Celeste promised it would mean? Now Principal Hansen slides a second sheet of paper toward you.

"Do you recognize this?" she asks.

It's a photocopy of a withdrawal slip taking $517 out of the class bank account. There are two signatures on it. Yours and Celeste's.

"I . . . I never saw this before in my life."

Principal Hansen places the two sheets of paper next to each other. "Look at the two withdrawal slips. Your signature is almost identical on both. Now look at Celeste's signature on the withdrawal slip and this copy of her signature that I just asked her to sign."

Principal Hansen slides a third piece of paper toward me. On it is Celeste's signature.

"Celeste Van Warner was just here," Principal Hansen explains. "I asked her to sign her name on this piece of paper. If you compare this signature to the signature on the withdrawal slip, does it look familiar?

The two signatures look vaguely similar. But the one on the withdrawal slip is rougher, as if a child scrawled it.

You look up and straight into Principal Hansen's eyes.

"Do you want to change your story?" she asks.

"Absolutely not. I never saw that withdrawal slip before in my life. Whoever did it must have forged my signature."

Principal Hansen presses her lips together and looks disappointed. It's obvious that she doesn't believe you.

"On each withdrawal slip *your* signature looks very similar," she says. "The only signature that looks forged is Celeste's."

Your stomach tightens and you start to feel sick. Everything has been turned inside out. If anything, you thought you would have been a hero for replacing the missing class money with your own. Instead you're being accused of stealing the money in the first place!

"Celeste just told me that you came to her and admitted that you took the skating money," Principal Hansen says.

You feel your jaw go slack and your whole body go weak. As if every drop of blood just drained out. "That's not true . . ." Your voice cracks and comes out like a whimper.

"Celeste says she encouraged you to take the money out of your account and use it to pay for the skating party."

"No," you whisper.

Principal Hansen points at the deposit and withdrawal slips. "Then how do you explain this?"

You remember the afternoon Celeste came to your house and put makeup on you, and how much fun you had . . . and how she insisted on practicing signatures. Even then she had it all planned. You gaze across the desk at your principal. "You'd never believe me."

Principal Hansen leans back in her chair and stares at you. Having done nothing to be ashamed about, you look right back at her. But you can feel tears welling up and spilling out of your eyes. Only they're stupid tears. Tears that spring up for the wrong reason.

Principal Hansen lets out a long, deep breath. "Maybe I won't believe you, but I want you to tell me."

So you tell her the whole story. How Celeste became your friend and made you feel better about yourself than you ever imagined you could feel. How thanks to her you did things you never thought you'd do, wore clothes you never thought you'd wear, and made friends you never thought you'd make. How you gained the confidence to do things you never dreamed you'd do. Like speaking your mind and admitting when you'd made a mistake. How you truly don't know what happened to the class's money, but you're not sorry you used yours to pay for the skating party. Because even though it didn't turn out the way you'd wanted, you learned something important and had a good time anyway.

Principal Hansen taps her pencil against the desk and looks over the papers. "The skating party cost three hundred dollars. Five hundred and seventeen was taken out of the class account."

More than enough for a pretty pink skating outfit, you think ruefully, blotting the tears out of your eyes and feeling them get dry again. Despite everything you feel good inside. You've done nothing wrong. "I don't know what happened to it," you reply. "I never saw or touched any of that money. Not one penny."

Once again, Principal Hansen gazes at you. This time for quite a while. Her lips part. She hesitates, then says, "You'll have to resign as co-treasurer."

You don't want that job anymore anyway. "Okay."

Principal Hansen frowns. "All right, Lauren. You can go."

chapter
thirty-one

At lunch you sit with Tara in the land of the socially inferior. Over toward the middle of the cafeteria Celeste now sits at the center of the DYWYWM table. She is clearly the new queen. Judy Knight sits on one side of her, and Shelby Kirk sits on the other. Even Stephanie Eisley is there, still clinging to her wanna-be spot near the end of the table.

Krista isn't in the cafeteria. You wonder if she is hiding at home with a pretend stomachache. Or maybe she has exiled herself to the library. Maybe that's what you should have done, too. Since your meeting this morning with Principal Hansen your emotions have been all over the place. A graph of them would look like a major earthquake on the Richter scale, or the jagged edges of a broken window. Spikes going high when you've felt good because you know inside you've done nothing wrong. Then deep valleys of despair when you catch someone in class giving you a curious look. You're fairly certain they're wondering if you're really a thief. The story of the stolen class funds, or various forms of it, has spread all over school. It isn't hard to guess who's been spreading it.

And now, here in the crowded cafeteria, you feel lower than ever. The kids glance from their tables at you. You stare down at your oily tuna sandwich. You chose not to buy lunch today just because you didn't want anyone to think you were buying it with class money. You have less than no appetite. They must all despise and hate you. What could possibly be lower than stealing school money? Maybe you could convince your mom to send you to the parochial school in town. Or would the story just follow you there, too?

"What's wrong?" Tara says.

"Do you have to ask?" you moan. "I feel like killing myself."

"Hold it," Tara says. "You're only supposed to say that if you've done something wrong. Not if you're innocent."

"How do you know I'm innocent?" you ask.

"Oh, give me a break, Lauren," Tara snorts. "I'm your friend, dummy. You'd never do something like that."

"But *they* don't know that." You tilt your head at the rest of the cafeteria.

"Who cares about them?" Tara asks.

"I do."

"Well, you shouldn't."

You give her a sad look. Maybe you shouldn't care, but you do. It's something Tara will never understand. It's something you're not even sure *you* understand. You just know it's a lot more important to you than it is to her.

But that doesn't stop Tara from trying to cheer you up. "Come on, Lauren, how long have we known each other? Since second grade? You're the most honest person I know. And, no offense, but you couldn't have come up with a plan like that in a million years."

"Thanks." You give her a crooked smile.

"I *told* you I didn't trust that girl." Tara chews pensively on her jerky. "I knew there was something bad about her. I could see it."

"How come I couldn't?" you ask.

"You could've if you'd wanted to. You just didn't want to."

Tara's right, but what difference does it make now?

thirty-two

Rob comes out of the lunch line with a tray. He swivels his head to the right and then left, as if looking for someone to sit with. You quickly look down again and feel your face begin to burn. Now that this story about you taking the class money is going around, you might as well forget about him, too. You really have to hand it to Celeste. She not only knew how to get what she wanted. She knew how to make sure she was the *only* one who got it. Severely cold-blooded.

"What a day, huh?"

You look up into Rob's face as he puts his tray down and sits across from you. This is a total shock. And what does he mean? Did something else happen today that you haven't heard about?

"You believe that Lauren took that money?" Tara asks.

"Tara!" you gasp, and feel your face instantly grow flushed.

"Let him answer," Tara says.

Rob shakes his head. "Not a chance."

Tara turns to you. "See, Lauren? Your *real* friends know the truth."

You look at Rob, not knowing what to say. He looks back at you. "It's one of those stories that sounds really juicy until you stop and think about it. Then you realize it doesn't make any sense."

You feel your eyes begin to get watery, but this time you manage to blink back the tears. "Thanks, Rob."

Someone else slides down the table and sits next to you. It's . . . Krista?

"I just talked to Principal Hansen," she announces. "She told me about your resigning as class treasurer. I said no way. If you resign, I resign."

"Hey, me, too," adds Rob.

You're totally stunned. Like, in shock. "Why?" you finally manage to croak.

"Oh, come on, Lauren," Krista goes, like its completely obvious. "I know you. We *grew* up together."

chapter
thirty-three

You wish you could report that Celeste got caught or punished or hit by a car. But nothing bad has happened to her. She still sits every day at the DYWYWM table with Shelby, and Stephanie and the others. She did resign as class treasurer, saying that she did so because she couldn't get along with Krista. And Principal Hansen did reinstate you to the position after Krista, Rob, and Judy all said that's what they wanted.

You still sit with Tara at your table at the edge of the cafeteria. Sometimes Rob sits with you. Sometimes he sits with some other boys. Sometimes Krista and Judy sit with you. Sometimes they don't.

In a strange way, what Celeste predicted has partly come true. The popular crowd has broken up. The A-list girls have spread out. Celeste reigns over the old DYWYWM table, but there are days now when that table is half empty and there is elbowroom to spare.

One morning in the hall before homeroom, you saw

Celeste at the locker of a girl named Robin Jeffers. Robin is tall and gawky, with long brown hair that she always parts in the middle. She's quiet and has only one or two friends, and most kids would never suspect that she is a musical genius on the cello. You watched as Robin slid a homework sheet out of her notebook and gave it to Celeste. Then Celeste put her hand on Robin's shoulder and spoke softly and meaningfully. You caught the yearning, envious look in Robin's eyes as she watched Celeste go off down the hall.

If you knew Robin better, perhaps you could go over and say something. Instead you will keep an eye on her. It may not be any of your business. Maybe it would be better to let Robin learn the same lesson you learned. But you don't think you can allow that to happen. You're not that kind of person. And that's good.

Once in a while you still feel like crying. Because Celeste deceived you and used you. And because you let her do it.

But more often now you're pretty happy. You wear makeup when you feel like it. And the other day you came to school in the slinkiest pink tank top your crazy aunt Sarah from California sent. When Shelby and Stephanie saw you, they whispered to each other. And you just smiled because it didn't bother you at all. They're not your friends and you don't care what they think. You just feel lucky that you do have a few good real friends. You care about them and you know they care about you. It's something you feel confident about. And that is what's truly important.

Lunchtime in the cafeteria. You are not happy, nor are you sitting where you want to be.

The center of the cafeteria is Krista Rice's realm. Her table is jammed so tightly with girls that, if one of them sneezed, the wanna-bes at the ends would fall off their seats and tumble to the floor. Krista sits in the middle of these girls. She is certainly one of the prettiest girls in your grade, but there is something about her that the other pretty girls don't have. Krista is the ultimate "Don't-You-Wish-You-Were-Me" girl.